The
Keeneland Association
Library

The Keeneland Association Library

A Guide to the Collection
by
Amelia King Buckley

University of Kentucky Press
1958

The publication of this book has been possible partly by reason of a grant from The Keeneland Association

Foreword

WHEN KEENELAND accepted the obligation to maintain an organized library on Thoroughbred racing and associated subjects, it was not responding to popular demand, since there was no general demand for information in such a specialized field. Rather, it was establishing a broad inventory of reference material for horsemen, a few hobbyists, and a few scholars. In a broader sense, it was storing up information against the day when racing, as the most nearly universal of the great spectator sports and as a large industry affecting social and economic life, would be called upon to furnish data for research in genetics, probability theory, economics, manners and morals, history, law, physiology, psychology, and other fields of inquiry.

The opportunity for such studies has been only dimly appreciated, partly because horsemen themselves are too entangled with detail to search for generality and are untrained for such work; partly because the scholar with time for research has been unaware of the possibilities in available data; and, of course, partly because so few students have addressed themselves to the task of assaying the abundant ore in one of mankind's oldest and most important forms of recreation.

A catalog listing the resources of the Keeneland Association Library is a contribution to numerous fields of knowledge. It provides a handbook in a highly specialized and relatively obscure branch of library science. It challenges the student of genetics, probability mathematics, and population statistics. Not altogether incidentally, it offers the historian a list of sources which may be absent from much larger but less specialized libraries. The old

Spirit of the Times, for instance, provides one of the most faithful records of American life and manners in the nineteenth century.

This unique work will, at the least, prove useful to writers, turf historians, folklorists, librarians, booksellers, publishers, occasional students, and the scattered few whose pleasure it is to collect and pore over the literary treasures and reference materials of Thoroughbred racing and breeding. Conceivably, it may draw the attention of scholars in many fields to a tremendous store of raw material awaiting the research worker. But even if Mrs. Buckley's work serves only as a guide to a comprehensive collection, it remains unique and valuable.

Lexington, Kentucky February 11, 1958

Joseph A. Estes

Acknowledgments

IT IS WITH sincerest appreciation that I acknowledge the consideration in time, technical advice, and sustaining encouragement which Dr. Edward J. Humeston, Jr., head of the department of library science of the University of Kentucky, and Mrs. Emma Lou Lecky and Miss Laura K. Martin, professors in that department, have given me. Miss Norma Cass, head of the reference department, and Miss Jacqueline Bull, head of the archives department, of the Margaret I. King Library of the University of Kentucky have been more than generous with their assistance in the development of this study.

I was most fortunate in having the interest and aid of W. T. Bishop, general manager of Keeneland Race Course, and Joseph A. Estes, editor of *The Blood-Horse,* both of whom were most cordial in sharing their time and store of knowledge about the racetrack and the library.

Without the information gleaned from lawyers, public librarians, track managers, horse trainers, magazine editors, bookdealers at home and abroad, and forbearing friends, the study would have been the poorer, and I am happy to express my thanks to each of them.

A. K. B.

Contents

Introduction

THE KEENELAND Association Library is a research library in Thoroughbred racing, breeding, and related subjects, and is located at the Keeneland Race Course, Lexington, Kentucky. Keeneland was organized for operation on a wholly nonprofit basis, with all returns beyond maintenance expenses being devoted to charity, education, and research. Because of the unique philosophy of its organizers, education and research have been emphasized from the outset. It is the only racetrack in the United States which maintains, provides service in, and makes available to the public a comprehensive library of turf literature.[1]

The library was begun in 1939 with the gift of William Arnold Hanger. No library had been anticipated in the original plans of the organizers of the track, but as the entire Keeneland picture developed, such a library seemed suitable and appropriate at a racetrack dedicated to the betterment of the sport. When Mr. Hanger, one of the stanchest and most imaginative supporters of the new track, offered a collection of books to the association for the establishment of a library at Keeneland, it was readily accepted. The board was quick to sense the benefit to Thoroughbred racing and breeding interests to be derived from such a library at the racecourse. It promised to be a fitting and well-placed adjunct to the whole establishment.

As a nucleus for the proposed library, Mr. Hanger purchased

[1] In April, 1957, Monmouth Park Jockey Club purchased the turf library of the late John Lawrence O'Connor. It was stated at that time the library would be established at Monmouth Park Race Track as a memorial to Mr. O'Connor.

the carefully selected turf library of Robert James Turnbull, a New York lawyer and bibliophile. Numbering approximately 2,000 volumes, this collection was a sound foundation with which to begin, for Mr. Turnbull had spent twenty-five years buying, discarding, and replacing books which emphasized the historical aspects of Thoroughbred racing and breeding. Comparison with other collections in the field reveals how thoughtfully and carefully this one was assembled. Mr. Turnbull not only knew the desirable familiar titles, but exercised rare discernment in searching for less well known works. If a well-known title is missing, one may believe that this is because he never found a copy of it which met his standards.

After Mr. Hanger's original gift was housed, other owners of turf libraries made gifts of books from their collections to the new Keeneland library. The late Robert Livingston Gerry, member of the Jockey Club, Thoroughbred breeder, and owner of the experimental Aknusti Stud in the Catskill Mountains, was the first to make such a gift, in March, 1941. In addition to a large number of finely bound and rare volumes, there were pamphlets and materials of an ephemeral nature covering the widest range within the field. Sales catalogs of yearlings and breeding stock, broadsides and leaflets, and booklets and pamphlets concerning breeding farms provide a revealing picture of the Thoroughbred horse of an earlier day. Mr. Gerry's preservation of many catalogs attests to his appreciation of their usefulness in a research library. This portion of his gift has formed a fine nucleus for the present pamphlet file.

Pierre Lorillard, grandson of the founder of Rancocas Stud at Jobstown, New Jersey, and presiding steward at Keeneland for several years, donated approximately 100 volumes from his family's library in the summer of 1942. Later individual gifts of titles of local interest have added material that otherwise would be difficult to acquire. A copy of Benjamin Gratz Bruce's *Memoir of Lexington* is an example of this kind of gift, as is the two-volume *Stallion Register* by William Treacy and Kenner Walker. Leonard Sutcliffe, America's foremost photographer of the Thor-

oughbred horse in the 1920's and 1930's, assembled to special
order his albums of *Famous Stallions* and *Famous Mares*. The
library's copies, which otherwise would have been almost impos-
sible to obtain, were a gift from the family for whom they had
been made.

In January, 1954, files of the three American sporting papers
loosely called *Spirit of the Times*, covering the years 1836-1892,
were given the library. It has been written that "No sporting
library is complete without a file of the *Spirit of the Times*, as
during its publication it provided a chronicle of the events in its
world which was complete, conscientious, admirable, and for the
period unequaled. In the history of sporting journalism it must
on this account, occupy a distinguished place."[2] The library's file
contains volumes 5-31 of the "old" *Spirit of the Times*, volumes
1-6 of *Porter's Spirit of the Times*, and volumes 1-104, 106-122,
125, and 126 of *Wilkes' Spirit of the Times* (later, "Wilkes'" was
dropped from the title and the paper appeared until its merger
as *Spirit of the Times*).

The value of the library has steadily increased with the
growth of its collections and with their more thorough analysis,
cataloging, and evaluation. In addition, the increase in horse
breeding as an industry and of racing as a spectator sport requires
more intensive research on the part of a larger number of people.
This would indicate a growing demand for the service which such
a library as Keeneland's can offer, situated as it is at a racetrack
in the heart of a racing and breeding country and in one of the
most important bloodstock sales centers in the world.[3]

Although horseracing as a sport in the United States dates
from the seventeenth century, collections of the literature of
Thoroughbred racing are not numerous. Most of them have been
made by private individuals and therefore are not generally

[2] *The Sporting Library of the Late George B. Raymond* . . . (1926),
Item 164.
[3] Triangle Publications, *American Racing Manual* (1953-58). The
number of breeding farms has increased from more than 1,261 in 1952
to more than 1,645 in 1957. Attendance in 1952 at racetracks for Thoroughbred racing was 26,434,903. By 1957 it had risen to 30,617,824.

accessible. So far as can be ascertained, the Keeneland library is the only library which has extensive material on the subject, available to anyone for use the year around. It may be consulted at all times by correspondence and telephone.

An annotated guide to the books on Thoroughbred racing, breeding, and related subjects which comprise the collection at Keeneland seems desirable for the use of lay persons and librarians interested in the contents of this specialized library. Such a guide, it is hoped, will be of great benefit to all persons interested in tapping the resources of this collection.

The use for which this guide is intended has been a determining factor in its construction. It is designed not as a definitive bibliography in the subjects of Thoroughbred racing and breeding but as a guidebook to a collection of turf literature to be found in one library. It is an alphabetical author arrangement of the titles in the library's catalog as of June 1, 1958. Included are more than 900 monograph titles, of which more than 140 are in foreign languages, chiefly French, and more than 100 serial titles. Other types of material listed are selected sales catalogs, private studbooks (as distinguished from those listed as continuations), bound pamphlets, and a limited amount of manuscript material.

The complete file of the sales catalogs of The Breeders' Sales Company, an organization closely linked to Keeneland, is entered in the guide. Individual sales catalogs have not been entered, although the library has many of them and continues to add them to its collection. Through the years there have been dispersal sales of historic interest to Thoroughbred racing and breeding. If a catalog of such a sale is in the library's collection, it is entered under the name of the stud owner. An example of this is the dispersal sale catalog of August Belmont's Nursery Stud issued in 1891. The catalog included Mr. Belmont's breeding theories and has more interest for the researcher than the average sales catalog.

Private studbooks, on the other hand, are included in the guide, being entered by the name of the stud owner, who in most cases was not the compiler. Issued at irregular intervals, these studbooks constitute reference material on a particular farm's breeding pattern.

Aside from the general run of sales catalogs, other materials excluded from the guide are pamphlets, microfilms and recordings, the photographic negative collection, and a very few titles on unrelated subjects which were in the original gift. Materials in the pamphlet file may be located through the pamphlet catalog, which is arranged by subject. Microfilmed books and recordings of Thoroughbred sales and turf events are not numerous in the collection, as yet, and the card catalog of the extensive photographic negative collection must of necessity be its guide.

As has been noted, the guide is arranged alphabetically by author. A title with author unknown is placed in the arrangement alphabetically by first word (article excluded) of the title. Serials are entered in the same manner. Entries include information from the title page of the book, which with few exceptions will include the author, title, edition (if that can be determined), place of publication, publisher, date, number of pages or volumes as the case may be, and illustrations, if any. Clippings, letters, and manuscript notes accompanying the volume which add pertinent information are referred to in a note following the completion of the entry.

The writer has attempted a thorough search in the case of each incomplete entry and has made a reference check as far as possible in the case of all others. It is hoped that those using the guide will report all errors, the present writer trusting, as did a turf writer in 1865, "that those who in their leisure hours may condescend to peruse [it] will make allowances for any errors which may creep in, or delusions under which the author may labour; and as the poet said, remember that

'Everything has faults; nor is't unknown,
That harps and fiddles often lose their tone;
And wayward voices, at their owners' call,
With all their best endeavours only squall:
Dogs blink their covey, flints withhold the spark,
And double barrels (d— them!) miss their mark.'"

The Cook Negatives

A SAMPLING OF

PHOTOGRAPHS TAKEN BY

Charles Christian Cook

from 1901 to 1951

THIRTY SCENES FROM THE
COOK NEGATIVE COLLECTION IN
The Keeneland Association Library

TOP: The start of the Turf Congress Handicap, Hawthorne Park, Chicago, June 6, 1901; J. J. Holtman, starter. The earliest dated negative in the Cook Collection. BOTTOM: *Beldame,* Frank O'Neill up, an outstanding race mare bred by August Belmont and foaled in 1901.

TOP: The entrance to the Crescent City Jockey Club, New Orleans, 1904. BOTTOM: *Sysonby*, left standing at the post at the start, coming on to win the Great Republic Stakes, Saratoga, August 12, 1905; *Oiseau*, second; *Broomstick*, third.

TOP: A steeplechase at Belmont Park, October 8, 1905. "Every position of a horse taking a jump" (Cook's note). BOTTOM: Mrs. Payne Whitney, 1906. The first woman to be honored by the Thoroughbred Club of America, at its annual testimonial dinner October 13, 1938, Lexington.

TOP: Copper magnate Jesse Lewisohn and actress Lillian Russell at Saratoga, 1906. BOTTOM: A steeplechase at Sheepshead Bay, September 12, 1908. "This photo won the Grand Prize in a contest at Grand Central Palace, 1915. 2500 competing" (Cook's note).

TOP: Gamecocks in flight, about to strike. BOTTOM: John Oliver (Jack) Keene (*center*), part of whose Keeneland Stud became the site of the Keeneland Race Course; William M. Pinkerton (*right*) of the famous detective agency.

TOP: Theodore Roosevelt at a cavalry review. BOTTOM: John E. Madden (*left*) of Hamburg Place, Lexington, a leading breeder of the first quarter of the twentieth century; Samuel C. Hildreth (*center*), an equally outstanding trainer of the period.

TOP: An international polo match, the United States versus England, at Meadow Brook, Westbury, Long Island, 1911. BOTTOM: Orrin Davenport of the Barnum and Bailey Circus, in a turn from *May* (white) to *Flora* (dapple), *circa* 1913.

TOP: The clowns with the Ringling Brothers' Circus. BOTTOM: August Belmont, II (*left*), chairman of the Jockey Club; Mr. and Mrs. John Sanford, millionaire carpet manufacturer and sportsman, former New York racing commissioner and member of Congress.

TOP: "Cowboy philosopher" Will Rogers on his roping horse *Dopey*, 1917. BOTTOM: Charles Christian Cook, in his uniform as commander of an aerophotographic group in France during World War I. One of the nation's first war aerial photographers.

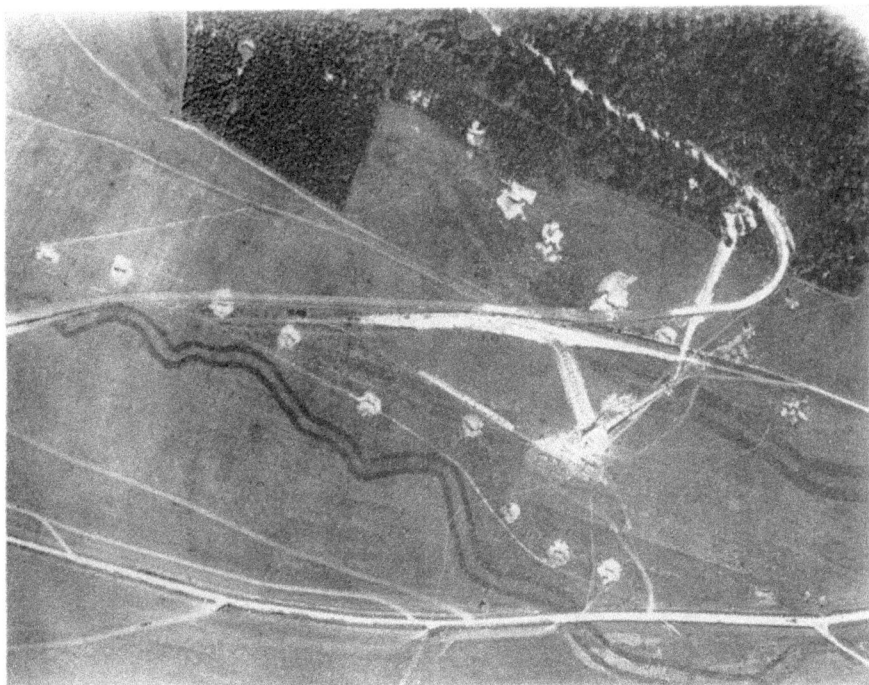

TOP: An aerial view "somewhere at the front," August, 1918. Note the clear detail obtained with primitive equipment. BOTTOM: *Exterminator*, the Kentucky Derby winner, and *Sun Briar* (on rail), both owned by Willis Sharpe Kilmer, working out at Saratoga, 1919.

TOP: *Man o' War,* "the most renowned stallion in the history of Thoroughbred racing," in his only loss—to *Upset,* in the Sanford Stakes, Saratoga, August 13, 1919. BOTTOM: Henry Carnegie Phipps (*left*), and his trainer, James (Sunny Jim) Fitzsimmons (*center*).

TOP: The British champion *Papyrus*, Steve Donoghue up (leading), and the American champion *Zev*, Earl Sande up, before the start of the Belmont International Race, October 20, 1923. *Zev* won easily. BOTTOM: The French champion *Epinard*, Everett Haynes up, September, 1924.

TOP: The Australian horse *Phar Lap*, who died of colic in California, mounted by a taxidermist and displayed at Belmont Park September 17, 1932. BOTTOM: Mr. and Mrs. Franklin Delano Roosevelt at Saratoga; on the running board, George H. Bull, president of Saratoga.

TOP: Mrs. Payne Whitney's *Twenty Grand* defeating her nephew C. V. Whitney's *Equipoise,* in the Junior Champion Stakes, Aqueduct, October 4, 1930. BOTTOM: Robert J. Kleberg, Jr. (*right*), of King Ranch, Texas, and his trainer, Max Hirsch, at Hialeah.

THE JOCKEY CLUB GOLD CUP
Belmont Park, N.Y. $50,000 added   October 13, 1951
G.V. Whitney's   David Gorman . up
S.E.Veitch.trainer COUNTERPOINT Two miles in 3:21:3
Hill Prince(2nd)   Kiss Me Kate(3rd)
Presentation by George D.Widener

Seasons Greetings
1951-'52
from;

TOP: Joseph E. Widener, chairman of the Jockey Club, presenting the Futurity Trophy to Hal Price Headley, first president of Keeneland, and his trainer, Duval A. Headley, current president, Belmont Park, October 2, 1937. BOTTOM: The latest dated negative in the Cook Collection.

Note on the Cook Negatives

THE KEENELAND Association Library, through the cooperation of William Arnold Hanger, in 1954 acquired the invaluable photographic negative collection of the late Charles Christian Cook. Mr. Cook was one of the first photographers in this country to specialize in racing and racetrack scenes, and his work covered the sport from the early 1900's to midcentury. Roughly 15,000 negatives, many of them glass, comprise the collection, which is cataloged as a separate entity and will remain as such.

Although the major portion of the negatives were made at New York tracks (Mr. Cook's first picture in the East was made at Saratoga in July, 1904) and at Hialeah, where he was track photographer through the 1942 season, there are negatives of Louisiana, Arkansas, Chicago, and Maryland tracks, some of which are no longer in operation. Racing, track scenes, the horses, owners, trainers, riders, and those persons otherwise interested in the sport are all represented in the negatives. A fine series of polo pictures, including international matches and women's polo, along with a comprehensive steeplechase group are also to be found in the collection.

Not directly related to racing, but of great value in themselves, are other negatives in the collection representing Mr. Cook's work in France during World War I and his photographs for the Ringling Brothers' Circus. In 1917 he became one of the first aerial photographers. He was in command of an aerophotographic group in France, and after the signing of the Armistice he was required to remain abroad to photograph the Hindenburg Line from Coblenz to Cologne. This work is filed in Washington, but the Keeneland collection includes more than 100 negatives made during his army service. For fourteen years Mr. Cook photographed extensively for the Ringling Brothers' Circus. Much of this work was done at the circus winter quarters in Bridgeport, Connecticut. It was here that Alf Ringling had constructed a miniature jungle for authentic backgrounds for the wild animals which Mr. Cook "shot." Several hundred negatives depicting all phases of circus life comprise a pictorial account of a form of entertainment rapidly disappearing from the American scene.

A pastime from behind the American scene, so to speak, is depicted in sixteen negatives of cockfighting. This sport was closely associated with racing in England from the earliest days, but in 1840 legislation was passed against it and the *Racing Calendar* no longer carried the item "Cocking in Great Britain."[4] However, as late as the early 1900's game chickens were advertised for sale in *The Thoroughbred Record* of Lexington, Kentucky. The fact that such an advertisement appeared in the then old and established racing and breeding magazine would indicate that cockfighting and horseracing in this country continued to be companionable.[5] It seems most significant, therefore, that in this library is to be found a photographic record of a sport so closely associated with horseracing.

[4]Charles Mathew Prior, *The History of the Racing Calendar* . . . (London, The "Sporting Life," 1926), 198.
[5] *The Thoroughbred Record,* LXI (March, 1905), 132.

Guide to the Collection

A. D. L. *See* HUSHED Up. By A. D. L. . . .

ABBILDUNGEN Königlich Württembergischer Gestütts Pferde von Orientalischen Racen. Herausgegeben von dem Königlichen Lithographischen Institut. Stuttgart, Ebner, 1823 [1824] 1 v. (unpaged) 21 plates (3 col.)

> Large oblong folio, captions in French and German. Beneath the 3 colored plates: "Peint d'après nature par A. Adam, 1830."

ABOU BEKR IBN BEDR. Le Nâcérî. La Perfection des Deux Arts, ou Traité Complet d'Hippologie et d'Hippiatrie Arabes; Ouvrage Publié par Ordre et Sous les Auspices du Ministère de l'Intérieur, de l'Agriculture et du Commerce. Traduit de l'Arabe d'Abou Bekr Ibn Bedr, par M. Perron . . . Paris, Huzard, 1852-60. 3 v. illus.

ACTON (C. R.). Silk and Spur. By C. R. Acton . . . London, Richards [1935] x, 322 p. plates, ports.

ADAMS (John). An Analysis of Horsemanship; Teaching the Whole Art of Riding, in the Manege, Military, Hunting, Racing, and Travelling System. Together With the Method of Breaking Horses, for Every Purpose to Which Those Noble Animals Are Adapted. By John Adams . . . London, Cundee, 1805. 3 v. front. (port.), plates. *Plates engraved from paintings by J. Sartorius.*

The ADMIRAL. *See* STODDART (Joseph).

AGA KHAN. The Sheshoon, Ballymany, Gilltown, Ongar and Sallymount Studs. Manager Cyril Hall . . . [Dublin, Brindley, 1956] 86 [6] p. *Library has: Supplement, 1956; Stud Book, 1957.*

ALBIGNY (G. D'). Les Paris aux Courses. Manuel des Meilleurs Systèmes Pour le Jeu aux Courses. Paris, Mathurins, 1902. 143 [1] p. tables.

[ALKEN (Henry Thomas).] The Beauties & Defects in the Figure of the Horse Comparatively Delineated in a Series of Engravings. Boston, Carter, 1830. 18 plates (unpaged)

Each plate accompanied by a leaf with descriptive letterpress. Believed to be an American piracy of Alken's earlier work published in 1816.

ALLEN (John). Principles of Modern Riding, for Gentlemen; in Which the Late Improvements of the Manege and Military Systems Are Applied to Practise on the Promenade, the Road, the Field, and the Course. By John Allen . . . London, Tegg, 1825. xiv, 286 p. plates.

[ALLISON (William).] "Blairmount?" A Turf Mystery. By Blinkhoolie . . . London, International Horse Agency, 1909. 227 p. front., facs.

ALLISON (William). The British Thoroughbred Horse. His History & Breeding Together With an Exposition of the Figure System. By William Allison . . . With Coloured Frontispiece and Ten Other Illustrations. London, Richards, 1901. xiii, 360, 183 [1] p. tables. *Supplement paged separately.*

ALLISON (William). Memories of Men and Horses. By William Allison . . . London, Richards, 1922. 341 p. front. (port.), plates, ports.

ALLISON (William). "My Kingdom for a Horse!" Yorkshire, Rugby, Balliol, the Bar, Bloodstock and Journalistic Recollections. By William Allison . . . London, Richards, 1919. 352 p. front. (port.), plates, ports.

AMERICAN Horse Breeder. Illustrated Journal for Horse Lovers . . . Boston, 1882-1935. illus. weekly. *Library has: v. 26-28 (1908-10)*

The AMERICAN Jockey Club. [New York, Thitchener, 1867] 79 p. *Directory and Rules of Racing.*

AMERICAN Race Horses. . . . A Review of the Breeding and the Performances of the Outstanding Thoroughbreds of the Year Engaged in Racing, Steeplechasing and Hunt Races . . . [New York] Sagamore Press [1936-] illus. annual. *Editor varies. Publisher varies. Library has: 1936 to date.*

The AMERICAN Racing Calendar. For . . . Being an Appendix to the American Turf Register and Sporting Magazine, for the Current Year. New York, 18 - . *Library has: 1840-41.*

AMERICAN Racing Calendar and Trotting Record . . . New York, 1858- . 2 v. *"Compiled from 'Porter's Spirit of the Times.'" Library has: 1858-59.*

AMERICAN Racing Calendar for . . . Containing a Complete Digest of All Turf Events in the United States and the Canadas During . . . Entries for the Stakes in . . . the Winners of the Principal Races in America and England From Their Commencement; the Racing Colors of the Leading Turfmen . . . List of Thoroughbred Foals of . . . etc., etc. New York, Turf, Field and Farm, 1873- . *Library has: 1873; 1876, pt. 1.*

AMERICAN Racing Manual. For . . . A Book of Reference . . . for Persons Interested in the Affairs of the Turf . . . Chicago, Daily Racing Form Publishing Co. etc., 1906- . illus. annual. *Library has: 1906 to date.*

The AMERICAN Racing Record and Turf Guide. For . . . A Complete Record of the Racing in the United States During . . . With an Index . . . Laws of Racing Used by the Different Jockey Clubs, etc. Edited and Published by W. G. Dorling. New York, 1871- . *Library has: 1871-72, 1875-76. In 1875-76 The American Racing Record was published by the* Spirit of the Times.

AMERICAN Sporting Manual . . . A Book of Reference . . . of All Sporting Records. Five Up to Date Tables as Used by the Handicappers of Racing . . . Bookmaking Percentages, Track Records . . . The Pugilistic Record of . . . Records to Date of Harness Racing, Billiards, etc. Edited by F. H. Brunell. Chicago, Daily Racing Form Publishing Co., 18 - . *Library has: 1904-05.*

The AMERICAN Stud Book. The American Stud Book . . . Revised in 1884 With Supplementary Index. New York, 1884- .

Library has: 1884 to date; Supplements for v. 16 to date. 1st 6 volumes by Bruce, volume 7 (1898) to date by the Jockey Club.

The AMERICAN Stud Book. 1868. *See* BRUCE (Sanders Dewees).

The AMERICAN Stud Book. 1873. *See* BRUCE (Sanders Dewees).

AMERICAN Thoroughbred Breeders Association. Statistical Summary of . . . Lexington, Ky., 1952- . annual. *Library has: 1952 to date.*

AMERICAN Trotting Register Association. Index-Digest of Wallace's American Trotting Register (Volumes One to Ten Inclusive) Containing Complete Alphabetical Lists, With Condensed Pedigrees of All Standard Stallions, Standard Mares, Geldings, and Non-Standard Animals . . . With an Appendix Containing . . . the Trotting Rules and Regulations; Registration Rules and Regulations etc., etc. Des Moines, Mills, 1892. 714 p.

AMERICAN Turf Register. A Correct Synopsis of Turf Events in the United States Embracing Running, Trotting and Pacing, for . . . Carefully Compiled From Official Records. And an Appendix, Containing Useful Notes on the Breeding . . . of Stock; Together With Tables of Winning Horses; Entries for . . . and Thereafter . . . New York, Turf, Field and Farm, 1871- . *Library has: 1871-73.*

AMERICAN Turf Register and Racing and Trotting Calendar. Containing Complete and Correct Reports of All the Races and Trots in the United States and Canada During the Year . . . Also Alphabetical Lists of Winning Horses in Racing and Trotting. New York, Richards, 18 - . *Library has: 1845-47, 1849, 1852-55, 1857-60.*

AMERICAN Turf Register and Racing Calendar. A Correct Synopsis of Turf Events in the United States and the Dominion of Canada, Embracing Running, Trotting and Pacing for . . . Carefully Compiled From Official Records and an Appendix . . . New York, Turf, Field and Farm, 18 - . *Library has: 1876.*

The AMERICAN Turf Register and Sporting Magazine. 1829-44. 15 v. illus. *Place and publisher vary.*

ANALYST. *See* HIGGINS (Francis).

ANDERSON (Clarence William). Big Red. Text and Pictures by C. W. Anderson. New York, Macmillan, 1943. 64 p. illus.

ANDERSON (James Douglas). Making the American Thoroughbred Especially in Tennessee, 1800-1845. By James Douglas Anderson. Including Reminiscences of the Turf. By Balie Peyton. With Notes by the Author. Norwood, Mass., Plimpton Press, 1916. xv, 300 p. ports.

[ANDERSON (Jesse Sylvester).] The Turf in Caricature. By VET. New York, Anderson [19–] 23 plates (unpaged) *Cover title only. Cartoons of jockeys and other racetrack personages.*

ANECDOTES on the Origin and Antiquity of Horse-Racing, From the Earliest Times. London, Gosden, 1825. 57 p. illus.

ANNALS of the Turf. 1735-1871. By P. J. 3 v. *Handwritten.*

ANTWERP and Lamplighter. [Pseud.] Modern Pedigrees. By Antwerp and Lamplighter. New York, Metropolitan Job Printing Co. [1895] 9 p. 43 tables in folder.

[APPERLY (Charles James).] The Chace, the Turf, and the Road. By Nimrod. With Illustrations by Henry Alken, and a Portrait by D. Maclise . . . London, Murray, 1837. xx, 301 p. front. (port.), plates.

[APPERLY (Charles James).] The Life of a Sportsman. By Nimrod . . . With Thirty-Six Coloured Illustrations by Henry Alken. London, Paul, 1914. xi, 400 [1] p. plates (col.) *Added eng. title page.*

APPERLY (Charles James). My Life and Times. By Nimrod (Charles James Apperly). Edited With Additions by E. D.

APPERLY (Charles James). *Continued:*
Cuming . . . London, Blackwood, 1927. xviii, 341 p. plates, ports. (part col.) *Portions first published in* Fraser's Magazine *1842-* .

APPERLY (Charles James). Nemrod ou L'Amateur des Chevaux de Courses. Observations sur les Méthodes les Plus Nouvelles de Propager, d'Élever, de Dresser et de Monter les Chevaux de Courses. Par Charles-James Apperly . . . Paris, l'auteur, 1838. viii, 258 (i.e. 250) p. plates.

APPERLY (Charles James). Nimrod Abroad. By C. J. Apperly . . . London, Colburn, 1843. 2 v.

[APPERLY (Charles James).] The Turf. By Nimrod. New York, Brentano, 1901. x, 195 p. illus. (The Sportsman's Classics)

ARCARO (George Edward). The Art of Race Riding. By Eddie Arcaro. With Whitney Tower and a Portfolio of Drawings by Robert Riger. New York, Wright Lithographing Co. [1957] 31 p. illus. (col.), 10 plates (in portfolio) *"This is copy 150 of an edition of 500." First appeared as a series in* Sports Illustrated.

ARCARO (George Edward). I Ride to Win! By Eddie Arcaro as Told to Jack O'Hara. New York, Greenberg, 1951. xii, 273 p. plates, ports., facs.

ARIEL. [Pseud.] Astronomy Applied to Horse Racing. A Sure Guide to Successful Speculation on the Turf . . . By Ariel. [Poona, Israelite Press, 1919?] 285 p. tables.

ARMSTRONG (   ). Turf Tales. By Captain Armstrong . . . London, Lucas, 1891. *Library has: v. 1.*

ASTLEY (Sir John Dugdale). Fifty Years of My Life in the World of Sport at Home and Abroad. By Sir John Dugdale Astley . . . London, Hurst, 1894. 2 v. illus.

AUBRY (Charles). Histoire Pittoresque de l'Equitation Ancienne et Moderne. Dédiée à MM. les Officiers-élèves de l'École Royale de Cavalerie. Par Charles Aubry Peintre Professeur à Cette École. Paris, Motte, 1833 [1834] 1 v. (unpaged) plates. *Printed on one side of leaf only.*

The "AUSTRALASIAN." Stallion Register, 1927, Containing the Tabulated Pedigrees, Racing Performances, and Stud Record of the Principal Sires at the Stud in Australia, Together With an Appendix Giving Short Pedigrees of Many Additional Stallions. Melbourne, 1927. xx, 114 p. illus.

The AUSTRALASIAN Turf Register. (With Which Is Incorporated the Australian Racing Chronicle) Containing Results of All Registered Australian and Principal New Zealand Meetings of the Past Season, and Handicaps for Principal Events . . . Melbourne, Argus & Australasian [1866?-] *Library has: v. 48-78 (1913-44)*

The AUSTRALIAN Stud Book. Containing Pedigrees of Racehorses, etc. From the Earliest Accounts to the Year . . . Inclusive . . . Compiled and Published Under the Direction of, and Obtainable From the Australian Jockey Club . . . Sydney, Bloxham, 1878- . *Library has: v. 1-11, 13-19.*

[BADCOCK (John).] Conversations on Conditioning. The Grooms' Oracle, and Pocket Stable Directory; in Which the Management of Horses Generally, as to Health, Dieting, and Exercise, Are Considered, in a Series of Familiar Dialogues, Between Two Grooms Engaged in Training Horses to Their Work. With Notes and an Appendix, Including Extracts From the Receipt Book of John Hinds [pseud.] . . . London, Sherwood, 1829. xii, 274 p. front. (col.), illus.

[BADCOCK (John).] Farriery, Taught on a New and Easy Plan; Being a Treatise on the Diseases and Accidents of the Horse; With Instructions to the Shoeing-Smith, Farrier, and Groom. Preceded by a Popular Description of the Animal Functions in Health and How These Are to Be Restored When Disordered. By John Hinds [pseud.] . . . With Considerable Additions and Improvements, Particularly Adapted to This Country. By Thomas M. Smith . . . With a Supplement: Comprising an Essay on Domestic Animals, Especially the Horse . . . Together With Trotting and Racing Tables . . . Pedigrees of Winning Horses Since 1839 . . . With Useful Calving and Lambing Tables, etc. etc. By J. S. Skinner . . . Philadelphia, Lippincott, 1867. xiv, 224 p.; vi, 106 p. illus. *Supplement paged separately.*

[BADCOCK (John).] The Veterinary Surgeon; or, Farriery Taught on a New and Easy Plan: Being a Treatise on All the Diseases and Accidents to Which the Horse Is Liable . . . With Instructions to the Shoeing-Smith, Farrier, and Groom . . . Preceded by a Popular Description of the Animal Functions in Health . . . By John Hinds [pseud.] . . . With Considerable Additions and Improvements, Particularly Adapted to This Country. By Thomas M. Smith . . . Philadelphia, Grigg, 1830. xiv, 284 p. 3 plates.

BAILY'S Magazine of Sports & Pastimes. London, Baily Brothers [etc.] 1860-1926. weekly. *Library has: partial file 1869-1922. Publisher and title vary.*

BAILY'S Racing Register. From the Earliest Records to the Close of the Year 1842 . . . London, Baily Brothers, 1845. 3 v.

BALL (Richard). Penny Farthing. By Richard Ball. Pencil Drawings by G. D. Armour. London, Country Life [1931] ix, 162 [1] p. illus.

[BANKS (Fred S.).] Index of Engravings With the Names of the Artists in The Sporting Magazine From the Year 1792 to 1870 . . . London, Vinton [1892] 116 p. front., illus. *"Published for Walter Gilbey." "Introduction by the Hon. Francis Lawley."*

BARANOWSKI (Zdzislaw). The International Horseman's Dictionary. English; French; German. London, Museum Press [1955] 176 p. front. (port.), plates.

BARNES (William Sudduth). Souvenir Catalogue of the Thoroughbreds (Stallions and Mares) Belonging to the Melbourne Stud. The Property of William S. Barnes, Lexington, Fayette County, Kentucky. Compiled and Written by John K. Stringfield. Cincinnati, O., 1901. viii, 252 [2] p. front. (port.), illus.

[BARROW (Albert Stewart).] Between the Flags. By "Sabretache" of The Tatler . . . London, Odhams Press [1930?] 255 p.

BATESON (William). Mendel's Principles of Heredity. By W. Bateson . . . Cambridge, University Press, 1913. xiv, 413 p. illus., plates (fold. col.)

BATTELL (Joseph). American Stallion Register Including All Stallions Prominent in the Breeding of the American Roadster, Trotter and Pacer From the Earliest Records to 1902 . . . Compiled From Original Sources With Many Pedigrees, Hitherto Incorrectly Recorded, Corrected (in All Cases the Evidence Upon Which This Is Done Being Given), and Many More Pedigrees Extended . . . By Joseph Battell . . . Middlebury, Vt., American Publishing Co., 1909-36. 5 v. illus.

Bound with v. 5: *The Horse,* 318 p. Paged separately and comprised chiefly of excerpts from other writers on the horse, etc.

BAYLES (F. H.). The Race Courses Atlas of Great Britain and Ireland. Illustrated With Sixty Coloured Descriptive Diagrams . . . London, Faux, 1903. xii, 116 p. front., maps.

BAYLISS (Marguerite Farlee). The Matriarchy of the American Turf. 1875-1930. By M. F. Bayliss. [New York] Privately Printed for Robert L. Gerry, 1931. xxii, 468 p. front., plates. *Foreword by Robert L. Gerry.*

BEAUMONT (Gerald). Riders Up! By Gerald Beaumont. New York, Appleton, 1922. 330 [1] p.

BECKER (Friedrich S.). The Breed of the Racehorse. Its Developments and Transformations. By Friedrich Becker . . . London, British Bloodstock Agency [1936] 267 p. front., illus., charts (part fold.)

BECKER (Friedrich S.). Charts of the Successful Sire Lines and a Comprehensive Index Showing the Tail Male Descent of the Chief Winning Brood Mares Covering the Period From 1700 to 1914. Compiled by F. S. Becker ("Boulanger") London, Sporting Life, 1915. iv, 39 p. 14 charts (part fold.)

BECKER (Friedrich S.). The Successful Female Lines in the Breeding of the Thoroughbred Horse. By Friedrich Becker. Hamburg, Rademacher, 1922. xlii, 162 p. tables. *Supplement I (1921-22) Text in English and German.*

BEDOUT (L.). Notes sur la Méthode de Classification Créée par Bruce Lowe Dans Son Application aux Grandes Épreuves Françaises. Par L. Bedout. (Publiées par le Jockey les 27, 28, 29, 30 et 31 Décembre 1897.) Paris, Legoupy, 1898. 47 [2] p. tables. *"First Edition."*

BEERY (Jesse). The Thoroughbreds. Jesse Beery . . . [Pleasant Hill, O., 1912] 197 p.

BELLAIRS (Archie). The God of the Turf. By Archie Bellairs. London, Federation Press [1924] 156 p.

BELLINGHAM (Cathal). Confessions of a Turf Crook. Told by Himself. Edited by Cathal Bellingham. London, Allan [1924] ix, 179 p. front. *"First Edition."*

[BELLOCQ (Pierre Émile).] Peb's Equine Comedy. 150 Hilarious Cartoons of Horses . . . and Their, Alas, Poor Human Fans From The Morning Telegraph and Daily Racing Form. New York, Random House [1957] 1 v. (unpaged) *"First printing."*

BELMONT (August). Nursery Stud Thoroughbreds. Property of August Belmont, Lexington, Kentucky. [New York, Polhemus] 1902. 177 p. illus. *Library has the catalog for 1906 also.*

BELMONT (August). Nursery Stud Yearlings. 1920. Bred by Major August Belmont in France and Kentucky. E. F. Simms, Henry Oliver. [Lexington, Ky., Cromwell, 1920] 49 p.

BELMONT (August). Reprint of Catalogue and Account of Sale and Dispersion of the Nursery Stud. Presented to Pierre Lorillard With Compliments of the Owner's Sons, Perry Belmont, August Belmont, Oliver H. P. Belmont. [n.p., n.d.] 1 v. (unpaged) front. (port.), plates.

Hand-lettered and hand-colored title page. The catalogue includes an account first printed in the *Spirit of the Times* in 1891-92 of Mr. Belmont's breeding theories, a description of the Nursery Stud Farm at Babylon, Long Island, and the sale of the thoroughbred horses.

BERENGER (Richard). The History and Art of Horsemanship. By Richard Berenger . . . London, Davies, 1771. 2 v. in 1. front., plates.

BERTERÈCHE DE MENDITTE (Pierre Jean Baptiste Édouard, Comte de). Les Courses de Résistance. Par Comte de Berterèche de Menditte. Clermont-Ferrand, Bellet, 1903. xx, 146 p.

[BERTRAM (James Glass).] Sporting Anecdotes Being Anecdotal Annals, Descriptions, Tales and Incidents of Horse-Racing, Betting, Card-Playing, Pugilism, Gambling, Cock-Fighting, Pedestrianism, Fox-Hunting, Angling, Shooting, and Other Sports. Now First Collected and Edited by "Ellangowan." London, Hamilton, 1889. 352 p.

BERTRAND (Léon). L'Hippodrome. Annales des Courses en France. Années 1845-1856. Publié sur les Documents de la Société d'Encouragement et du Ministère de l'Agriculture et du Commerce, par M. Léon Bertrand . . . Paris, au Bureau du Journal des Chasseurs, 1851-56. 2 v. *No more published?*

BETTS (Tony). [Pseud.] Across the Board. By Tony Betts. New York, Citadel [1956] 320 p. illus. *Real name: Anthony Zito.*

[BINDLEY (Charles).] A Treatise on the Proper Condition for All Horses. By Harry Hieover [pseud.] . . . Third Edition. London, Newby, 1857. xiv, 204 p. 2 plates by the author.

BIRCH (Frank Louis). Pedigrees of 150 Leading Winners 1912-1925. (Compiled by F. L. Birch) . . . London, Thoroughbred Breeders Association [1926] xii, 44 p.

BIRCH (Frank Louis) and Birch (Franklin Edwin). Pedigrees of 400 Leading Winners 1912-1946. Compiled by F. L. and F. E. Birch. Introduction by the Earl of Rosebery . . . London, Thoroughbred Breeders Association, 1947. xxxv, 129 p.

BIRCH (Franklin Edwin). Pedigrees of Leading Winners 1947-1953. Compiled by F. E. Birch . . . London, Thoroughbred Breeders Association, 1954. xxv, 51 p.

BIRCH (John). Examples of Stables, Hunting-Boxes, Kennels, Racing Establishments, etc. By John Birch . . . London, Blackwood, 1892. 64 p. plates (part fold.)

BIRD (Thomas Henry). Admiral Rous and the English Turf, 1795-1877. By T. H. Bird. London, Putnam [1939] x, 331 [1] p. front. (port.), illus., ports.

BLACK (Robert). Horse-Racing in England. A Synoptical Review. By Robert Black . . . London, Bentley, 1893. xv, 356 p.

BLACK (Robert). Horse-Racing in France. A History. By Robert Black . . . London, Low, 1886. x [1] 387 p. *Bibliography: p. [xi]*

BLACK (Robert). The Jockey Club and Its Founders in Three Periods. By Robert Black . . . London, Smith, 1891. x [1] 420 p.

BLAINE (Delabere Pritchett). An Encyclopaedia of Rural Sports, or Complete Account (Historical, Practical, and Descriptive) of Hunting, Shooting, Fishing, Racing, etc. etc. By Delabere P. Blaine . . . A New Edition, Revised and Corrected. Illustrated by Above Six Hundred Engravings on Wood by R. Branston From Drawings by Leech, Alken, T. Landseer, Dickes, etc. London, Longmans, 1870. xiii, 1246 p. illus., plates.

BLAKE (Charles W.). Caps and Jackets of the Modern Turf. Edited by Chas. W. Blake, Illustrated by John Sturgess. [London] Strand Publishing Co. [1885] 1 v. (unpaged) 16 plates (col.) *48 owners represented.*

BLANC (Edmond). Haras de Jardy à M. Edmond Blanc. [n.p.] 1905. 92 p. illus., charts (fold.) *Tipped in: "La Fouilleuse. Chevaux à l'Entraînement Appartenant à M. Edmond Blanc." [n.p., n.d.]*

BLANCHARD (Elizabeth Amis Cameron) and Wellman (Manly Wade). The Life and Times of Sir Archie. The Story of America's Greatest Thoroughbred, 1805-1833. By Elizabeth Amis Cameron Blanchard and Manly Wade Wellman. Chapel Hill, N. C., University of North Carolina Press [1958] xiii, 232 p. front. (col.), plates (part col.)

BLAND (Ernest). Flat-Racing Since 1900. Edited by Ernest Bland With a Foreword by the Earl of Rosebery . . . London, Dakers [1950] xii, 339 (i.e. 355) p. illus., ports., tables.

BLEW (William Charles Arlington). A History of Steeple-Chasing. By William C. A. Blew . . . With 28 Illustrations Chiefly Drawn by Henry Alken, 12 of Which Are Coloured by Hand. London, Nimmo, 1901. xii, 334 p. plates (part col.) *Appendix: Colours of Riders, p. 311.*

BLEW (William Charles Arlington). Racing. Famous Racehorses, Horse Owners, Trainers, Jockeys, Steeplechasing, Bookmakers, Betting Men, Turf Finance, Touts, and Tipsters, etc. By W. A. C. Blew . . . London, Everett, 1900. 215 p.

BLINKHOOLIE. *See* ALLISON (William).

The BLOOD-HORSE. Devoted to the Turf. Lexington, Ky., 1928- . illus. weekly. *Library has: 1928 to date. Monthly September 1928–May 1929, weekly thereafter.*

The BLOOD-HORSE. Five Years of Speed (1945-1949) and a Supplement Covering the First Six Months of 1950. A Register of Sires and Dams of Horses Winning in Record Time on North American Race Courses. Compiled and Published by The Blood-Horse. Lexington, Ky. [1950] 50 p.

The BLOOD-HORSE. Sires of American Thoroughbreds. Revised Edition . . . [Lexington, Ky.] 1951. 151 p.

The BLOOD-HORSE. Stakes Winners of . . . Lexington, Ky., 1929- . *Library has: 1940, 1941, 1947, 1949, 1940-50 (bound together), 1951.*

The BLOOD-HORSE. Stallion Register. A Compilation of Pedigrees, Racing and Stud Records of Thoroughbred Stallions at Service in North America, Together With Various Other Pertinent Information. Compiled and Published by The Blood-Horse. Lexington, Ky., 1950. vi, 191 p. illus.

The BLOOD-HORSE. Stallion Register and Mating Book. A Looseleaf Compilation of Pedigrees, Racing and Stud Records of Thoroughbred Stallions at Service in North America, Together With Various Other Pertinent Information. Compiled and Published by The Blood-Horse, Edited by Mrs. Joe H. Palmer. Lexington, Ky. [1954] 1 v. (loose-leaf) *Revised annually.*

The BLOOD-HORSE. Thoroughbred Broodmare Records, 1935-1939. Compiled and Published for the Subscribers by The Blood-Horse. Lexington, Ky., 1940. xiv, 846 p. *Of 250 copies, 211 were for subscribers.*

The BLOOD-HORSE. Thoroughbred Sires and Dams . . . Compiled and Published by The Blood-Horse. Lexington, Ky., 1941- . annual. *Library has: 1941 to date.*

The BLOODSTOCK Breeder's Review. Edited and Published by The British Bloodstock Agency. London, 1912- . illus. quarterly (April, July, October, December) 1912-18; annual 1919 to date. *Library has: 1912 to date.*

BLOSSOM (Henry Martyn). Checkers. A Hard-Luck Story. By Henry M. Blossom, Jr. Chicago, Stone, 1904. 239 p. illus.

BLUNT (Lady Anne). Bedouin Tribes of the Euphrates. By Lady Anne Blunt. Edited, With a Preface and Some Account of the Arabs and Their Horses by W. S. B. Map and Sketches by the Author. New York, Harper, 1879. 445 p. front., plates, fold. map and table. *W. S. B.: Wilfred Scawen Blunt. Full name: Anne Isabella Noel (King Noel) Blunt, Baroness Wentworth.*

BOARDMAN (Samuel Lane). Handbook of the Turf. A Treasury of Information for Horsemen Embracing a Compendium of All Racing and Trotting Rules; Laws of the States in Their Relation to Horses and Racing; a Glossary of Scientific Terms; the Catch-Words and Phrases Used by Great Drivers, With Miscellaneous Information About Horses, Tracks and Racing. By Samuel L. Boardman . . . New York, Judd, 1900. x, 303 p.

BOBIŃSKI (Kazimierz). Family Tables of Race Horses. Compiled by Captain Kazimierz Bobiński . . . London, Zamoyski, 1953. 1 v. (unpaged) tables. *Index in separate volume; 1st supp. 1954, 2d supp. 1955, 3d supp. 1956, 4th supp. 1957.*

BORDEN (Spencer). The Arab Horse. By Spencer Borden. Many Illustrations From Photographs. New York, Doubleday, 1906. xx, 104 p. front., plates. *Preface by Henry Fairfield Osborne.*

BOUCAUT (Sir James Penn). The Arab, the Horse of the Future. By the Hon. Sir James Penn Boucaut . . . Preface by Sir Walter Gilbey . . . London, Gay, 1905. xx, 249 p. front., plates.

BOUCAUT (Sir James Penn). The Arab, the Thoroughbred, and the Turf. By the Hon. Sir James Penn Boucaut . . . With a Foreword by the Rt. Hon. Sir George H. Reid . . . London, Bird, 1912. xi, 222 p.

BOUYSSONIE (Jean) and Capitan (Louis). . . . Un Atelier d'Art Préhistorique Limeuil, Son Gisement à Gravures sur Pierres de l'Age du Renne. Par le Docteur L. Capitan . . . et l'Abbé Jean Bouyssonie . . . Paris, Nourry, 1924. 41 p. (Publications de l'Institut International d'Anthropologie, No. 1) *Descriptive text with plates following on unnumbered pages.*

BOVILL (Mai). 'Roddy Owen' . . . A Memoir by His Sister Mai Bovill and G. R. Askwith . . . London, Murray, 1897. viii [1] 279 p.   front. (port.), plates, ports., maps.

BRADLEY (Edward Riley). Catalogue of Thoroughbreds Native and Imported. Idle Hour Stock Farm, Lexington, Kentucky, U. S. A. E. R. Bradley, Proprietor, 1919. [Lexington, Ky., Cromwell, 1919] 126 p. illus. *Illustrations unpaged at end.*

BRADLEY (Edward Riley). Idle Hour Stock Farm Company, Inc. Lexington, Kentucky, U. S. A. Catalogue of Blood Stock Holdings, 1922. [n.p., 1922?] 157 p. illus. *Includes Dairy Department.*

BRADLEY (Edward Riley). Idle Hour Stock Farm Company, Incorporated. Lexington, Kentucky, U. S. A. Catalogue of Blood Stock Holdings, 1926. Established 1906. E. R. Bradley. [Cleveland, O., Judson, 1926?]   157 p. front. (port.), illus. *"Compiled and edited by Thos. S. Bohne."*

The BREEDERS' Sales Company. Thoroughbred Sales Catalogue. Lexington, Ky., 1944- . semi-annual. *Library has: 1944 to date. Issued for summer and fall sales annually.*

BREITIGAM (Gerald B.). Morvich. An Autobiography of a Horse. By Gerald B. Breitigam . . . New York, Rotary Press [1922] 64 p. illus.

BRIGNAC (François de). Mères de Gagnants de Toutes les Courses Plates Courues en France de 1916 à 1940. Présenté par François de Brignac . . . Paris, Pailhé, 1942. 283 [1] p.

[BRIGNAC (François de).] Mères de Gagnants en France 1941 à 1955 Présenté par G. C. Sale et M. R. Ross (British Bloodstock Agency). London, 1956. iv, 316 p.

BRINLEY (Francis). Life of William T. Porter. By Francis Brinley. New York, Appleton, 1860. vii, 273 p. front. (port.)

The BRITISH Racehorse. London, 1949- . illus. Issued five times a year. *Library has: 1949 to date. Cover illus. (col.) notable.*

BROLASKI (Harry). Easy Money. Being the Experiences of a Reformed Gambler. All Gambling Tricks Exposed. By Harry Brolaski. Cleveland, O., Searchlight Press, 1911. 328 p. front. (port.), illus., ports., facs.

BROOKE (Geoffrey Francis Heremon). Training Young Horses to Jump. By Geoffrey Brooke . . . Preface by Colonel J. Vaughan . . . With Three Plates in Colour and 34 Illustrations in Black and White. New York, Dutton, 1913. xi, 118 p. front. (col.), illus.

BROWN (C. F.). The Turf Expositor; Containing the Origin of Horse Racing, Breeding for the Turf, Training, Trainers, Jockeys; Cocktails, and the System of Cocktail Racing Illustrated; the Turf and Its Abuses; the Science of Betting Money, so as Always to Come Off a Winner, Elucidated by a Variety of Examples; the Rules and Laws of Horse Racing; and Every Other Information Connected With the Operations of the Turf. By C. F. Brown. London, Sherwood, 1829. x, 180 p.

BROWN (Sara Lowe). Rarey, the Horse's Master and Friend. Sara Lowe Brown. Reprinted From Ohio Archaeological and Historical Society Publications, October, 1916. Columbus, O., Heer, 1916. 57 p. front. (port.), illus., facs.

BROWN (Thomas). Biographical Sketches and Authentic Anecdotes of Horses, and the Allied Species. Illustrated by Portraits, on Steel, of Celebrated and Remarkable Horses. By Captain Thomas Brown . . . Edinburgh, Lizars, 1830. 580 p. plates.

[BROWNE (Hablot Knight).] The Derby Day. By Phiz. The Road and the Course. A Series of Eight Illustrations . . . London, Fores [n.d.] Eight double-page plates in color.

BROWNE (T. H.). History of the English Turf. 1904-1930. By Captain T. H. Browne . . . Supplementary to History of the English Turf by Sir T. A. Cook. London, Virtue, 1931. 2 v. (paged continuously) illus.

BRUCE (Benjamin Gratz). Memoir of Lexington. By B. G. Bruce. [n.p., 188–] 51 p. *First appeared in* The Livestock Record, *v. 12 (1880), p. 376; v. 13 (1881), p. 104.*

BRUCE (Sanders Dewees). The American Stud Book: Containing Full Pedigrees of All the Imported Thoroughbred Stallions and Mares, With Their Produce . . . From the Earliest Accounts of Racing in America, to the End of the Year

BRUCE (Sanders Dewees). *Continued:*
1867 . . . With an Appendix . . . By S. D. Bruce . . .
Volume I, A to L. Chicago, Myers, 1868. 649 p. 20 plates.
Vol. I only published. Plates lacking in Library's copy.

BRUCE (Sanders Dewees). The American Stud Book: Containing Full Pedigrees of All the Imported Thorough-bred Stallions and Mares, With Their Produce . . . From the Earliest Account of Racing in America to the End of the Year 1872 . . . With an Appendix . . . By S. D. Bruce . . . New York, the author, 1873. 2 v.

BRUCE (Sanders Dewees). The Horse-Breeder's Guide and Hand Book. Embracing One Hundred Tabulated Pedigrees of the Principal Sires, With Full Performances of Each and Best of Their Get, Covering the Season of 1883, With a Few of the Distinguished Dead Ones. By S. D. Bruce . . . [New York] Turf, Field and Farm, 1883. xii, 205 p.

BRUCE (Sanders Dewees). The Thoroughbred Horse. His Origin, How to Breed and How Select Him. With the Horse Breeders' Guide. Embracing One Hundred Tabulated Pedigrees of the Principal Sires, With Full Performances of Each and Best of Their Get, Covering the Season of 1892. By S. D. Bruce . . . New York, Turf, Field and Farm, 1892. xii, 316 [2] p.

BRUNELL (Frank H.). Chicago Racing Form. (Special Edition) Charts of American Racing. Edited by F. H. Brunell . . . With a Full and Complete Index. Chicago, Daily Racing Form Co., 1898- . *Library has: 1898.*

BRUNELL (Frank H.). Racing Form (Monthly Edition) Charts of American Racing From Jan. 1, 1900 to [Dec. 31, 1924] Inclusive. Edited by F. H. Brunell . . . With a Full and Complete Index. Chicago, Daily Racing Form Publishing Co., 1900-1924. *Library has: 1900, 1903, 1907-09, 1912-24.* *See* TRIANGLE Publications.

BRYON (Thomas J.). Calendrier des Courses de Chevaux, ou "Racing Calendar" Français; Relation Détailée de Toutes les Courses (à Peu d'Exceptions) Qui Ont Eu Lieu en France Depuis 1776 Jusqu'à la Fin de 1833, par T. Bryon . . . Paris, Galignani, 1834. cxix, 612 p. *Library has: v. 1 only.*

[BRYON (Thomas J.)] The French Stud-Book Containing in French and English the Pedigree of Every Horse, Mare, etc., of Note Known in This Country Together With Some Account of the Foreign Horses and Mares From Whence Is Derived the Present Breed of Racers in France and England. Dedicated by Permission to His Royal Highness the Dauphin. Paris, Didot, 1828. xxiii, 104, 104 p. *Opposite pages numbered in duplicate. Text in French and English. Added title page in French.*

BRYON (Thomas J.). Manuel de l'Amateur des Courses, Contenant les Règles qui Sont Observées en Angleterre aux Courses de Chevaux; Suivi des Calculs Mathématiques de T. Gard, Pour Parier et Servir de Guide aux Amateurs de Courses de Paris . . . Thomas Bryon. [Paris, Firmin Didot, 1827] xvii, 90 [1] p. front., tables. *Text in English and French. Added title page in English.*

BUCK (Charles Neville). Sandollar. By Charles Neville Buck. New York, Chelsea House [1926] 308 p.

BUCK (Frederick Silas). Horse Race Betting. A Complete Account of Pari-Mutuel and Bookmaking Operations. By Fred S. Buck. New York, Greenberg [1946] x, 149 p. illus., tables, facs.

BUCK (H. A.) and Burke (J. J.). Horses in Training. Embracing All Horses Engaged in Stakes on Eastern Courses

BUCK (H. A.). *Continued:*
Including Two-Year-Olds. Published by H. A. Buck and J. J. Burke . . . New York, [18 -] *Library has: 1891, 1898-1908, 1910, 1928-42.*

BUCKMAN-LINARD (Sara). My Horse; My Love. By Sara Buckman-Linard . . . London, Unwin, 1898. xii, 227 p. illus., facs.

BUDGELL (Eustace). A Poem Upon His Majesty's Late Journey to Cambridge and Newmarket. By Eustace Budgell Esq; of the Inner Temple. London, Motte, 1728. 20 p.

BUFFARD (Paul Jules Victor). L'Élevage et les Courses de Chevaux en France et à l'Étranger. Étude d'Économie Financière et Rurale par Paul Buffard . . . Paris, Boyer, 1900. 260 p.

BULLETIN Hebdomadaire . . . du Journal des Haras, des Chasses et des Courses de Chevaux. Paris, 1834-35. Nos. 1-53 (Apr. 6, 1834–Mar. 29, 1835) *Editor: Le Comte Jean Baptiste Guillaume Achille de Montendre.*

BURCH (Preston Morris). Training Thoroughbred Horses. By Preston M. Burch With the Assistance of Alex Bower. Lexington, Ky., The Blood-Horse, 1953. x, 124 p. illus. *First appeared in* The Blood-Horse.

BURROWS (George Thomas). Cheshire Sports and Sportsmen. Including a History of the Chester Cup. By G. T. Burrows . . . Chester [England] Phillipson [1924?] 188 p. *Printed in newspaper columns, 1 column each page.*

[BURTON (John).] Anecdotes Relating to the Antiquity and Progress of Horse-Races, for Above Two Thousand Years. London, Bell, 1769. 35 p.

BUSBEY (Hamilton). Recollections of Men and Horses. By Hamilton Busbey . . . New York, Dodd, 1907. xii, 354 p. front. (port.), plates, ports.

BUSBEY (Hamilton). The Trotting and Pacing Horse in America. By Hamilton Busbey. New York, Macmillan, 1904. x, 369 p. front. (port.), ports. (American Sportsman's Library)

C. W. *See* PORTRAITS of Broodmares . . .

CADIOT (Pierre Juste). Roaring in Horses: Its Pathology and Treatment. By P. J. Cadiot . . . Translated From the Original by Thomas J. Watt Dollar . . . Illustrated by Eighteen Figures. New York, Jenkins, 1892. 78 p. illus.

The CALCUTTA Turf Club. The Racing Calendar . . . Races Past Under C. T. C. and W. I. T. C. Rules. Published by the Calcutta Turf Club . . . Calcutta, Spink, 18 - . *Library has: v. 19 (1906-07); v. 25 (1912-13)*

The CANADIAN Thoroughbred Stud Book . . . Compiled and Edited in the Office of the Canadian National Livestock Records. Ottawa, Canada. Published by The Canadian Thoroughbred Horse Society . . . Ottawa [19 -] *Library has: v. 7 (1942)*

CANTI (Enrico). Nel Mondo del Galoppo. La Storia del Puro Sangue. [Milano, Sabaini, 1950] 2 v. illus. *Special edition of 200 copies.*

CARSON (James Crawford Ledlie). The Form of the Horse, as It Lies Open to the Inspection of the Ordinary Observer. By James C. L. Carson . . . Dublin, Robertson, 1859. 139 p.

CARTER (William Giles Harding). The Horses of the World. The Development of Man's Companion in War Camp, on

CARTER (William Giles Harding). *Continued:*
Farm, in the Marts of Trade, and in the Field of Sports. By
Major General William Harding Carter, U. S. A. Paintings
by Edward Herbert Miner. With 95 Illustrations, Including
24 Pages of Color. Washington, National Geographic Society, 1923. 118 p. illus. (part col.)

CARVER (William). Practical Horse Farrier; or The Traveller's
Pocket Companion. Showing the Best Method to Preserve
the Horse in Health . . . Second Edition . . . Embellished
With Three Engravings. By William Carver . . . Philadelphia, McCarty, 1820. xxv, 251 p. plates.

CARY (Richard Leander). Sporting Ballads and Other Verse.
By R. L. Cary, Jr. "Hyder Ali" Chicago, Bentley [1903]
326 p. illus.

CARY (Richard Leander). Tales of the Turf and "Rank Out-
siders." By Richard L. Cary, Jr. (Hyder Ali) With Thirty-
One Original Illustrations by Gean Smith. Chicago, Schulte
[1891] 166 p. illus. *Poems.*

CATALOGUES (Miscellaneous). 1879-1886.
Bound together: Dixiana (yearling sale) 1885; Grinstead, J. A.
(bloodstock sale) 1882; Grinstead, J. A. (bloodstock sale) May
1, 1882; Bethune, J. G. (thoroughbred sale) June 17, 1879;
Keene, S. Y. (yearling sale) June 17, 1879; Sanford, M. H.
(yearling sale) June 19, 1879; Grinstead, J. A. (bloodstock sale)
n.d.; Sanford, M. H. (yearling sale) May 27, 1880; Grinstead,
J. A. (bloodstock sale) May 6, 1884; Nursery Stud (bloodstock
sale) June 1, 1883; Elmendorf Stud (stud book) 1882; Combi-
nation sale, May 12, 1884; Elmendorf Stud (yearling sale) May
13, 1885; Dixiana (colts and fillies) May 10, 1884; Woodburn
Farm (thoroughbred stock sale) May 14, 1885; Clay & Wood-
ford (yearling sale) May 12, 1885; Withers, Alfred (imported
stock sale) 1886; Rancocas Stud (yearling sale) June 15, 1885;
Belle Meade (yearling sale) April 30, 1885; Young, Milton
(race horses sale) December 19, 1885; Fleetwood Stud (stud
book) 1885; Elmendorf Stud (yearling sale) May 19, 1883;
Chinn & Morgan (thoroughbred stock sale) February 24, 1884.

CATER (Philip). The Great St. Derby Day; or, Evenings With My Lords Spiritual and Temporal, About the Horses and the Asses of the English Race Course . . . By Philip Cater . . . [n. p., 1850?] 64 p.

[CATERS (Baron Louis de).] Les Courses de Chevaux. Par Saint Georges. Préface de Fernand Vandérem. Ouvrage Orné de 64 Pages d'Illustrations Photographiques Hors Texte. Paris, Lafitte [1912] xii, 557 p. front. (port.), plates, ports. (Sports-Bibliothèque) *"Encyclopédie, Definitions: p. 411."* *"Carnet du Vétérinaire par M-J. Almy: p. 547."*

CAVAILHON (Édouard). Les Chevaux de Courses en 1889. Par Édouard Cavailhon. Tous les Renseignements Désirables sur les Chevaux, Qui Doivent Courier en 1889, Se Trouvent Dans Ce Volume. Dessins de Tristan Lacroix, Cotlison, Desmoulins. Paris [Balitout] 1889. 368 [1] p. front. (ports.), ports.

CAVAILHON (Édouard). Les Courses et les Paris. Paris, Dentu, 1885. 323 [1] p.

CAVAILHON (Édouard). . . . Les Haras de France. Les Haines Contre les Courses. Les Deux Haras de M. Lupin; le Haras de Lonray; le Haras de la Celle-Saint-Cloud; le Haras de la Chapelle; le Haras de Senailly; le Haras de Bois-Roussell. Variétés: Les Entraîneurs Qui Boivent; Compiègne et Chantilly; la Marquise Sportive. Paris, Dentu, 1886. xcvi, 272 p.

Il CAVALLO. Rivista Mensile Illustrata Disport e Allevamento Ippico . . . Milano, Societa Editrice Ippica, 1921- . illus. *Library has: v. 1-6 (1921-26)*

CAWTHORNE (George James) and Herod (Richard S.). Royal Ascot, Its History and Its Associations. By George James Cawthorne and Richard S. Herod. Revised and Enlarged . . . London, Treherne, 1902. xiii, 386 p. front. (port.), illus.

CECIL. *See* TONGUE (Cornelius).

CHAMBERLIN (Harry Dwight). Riding and Schooling Horses. By Harry D. Chamberlin . . . Introduction by Hon. John Cudahy. New York, Derrydale Press [1934] xiv, 199 [1] p. illus.

CHAMPION DE CRESPIGNY (Sir Claude). Forty Years of a Sportsman's Life. By Sir Claude Champion de Crespigny . . . London, Boon [1910] 318 p. front. (port.), ports.

CHAMPION DE CRESPIGNY (Sir Claude). Memoirs of Sir Claude Champion de Crespigny . . . Edited by George A. B. Dewar. With a Preface and Notes by the Duke of Beaufort . . . Second Edition. London, Lawrence, 1896. xiv, 371 [1] p. front. (port.)

CHAPMAN (John Kemble). Chapman's Racing Record and Sunday Times Sporting Companion for 1849-50, Carefully Compiled From Original Returns . . . The Performances of Two Year Olds in England, Ireland, and Scotland in 1849; the Results of Handicaps and Cups; the Winners of Royal Plates in 1849; Entries for the Derby, Oaks, and St. Leger, 1850 . . . Results of Matches in 1849; Racing Fixtures for 1850; Laws of Racing and Betting . . . Published for the Proprietors of "The Sunday Times," by John K. Chapman . . . [London, 1849] 136 p.

CHAPUS (Eugène). Le Turf, ou Les Courses de Chevaux en France et en Angleterre. Par E. Chapus. Deuxième Édition. Paris, Hachette, 1854. 396 p. *"Vocabulaire des Termes les Plus Usités sur le Turf": p. 370-77.*

A CHELTONIAN. [Pseud.] Autobiographies of the Archers, William (père), Fred and Charlie. By a Cheltonian . . . London, Brookes [1885] 54 p. front. (port.)

[CHENY (John).] An Historical List, or Account of All the Horse-Matches Run, and of All the Plates and Prizes Run for in England . . . in . . . Containing the Names of the Owners of the Horses etc. That Have Run, as Above, and the Names and Colours of the Horses Also . . . With a List Also of the Principal Cock-Matches of the Kingdom in the Year Above, and Who Were the Winners and Losers of Them. London, the author, 1727-50. 24 v.

Ms note in 1727 volume: "This is the first volume of Cheny's Historical List of Horse Matches Run—The series extended to twenty-four volumes ending at the year 1750. The work was continued by Reginald Heber of Fullwood Rents, Holborn. His first volume is for the year 1751. At page 236 of his third volume containing the list of matches run in 1753, there is an advertisement of his having 'purchased all the remaining Stock of Books of the late Mr. John Cheney.' I have not yet been able to ascertain the number of volumes to which Heber's work extended. I have the eleventh volume being a list of the Matches run in 1761. (Signed) E. D. 7 July 1885" The volume for 1737 contains the following ms note which appears to be in the same hand as that of the note in the 1727 volume: "A complete set of these books should contain 24 years. See Advertisement at the end of Heber's 5th volume. Heber's Volumes begin with 1751. If Cheny's ended with 1750 then they would begin with 1727 so that there would be five volumes wanting prior to these and seven subsequent."

CHESTER (Walter T.). Chester's Complete Trotting and Pacing Record, Containing Summaries of All Races Trotted or Paced in the United States or Canada, From the Earliest Dates to the Close of 1883. Compiled by Walter T. Chester. New York, 1884. 990 p. illus.

CHETWYND (Sir George). Racing Reminiscences and Experiences of the Turf. By Sir George Chetwynd . . . London, Longmans, 1891. 2 v.

CHIFNEY (Samuel). Genius Genuine, by Samuel Chifney, of Newmarket. A Fine Part in Riding a Race, Known Only to

CHIFNEY (Samuel). *Continued:*

the Author. Why There Are so Few Good Runners; or Why the Turf Horses Degenerate. A Guide to Recover Them to Their Strength and Speed . . . Likewise a Full Account of the Prince's Horse Escape Running at Newmarket on the 20th and 21st Days of October 1791. With Other Interesting Particulars. [London, Sheery] Sold Only for the Author, 232 Picadilly [1795] vii, 170 p.

Opp. title page: "From unforeseen circumstances the author has been prevented publishing this book at the time intended."

CHIFNEY (Samuel). Genius Genuine, by Samuel Chifney, of Newmarket. Containing a Statement of a Fine Part in Riding a Race; Known Only to the Author: Why the Turf Horses Degenerate, and How to Recover Them to Their Strength and Speed . . . Likewise, a Full Account of the Prince's Horse Escape's Running at Newmarket, on the 20th and 21st Days of October 1791; With Other Interesting Particulars. Twelve Years Ago the Author Would Not for One Thousand Guineas Have Made Known to Anyone Person the Information Contained in This Publication Respecting the Condition of Horses. London, Printed for the Author; and Sold by E. Chifney . . . 1803. vii, 130 p. *"Price £ 2."*

CHIFNEY (Samuel). The Narrative or Statement of Samuel Chifney, (Rider for Life to His Royal Highness the Prince of Wales) Containing a Full Account of the Running of His Royal Highness's Horse Escape, at Newmarket on the 20th and 21st days of October 1791, With Many Other Interesting Particulars; Addressed More Especially to Those Gentlemen Connected With the Turf; and Also to the Public in General. London, Taylor [1801?] 97 p.

Ms note: "May 28, 1933. This vol. is really the second edition. The first or (suppressed) edition is marked by the date of the affidavit Aug. 19, 1880. A copy of this first appeared in Rosebery sale June 28, 1933. R. J. T."

CHINN (Philip Thompson). Himyar Stud Incorporated. Lexington, Ky., Phil T. Chinn. [Lexington, Ky., Welsh] 1927. 141 p.

CHINN (Philip Thompson). Himyar Stud. Lexington, Kentucky. Apply to Mr. Phil T. Chinn . . . [Lexington, Ky., Welsh, 1920] 1 v. (unpaged)

CHISMON (William). Stallion Record: Being a Dictionary of Stallions of the XIX Century, Whose Names Are Found in Modern Pedigrees. Compiled by Wm. Chismon. Liverpool, Ratcliffe, 1901. 274 [3] p.

CHURCHILL (Seton). Betting and Gambling. By Major Seton Churchill . . . Second Edition . . . London, Nisbet, 1894. 212 p.

[CLARK (Bracy).] A Short History of the Celebrated Race-Horse, Eclipse. [London, Richards, 1835?] 4 p.

CLARK (Bracy). A Short History of the Horse, and Progress of Horse Knowledge. By Bracy Clark . . . London, Adlard, 1824. 56 p. front., diagr. *Bound in: Printed statement of Clark's intended publishing enterprises. Ms. date: 11/15-1809.*

CLARK (Bracy). Veterinary Pamphlets.

Cover title of eight pamphlets bound together. 1. An Essay on the Knowledge of the Ancients Respecting the Art of Shoeing the Horse, and of the Probable Period of the Commencement of This Art. By Bracy Clark . . . London, the author, 1831. 36 p. front. 2. On the Knowledge of the Age of the Horse by His Teeth. With Remarks. By Bracy Clark . . . London, Richards, 1826. 16 p. illus., tables. 3. Hippiatria; or the Surgery and Medicine of Horses. By Bracy Clark . . . London, Charles Clark, 1838. 50 p. 4. Pharmacopoeia Equina; or New Pharmacopoeia for Horses. By Bracy Clark . . . 3d ed. London, the author, 1833. 41 p. front. *Supplementary matter paged separately: 7 p.* 5. A Description of the Gripes of Horses, and of a Better Mode of Treating It; Also, Human Cholera Explained;

CLARK (Bracy). *Continued:*
Shewing Its Identity With the Above, and a More Successful Manner of Treating It; Its History, etc. By Bracy Clark . . . 2d ed. London [Mackintosh] 1837. 28 [2] p. 6. Disorders of the Foot of the Horse. By Bracy Clark . . . London, 1839- . *Variously paged. Essays on the same subject dating from 1834 to 1851.* 7. On the Vices of Horses. By B. C. London, 1839. *Variously paged.* 8. On Casting Horses for Operations With a Description of the New Casting Hobbles . . . By Bracy Clark . . . 2d ed. London, 1842. 4 p. plate. *First printed: 1814.*

[CLARK (Charles).] The Flying Scud. A Sporting Novel. By the Author of "Charlie Thornhill" . . . London, Bentley, 1867. 2 v.

CLAY (Mrs. John M.). The Sport of Kings. Racing Stories by Mrs. John M. Clay . . . New York, Broadway Publishing Co. [1912] 90 p. *Full name: Josephine Russell Clay.*

CLER (Albert). La Comédie à Cheval ou Manies et Travers du Monde Équestre, Jockey-Club, Cavalier, Maquignon, Olympique, etc., par Albert Cler. Illustrée par Mm. Charlet, T. Johannot, Eug. Giraud et A. Giroux. Paris, Bourdin [1842] 155 (i.e. 153) [1] p.

COATEN (Arthur Wells). Famous Horses of the British Turf. 1919-1923. Photography by W. A. Rouch. Edited by Arthur W. Coaten. London, Welbecson Press [1930] 95 p. plates.

COATEN (Arthur Wells). Famous Horses of the British Turf. 1924-1933. An Annual Illustrated Review of Racing in Great Britain. Edited by Arthur W. Coaten. London, Welbecson Press [1924-33] 10 v. plates. *No more published.*

COBBETT (Martin Richard). Racing Life and Racing Characters. By Martin Cobbett . . . London, Sands, 1903. viii, 344 p. ports. *Ports. are interspersed with advertising at the end of the text, unpaged.*

COBBETT (Martin Richard). Sporting Notions of Present Days and Past. By Martin Cobbett ("Geraint" of the Referee) . . . Edited by Alice Cobbett. London, Sands, 1908. vii, 366 p.

COBBETT (Martin Richard). Wayfaring Notions. By Martin Cobbett ("Geraint" of the "Referee") . . . Edited by Alice Cobbett. With a Portrait and Memoir of the Author. London, Sands, 1906. xxxii, 331 p. front. (port.)

CODRINGTON (William Stephen). Know Your Horse. A Guide to Selection and Care in Health and Disease. By Lt. Col. W. S. Codrington . . . New York, Coward-McCann [1958] xiv, 180 p. front., illus. *"New revised edition." Foreword by Pat Smythe.*

COLE (Edward W.). Racing Maxims and Methods of "Pittsburg Phil" [George E. Smith] Complete System as Employed by the Most Successful Speculator in the History of the American Turf. Condensed Wisdom of Twenty Years' Experience on the Track From the Only Personal Interviews Ever Given by the Famous Horseman. Edited and Published by Edward W. Cole . . . [New York, the author, 1908] 174 p. front. (port.), facs.

[COLLINS (Charles James?).] Bits of Turf. By Priam. London, "Racing Times" [1853] 95 p.

COLLINS (Charles James?). Dick Diminy; or, The Life and Adventures of a Jockey. By Priam (C. J. Collins). New and Revised Edition. London, Ward [1855] 256 p. *"Second edition."*

COLLINS (Digby). The Horse-Trainer's and Sportsman's Guide; With Additional Considerations on the Duties of Grooms, on Purchasing Bloodstock, and on Veterinary Examination. By Digby Collins. London, Longmans, 1865. xi, 254 p.

COLLINS (George E.). Tales of Pink and Silk. By George E. Collins ("Nimrod Junior") Illustrated by G. H. Jalland. London, Vinton, 1900. 136 p. front. (col.), illus.

"These stories have already appeared in the *Hull Weekly News,* and are now reprinted in collected form by permission of the proprietors."

COLOURS at a Glance of the Leading Owners . . . Manchester, the author [1889] 48 p. illus. (col.) *Cover title. Printed on one side only. "2nd edition revised and enlarged."*

[COLTON (Robert).] The Bye-Lanes and Downs of England, With Turf Scenes and Characters. By Sylvanus . . . London, Bentley, 1850. xvi, 348 p. front. (eng. port.)

COMMINGES (Marie Aymery, Comte de). Les Races Chevalines Françaises & Anglaises. Comte de Comminges. [Saumur] Robert [1913] 322 p. front. (map), plates. *"Bibliothèque de l'éleveur": p. 305-311.*

A COMPARATIVE View of the Form and Character of the English Racer and Saddle-Horse During the Last and Present Centuries. Illustrated by Eighteen Plates of Horses. London, Hookham, 1836. v, 153 p. plates.

COMSTOCK (Anthony). Gambling Outrages; or, Improving the Breed of Horses at the Expense of Public Morals. By Anthony Comstock . . . New York, American News Co., 1887. vii, 218 p.

CONSTABLE (Henry Strickland). Something About Horses, Sport and War. By H. Strickland Constable. London, Eden, 1891. [vii] 293 p.

CONTADES (Gérard, Comte de). Bibliographie Sportive. Les Courses de Chevaux en France (1651-1890) Comte G. de Contades. Paris, Rouquette, 1892. xxvi, 154 p. *"Tiré à 250 exemplaires . . . no. 67."*

COOK (Theodore Andrea). Eclipse & O'Kelly. Being a Complete History so Far as Is Known of That Celebrated English Thoroughbred Eclipse (1764-1789) of His Breeder the Duke of Cumberland & of His Subsequent Owners William Wildman, Dennis O'Kelly & Andrew O'Kelly Now for the First Time Set Forth From the Original Authorities & Family Memoranda. By Theodore Andrea Cook . . . London, Heinemann, 1907. xxx [1] 312 [1] p. front. (port.), plates.

COOK (Theodore Andrea). A History of the English Turf. By Theodore Andrea Cook . . . London, Virtue [1905?] 3 v. (paged continuously) illus.

COOPER (Edward Herbert). The Monk Wins. By Edward H. Cooper. Chicago, Stone, 1900. 351 p.

COOPER (Page). Great Horse Stories. Selected by Page Cooper. Drawings by Paul Brown. Garden City, N.Y., Doubleday, 1946. x, 366 p. illus. *"First edition."*

COOPER (Page) and Treat (Roger L.). Man o' War. By Page Cooper and Roger L. Treat . . . New York, Messner [1950] xiv, 230 p. illus., tables.

COPPERTHWAITE (R. H.). The Turf and the Racehorse Describing Trainers and Training, the Stud-Farm, the Sires and Brood-Mares of the Past and Present, and How to Breed and Rear the Racehorse. By R. H. Copperthwaite. London, Day, 1865. vi, 330 p.

CORBET (Henry). Tales and Traits of Sporting Life. By Henry Corbet. London, Rogerson, 1864. 202 p. front. (col.) *Added title page (col.)*

CORBIÈRE (Pierre). Étalons de Pur Sang de France. Paris, Legoupy, 1920- . *Library has: v. 1-3 only.*

COUSSELL (Ernest Edward). The Bruce Lowe Numbers of the Mares in Vol. XXI of the General Stud Book . . . Specially Compiled by E. E. Coussell for the International Horse Agency & Exchange . . . London, 1909. 268, 105 p. illus.

Pt. 1: Statistics. Pt. 2: "Photographs and tabulated figured pedigrees of nearly 50 of the leading stallions of the day. Together with many other particulars."

COUSTÉ (Henri Jean Paul). Une Foulée de Galop de Course. Deuxième Édition Augmentée d'une Étude sur les Fonctions et le Modèle de l'Arrière-Main. Réponses à le Critique. Paris, Lavauzelle, 1914. 84 p. illus., diagr.

COUSTÉ (Henri Jean Paul). Mechanics Applied to the Race Horse. (Une Foulée de Galop de Course) Second Edition. With a Study of the Construction and Functions of the Hind Legs. Replies to Criticisms. By Colonel H. Cousté. Translated by E. B. Cassatt. Paris, 1914, New York, 1916. 80 p. illus., diagr.

COX (Harding Edward de Fonblanque). The Amateur's Derby. A Sporting Novel. By Harding Cox . . . London, Cranton, 1924. 278 p.

COX (Harding Edward de Fonblanque). Chasing and Racing. Some Sporting Reminiscences. By Harding Cox. London, Lane, 1922. xiv, 282 p. front. (port.)

CRAFTY. See GÉRUSEZ (Victor).

CRAVEN (W. G.). The Royal Commission on the General Utility or Three-Parts Bred Horse. By W. G. Craven. London, Longmans, 1888. 23 p.

CREMIÈRE (Léon). Album du Centaure. 1866. Chevaux. [Paris] Cremière, 1866. 27 plates (col.) *Cover title.*

CRICKMORE (Henry G.). The American Turf, 1876. A Recapitulation of the Gross Earnings of All Sires, Horses & Stables, Number of Races Run, etc. Compiled by "Krik" of the New York World. [New York, Russell] 1877. 60 p.

[CRICKMORE (Henry G.).] Krik's Guide to the Turf. Part . . . Record of Races Run in the United States in . . . With Index . . . New York [1878-]

Library has: 1878-85. From 1878 to 1883 the guides were in 2 pts. bound together. In 1884-85 the guide was in one part only.

CRICKMORE (Henry G.). Racing Calendars . . . Compiled by H. G. Crickmore. New York, W. C. Whitney, Printer Not Publisher, 1901. 3 v. (1861-69)

CROSLAND (Thomas William Hodgson). Who Goes Racing. By T. W. H. Crosland . . . London, Collier, 1907. 189 p.

CULLEN (Clarence Louis). Taking Chances. By Clarence L. Cullen . . . New York, Log Cabin Press [1900?] 269 p.

The CULTIVATOR and Country Gentleman. Devoted to the Practise and Science of Agriculture and Horticulture at Large, and to All the Various Departments of Rural and Domestic Economy . . . Albany, N. Y., Tucker, 1866- . *Library has: v. 39 only (Jan. 1, 1874—Dec. 24, 1874) Title varies. Publisher varies.*

CULVER (Francis Barnum). Blooded Horses of Colonial Days. Class Horse Matches in America Before the Revolution. By Francis Barnum Culver. Baltimore, the author, 1922. 1 v. (variously paged) plates, facs. *"12 pages memorabilia following p. 96."*

CUMING (Edward William Dirom). British Sport Past and Present. By E. D. Cuming. With Illustrations by G. Denholm Armour. London, Hodder, 1909. xv, 271 p. plates (col.)

CURNIEU (Charles Louis Adélaïde Henri Mathevon, Baron de). Leçons de Science Hippique Générale ou, Traité Complet de l'Art de Connaitre, de Gouverner et d'Élever le Cheval. Par le B'on de Curnieu . . . Paris, Dumaine, 1855-60. 3 v. illus.

CUROT (Edmond). La Ferrure de Course du Galopeur & du Trotteur au Haras et à l'Entraînement. Anatomie—Physiologie—Hygiène—Pathologie du Pied. Par Ed. Curot . . . Préface de Frédéric Chapard . . . Avec 42 Illustrations. Paris, Laveur, 1908. xiv, 200 p. illus.

CUROT (Edmond). Galopeurs et Trotteurs. Hygiène—Élevage —Alimentation—Entraînement—Maladies. Par Ed. Curot . . . 72 Figures et Graphiques. Paris, Vigot, 1925. xvi, 623 p. illus.

CUROT (Edmond) and Fournier (Paul). Comment Nourrir le Pur Sang au Haras et à l'Entraînement? Par Ed. Curot . . . Paul Fournier (Ormonde) . . . Paris, Asselin, 1907. xv, 580 p.

CUROT (Edmond) and Fournier (Paul). Le Pur Sang. Hygiène, Lois Naturelles, Croisements. Élevage. Entraînement. Alimentation. Par Paul Fournier (Ormonde) . . . et Ed. Curot . . . Avec 26 Illustrations (Clichés du Sport Universel Illustré) Paris, Laveur, 1906. viii, 765 p. illus.

CURR (Edward Mickethwaite). Pure Saddle-Horses, and How to Breed Them in Australia. Together With a Consideration of the History and Merits of the English, Arab, Andalusian, & Australian Breeds of Horses. By Edward M. Curr. Melbourne, Wilson, 1863. xviii, 299 p.

CURZON (Louis Henry). The Blue Ribbon of the Turf . . . By Louis Henry Curzon . . . London, Chatto, 1890. x, 364 p. *Printed in blue.*

CURZON (Louis Henry). A Mirror of the Turf, or The Machinery of Horse-Racing Revealed Showing the Sport of Kings as It Is Today . . . By Louis Henry Curzon . . . London, Chapman, 1892. vii, 372 p.

CUSTANCE (Henry). Riding Recollections and Turf Stories. By Henry Custance. London, Arnold, 1894. xv, 304 p. front., plates. *"This is copy 146 of the large paper edition."*

DADD (George H.) The Modern Horse Doctor: Containing Practical Observations on the Causes, Nature, and Treatment of Disease and Lameness in Horses Embracing the Most Recent and Approved Methods . . . With Illustrations. By George H. Dadd . . . New York, Judd, 1865. 432 p. illus. *"Twelfth thousand."*

DAINGERFIELD (Keene). Training for Fun, and Profit—Maybe! By Keene Daingerfield, Jr. Lexington, Ky., Thoroughbred Record Co. [1942] ix, 250 p. front. (port.) *First edition.*

DAINGERFIELD (Keene). Training for Fun (and Profit, Maybe). By Keene Daingerfield, Jr. Illustrations John Zeigler . . . Lexington, Ky., Thoroughbred Record Co., 1948. xi, 230 p. front. (port.), illus. *Third edition.*

DARLING (Sam). Sam Darling's Reminiscences. With 8 Illustrations in Photogravure and 43 in Half-Tone. London, Mills [1914] xiii, 248 p. front. (port.), plates, port. *"This large paper edition is limited to seventy-five copies."*

DARVILL (Richard). A Treatise on the Care, Treatment, and Training of the English Race Horse. In a Series of Rough Notes; by R. Darvill . . . London, Ridgway, 1828-46. illus. *Library has: v. 1 (1828) 1st ed.; v. 2 (1846) 3d ed.*

DAUMAS (Melchior Joseph Eugène). Les Chevaux du Sahara. Par le Général Daumas . . . Ouvrage Publié Avec l'Autorisation du Ministre de la Guerre. Paris, Chamerot, 1851. vi, 384 p. *First edition.*

DAUMAS (Melchior Joseph Eugène). Les Chevaux du Sahara et les Moeurs du Désert. Par le Général E. Daumas. Huitième Édition, Revue et Augmentée Avec des Commentaires par l'Émir Abd-el-Kader. Publié Avec l'Approbation du Ministre de la Guerre. Paris, Lévy, 1881. xii, 527 p.

DAUMAS (Melchior Joseph Eugène). The Horses of the Sahara, and the Manners of the Desert. By E. Daumas . . . With Commentaries by the Emir Abd-El-Kader. Translated From the French by James Hutton (the Only Authorized Translation) London, Allen, 1863. xi, 355 p.

Tipped in: Presentation letter from James Hutton to E. C. Bayley describing his translation as an "Adaptation." He explains why it is "full of mistakes."

DAUMAS (Melchior Joseph Eugène). Principes Généraux du Cavalier Arabe. Par le Général E. Daumas. Quatrième Édition. Paris, Hachette, 1855. 63 p.

DAVIS (John H.). The American Turf. By John H. Davis. History of the Thoroughbred, Together With Personal Reminiscences by the Author, Who, in Turn, Has Been Jockey, Trainer and Owner. New York, Polhemus, 1907. 183 p. front. (port.)

DAWKINS (George Henry). Present Day Sires and the Figure System. One Hundred and Fifty Pedigrees of Horses Now at the Stud. By G. H. Dawkins. London, Cox, 1897. xi, 152 p.

DAY (John Isaac, Jr.) and Barber (Rowland) . . . Racing Almanac. By John I. Day, Jr. and Rowland Barber. General Editor: Van der Veer Varner . . . [New York, Dell] 1953. 224 p. *Specially bound for Hamburg Place.*

DAY (William). Le Cheval de Course à l'Entraînement Accompagné de Conseils Pour les Courses et de Projets de Réforme. Par William Day. Traduit de l'Anglais par le Vte de Hédouville. Paris, Plon, 1881. xi [5] 271 p. 3 comparative tables.

DAY (William). The Horse. How to Breed and Rear Him. Race-Horse. Hunter. Hack. Troop-Horse. Draught-Horse. Shire-Horse. Carriage-Horse. Pony. By William Day . . . London, Bentley, 1888. xxiii, 453 p.

DAY (William). The Racehorse in Training With Hints on Racing and Racing Reforms. By William Day. London, Chapman, 1880. viii, 323 p.

DAY (William). Turf Celebrities I Have Known. By William Day . . . London, White, 1891. 290 p. front. (port.)

DAY (William). William Day's Reminiscences of the Turf. With Anecdotes and Recollections of Its Principal Celebrities. Second Edition. London, Bentley, 1886. xiv, 466 p.

DAY (William) and Day (Alfred James). The Racehorse in Training. By William Day and Alfred J. Day . . . With a Three-Colour Frontispiece and 16 Half-Tone Plates. London, Cassell [1925] xviii, 213 [1] p. front. (col.), ports. *"Revised edition."*

DE GREY (Thomas). The Compleat Horseman and Expert Ferrier. In Two Bookes. The First, Shewing the Best Manner of Breeding Good Horses . . . The Second, Directing the Most Exact and Approved Manner How to Know and Cure All Maladies and Diseases in Horses . . . London, Harper, 1639. [xxvi] 356 [3] p. front., illus.

[DELAUNEY (Julien Félix).] Les Courses. Guide Pour Ga- gner. Historique–Vocabulaire–Fonctionnement–Sociétés de Courses–Propriétaires–Jockeys et Entraîneurs–Hippo- dromes–Couleurs des Jockeys. Manière de Parier. Par le Dr. Laun [pseud.] Paris, Delarue [1890?] 156 p.

DELISSER (George P.). How to Win at the Races: A Successful System of Making a Steady Income on the Turf. Discovered by G. P. Delisser . . . New York, Spruce Printing Co., 1889. 22 [1] p.

DENHARDT (Robert Moorman). The Horse of the Americas. Robert Moorman Denhardt. Norman, Okla., University of Oklahoma Press, 1949. xvii, 286 p. illus.

DENHARDT (Robert Moorman). Official Stud Book and Regis- try of the American Quarter Horse Association. Compiled and Edited by Robert M. Denhardt . . . Fort Worth, Texas [1941-] *Library has: v. 1, no. 1 (1941) only.*

DENMAN (John). . . . Betting Systematized. By John Den- man. London [the author] 1865. vii, 118 p. *"Printed for private circulation only."*

The DERBY Day. Or Won by a Neck. A Sporting Novel. (Never Before Printed) London, Hall, 1864. 171 p.

DE TRAFFORD (Sir Humphrey Francis). The Horses of the British Empire. Edited by Sir Humphrey F. de Trafford . . . London, Southwood [1907?] 2 v. plates. *Printed in double columns.*

DEY (Thomas Henry). Horses and Horse-Racing. A Useful Bro- chure for All Interested in Horses and Horse-Racing. Com- piled by Thomas Henry Dey. London, the author, 1908. 83 p.

DEY (Thomas Henry). Leaves From a Bookmaker's Book. By Thomas Henry Dey. London, Hutchinson [1910?] 384 p. front. (port.)

DEY (Thomas Henry). . . . The Opinions of a Betting Man. Being the Reprint of a Series of Articles That Have Appeared in "Dey's Daily." By Thomas Henry Dey. London, the author, 1908. 149 p. front. (port.) (Dey's Handy Handbooks for Sportsmen, no. 2)

DIBDIN (Charles). [The Elder, 1745-1814] The High-Mettled Racer. By the Late Charles Dibdin. To Which Are Added Many Interesting Anecdotes of the Race-Horse. Illustrated by Ten First Rate Engravings on Wood, by G. W. Bonner. From Designs by Robert Cruikshank. London, Kidd, 1831. 36 p. front., illus.

> p. 25: "The following interesting anecdotes of the race-horse, are extracted from Captain Thomas Brown's 'Biographical Sketches of Horses.'"

DIMON (John). American Horses and Horse Breeding. A Complete History of the Horse From the Remotest Period in His History to Date. The Horseman's Encyclopaedia and Standard Authority on Horses, Embracing Breeds, Families, Breeding, Training, Shoeing, and General Management. The Modern and Practical Horse Doctor on the Cause, Nature, Symptoms, and Treatment of Diseases of All Kinds . . . John Dimon. Hartford, Conn., the author, 1895. 449 p. front. (port.), illus.

DISNEY (John). The Laws of Gaming, Wagers, Horse-Racing, and Gaming Houses. By John Disney . . . London, Butterworth, 1806. xiii [7] 132 [8] p. *Index unpaged.*

DIXON (Henry Hall). Field and Fern, or Scottish Flocks & Herds. (North) By H. H. Dixon . . . London, Rogerson, 1865. 10 p., vi, 373 p. front. (port.), illus.

DIXON (Henry Hall). Field and Fern, or Scottish Flocks & Herds. (South) By H. H. Dixon . . . London, Rogerson, 1865. vi, 409 p. front. (port.), illus.

[DIXON (Henry Hall).] The Post and the Paddock, With Recollections of George IV, Sam Chifney, and Other Turf Celebrities. By The Druid. London, Rogerson, 1862. 376 p., xxxii. front. (port.), illus. *"Hunting Edition" "Miscellaneous verses, 1848-61."*

[DIXON (Henry Hall).] Saddle and Sirloin, or English Farm and Sporting Worthies, by The Druid . . . London, Rogerson, 1870. iv, 486 p. front. (port.)

[DIXON (Henry Hall).] Scott and Sebright, by The Druid . . . London, Rogerson, 1862. iii, vii, 426 p. front. (port.), illus.

[DIXON (Henry Hall).] Silk and Scarlet. By The Druid . . . London, Rogerson, 1859. iv, 398 p. front. (port.), illus. *"Presentation copies."*

DIXON (Sydenham). From Gladiateur to Persimmon. Turf Memories of Thirty Years. By Sydenham Dixon ('Vigilant' of "The Sportsman") With Illustrations in Colours. London, Richards, 1901. xiii, 307 [1] p. front., ports.

DIXON (William Scarth). The Influence of Racing and the Thoroughbred Horse on Light-Horse Breeding. By William Scarth Dixon. London, Blackett [1925?] xi, 247 p. front., plates.

DOBIE (James Frank). The Mustangs. By J. Frank Dobie. Illustrated by Charles Banks Wilson. London, Hammond [1954] xiv, 343 p. front. (col.), illus.

DODDS (E. King). Canadian Turf Recollections and Other Sketches by E. King Dodds . . . Toronto, the author, 1909. 304 p. front. (port.)

DODGE (Theodore Ayrault). Riders of Many Lands. By Theodore Ayrault Dodge . . . Illustrated With Numerous Drawings by Frederic Remington . . . New York, Harper, 1894. viii, 486 p. illus., plates.

DOLLAR (John A. W.). A Surgical Operating Table for the Horse. By Jno. A. W. Dollar . . . London, Gay, 1903. 42 p. illus.

DONCASTER Races. Names of Subscribers to the Assembly. Doncaster Races. 1799-1839.

> These are printed lists of subscribers and the Doncaster Racing Calendar. Ms list of total subscribers for each year on front flyleaf. Between 1826-27 *The York Courant* for Jan. 8, 1810, is tipped in. Later lists (1825-39) include picture of the Gold Cup.

DONOGHUE (Stephen). Just My Story. By Stephen Donoghue. With 4 Coloured and 49 Other Illustrations. London, Hutchinson [1923] viii, 287 p. front. (port. col.), plates (part col.), ports.

DORÉ (Gustave). Two Hundred Sketches Humorous and Grotesque. By Gustave Doré. London, Warne, 1867. 86 p. front., illus. *Title page vignette.*

DOWST (Robert Saunders) and Craig (Jay). Playing the Races. A Guide to the American Tracks. By Robert Saunders Dowst and Jay Craig. New York, Sun Dial [1940] vii, 183 p. *First published 1934. Glossary: p. 172-183.*

DOYLE (John Andrew). Essays on Various Subjects. By John Andrew Doyle . . . Edited by W. P. Ker. With an Introduction by the Right Hon. Sir William Anson . . . With Portrait. London, Murray, 1911. xxv, 333 p. front. (port.)

The DRUID. *See* DIXON (Henry Hall).

DUBOST (Antoine, ou Alexandre). Newmarket. Collection d'Onze Planches Lithographies, Representant la Vue de Newmarket, et la Vie du Cheval de Course Depuis l'Instant Où Il Est Dans le Haras Jusqu'á Celui de Sa Vente, Figure Sous les Formes des Plus Célèbres Chevaux de Course Anglais en 1809; Comprenant les Principaux Sites et Points de Vue de Newmarket; les Portraits de Plusieurs Amateurs de Course et des Plus Fameux Jockeys; Auxquels Sont Joints une Notice sur Newmarket et un Texte Explicatif des Planches, les Actes du Parlement d'Angleterre Relatifs aux Courses, les Règles des Courses en Général, et les Règles et Ordonnances du Jockey-Club; par A. Dubost . . . Paris, l'auteur, 1818 [cover 1825] 1 v. (unpaged) plates.

DUDLEY (William Stockton). Thoroughbreds Property of W. S. Dudley, Lexington, Ky. at Letton Vimont's Sunny Hill Farm, Millersburg, Ky. (Bourbon County) 1928. [Lexington, Cromwell, comp., 1928] 43 p. *Library has also: "Second Private Catalog. 1929" 60 p. illus.*

DU HAYS (Jean Charles Aimé). Les Courses en France en Belgique et à Bade. Origines, Performances, et Produits des Vainqueurs des Principaux Prix Dans Ces Diverses Contrées. Tableaux de Tous les Prix Groupés par Réunions de Courses. Par Charles du Hays. Paris, Goin, 1863. ii, 244 p. *Imprint covered by label: Paris, Tanera, 1864.*

DU HAYS (Jean Charles Aimé). Dictionnaire de la Race Pure Pour Remonter à l'Origine des Chevaux et Juments de Pur Sang Anglais Qui Ont Été Introduits en France, Belgique, Hollande et Tout le Continent Germanique, et des Individualités Célèbres Restées en Angleterre, Qui Ont Formé Illustré et Conservé Cette Race. Par Charles du Hays. Bruxelles, Parent, 1863. vii, 491 p.

DUPRÉ (François). . . . Haras d'Ouilly (Calvados) à M. François Dupré. 1956. [Alençon (Orne) France, 1956] 235 p.

DURAND (Sir Edward Percy Marion). Ponies' Progress. By Sir Edward Durand. With a Foreword by Captain C. T. I. Roark and One Chapter by W. F. Holman. Stable Plans by Horace Farquharson . . . New York, Scribner, 1935. 190 p. front., plates, diagr.

DUVAL (Clément). L'Entraînement du Cheval de Course. Illustrations Humoristiques par Malespina. Paris, Legoupy, 1924. 121 [3] p. illus.

EASBY Abbey Breeding Stud. Reprinted From "Bell's Life." With a Memoir of Mr. Jaques, Reprinted From the "British Farmer's Magazine," and an Account of the Presentation of His Portrait to Him by the "Richmondshire Agricultural Association." Extracted from the "Yorkshire Gazette." Richmond [England] Bell, 1860. 93 p. front., plates.

"Reminiscences of Easby Abbey. A Memento of the Festivities on the Occasion of the Celebration of the Twenty-First Anniversary of the Birthday of Leonard Jaques, September, 1860."

EDGAR (Patrick Nisbett). The American Race-Turf Register, Sportsman's Herald, and General Stud Book: Containing the Pedigrees of the Most Celebrated Horses, Mares, and Geldings, That Have Distinguished Themselves as Racers on the American Turf . . . The Whole Calculated for the Use and Information of Amateurs, Breeders, and Trainers . . . Compiled From the Papers, Letters, Memorandums, Stud-Books, and Newspapers, of the Most Celebrated and Distinguished Sportsmen; Also, From Other Sources of the Most Correct Information. By Patrick Nisbett Edgar . . . In Two Vols. . . . Vol. 1. New York, Press of Henry Mason, 1833. xvi, 601 [1] p. *No more published. Endorsement by W. T. Porter and Henry Mason, Sept. 1, 1833: p. [602]*

EDWARDS (Frederic). Brief Treatise on the Law of Gaming, Horse-Racing & Wagers; With a Collection of the Statutes

EDWARDS (Frederic). *Continued:*
in Force in Reference to Those Subjects; Together With
Practical Forms of Pleadings & Indictments, Adapted for
the General or Professional Reader. By Frederic Edwards
. . . London, Butterworth, 1839. xiv, 141 p.

EGAN (Pierce). Book of Sports, and Mirror of Life: Embracing
the Turf, the Chase, the Ring, and the Stage. Interspersed
With Original Memoirs of Sporting Men, etc. . . . Dedicated to George Osbaldeston . . . London, Tegg, 1832.
iv, 414 p. illus.

EGAN (Pierce). Sporting Anecdotes, Original and Selected; In-
cluding Numerous Characteristic Portraits of Persons in
Every Walk of Life, Who Have Acquired Notoriety From
Their Achievements on the Turf, at the Table, and in the
Diversions of the Field, With Sketches of the Various Ani-
mals of the Chase: To Which Is Added, an Account of
Noted Pedestrians, Trotting Matches, Cricketers, etc. The
Whole Forming a Complete Delineation of the Sporting
World. By Pierce Egan. Philadelphia, Carey, 1822. iv,
359 p. front.

L'ÉLEVEUR, Journal des Chevaux. Par An: 12 Francs. Paris,
May, 1834-35.

Library has: v. 1, no. 1-2 (May, June 1834) all published; v. 2,
no. 3-14 (Jan.-Dec. 1835). Each no. paged separately. Bound
together in one volume. Ms note: "Aug. 3, 1915. I have collected this volume as well as I could, never having seen another
copy I find it complete except that (1) There are no outside
covers except the title page of the volume. (2) The index referred to in the note (1) on page 1 of no. 14, Dec. 1835 does not
appear (perhaps never was added) Notes 15 & 16 in 1st no. are
bound in out of place. In no. 6 (p. 30-32) English notes have
been pasted over. They can be clearly read by holding the page
to the light. I can see no reason why this was done as the paper
is firm. Perhaps the former owner objected to English advs. in
the magazine, & perhaps the matter was not accurate. R. J. T."

ELLANGOWAN. *See* BERTRAM (James Glass).

ESTES (Joseph Alvie). Average-Earnings Index. Annual and Cumulative Progeny Indexes for Thoroughbred Sires Represented by Runners in North America in . . . , With Similar Records for Leading Sires of . . . in Great Britain, Ireland and in France. By J. A. Estes . . . Lexington, Ky., The Blood-Horse, 1949- . *Library has: 1949 to date.*

ESTES (Joseph Alvie). Thoroughbred Pedigrees. 1934. Tabulated Pedigrees of Prominent Race Horses and a Bloodline Analysis of Important Stallions at Stud in the United States. Edited by J. A. Estes . . . Lexington, Ky., A T B A, 1935. 64 p. tables.

ESTES (Joseph Alvie) and Palmer (Joseph Hill). An Introduction to the Thoroughbred Horse, Origin, Distribution, Breeding, Conformation, Uses. [Lexington, Ky., The Blood-Horse, 1942] 28 p. illus., diagr.

ÉTALONS de Pur Sang. Répertoire 1957 Contenant le Pedigree, les Performances et la Production de 155 Étalons Ainsi que la Liste des 82 Autres Étalons Devant Faire le Monte en France en 1957. Paris, Union Nationale Interprofessionnelle du Cheval [1956] 201 p. *G. Thibault, rédacteur. At head of title: Courses et Élevage Supplément aux nos. 8, 9, 10 et 11 de 1956.*

[ÉTREILLIS (Le Baron d').] Dictionnaire du Sport Français. Courses—Chevaux—Entraînement—Langue du Turf—Célébrités du Turf—Paris et Parieurs—Règlements—Hippodromes. Par Ned Pearson [pseud.] . . . Paris, Lorenz, 1872. 676 p.

FAIRFAX (Thomas). The Complete Sportsman; or, Country Gentleman's Recreation: Containing the Whole Arts . . . of Rearing and Backing Colts; of Managing Racehorses, Hunters, Etc.; of Horse-Racing . . . Together, With Several

FAIRFAX (Thomas). *Continued:*
Other Equally Curious Articles Too Numerous to Be Mentioned in This Title Page. By Thomas Fairfax . . . London, Cooke [1760?] vi, 240 p. front. (eng.)

FAIRFAX-BLAKEBOROUGH (John). The Analysis of the Turf or the Duties and Difficulties of Racing Officials, Owners, Trainers, Jockeys, Bookmakers and Bettors, With Stories of Horses and Courses. By J. Fairfax-Blakeborough . . . London, Allan, 1927. vii, 321 p. front., illus.

FAIRFAX-BLAKEBOROUGH (John). The Disappearance of Cropton. By J. Fairfax-Blakeborough . . . [London] Allan, 1933. 177 p.

FAIRFAX-BLAKEBOROUGH (John). Malton Memories and I'Anson Triumphs. Being the Sporting History of Malton From Earliest Times to the Present Day Together With the Lives and Times of the Scotts, I'Ansons, and Other Trainers, Jockeys, and Gentlemen Riders. By J. Fairfax-Blakeborough . . . With an Introduction by Mr. Arthur B. Portman "Audax" of "Horse and Hound." London, Bray, 1925. xv, 328 p. front. (port.), illus.

FAIRFAX-BLAKEBOROUGH (John). Northern Sport & Sportsmen. (Being the Story of the Hurworth Hunt and Other Packs, Together With Biographies of Northern Sportsmen and Sportswomen, Old Records, Diaries and Songs, Reminiscences and Illustrations, Collected From Many Sources.) Edited by J. Fairfax-Blakeborough . . . London, Hunter [1912] 152 p. illus., ports.

FAIRFAX-BLAKEBOROUGH (John). Paddock Personalities. Being Thirty Years' Turf Memories. By J. Fairfax-Blakeborough . . . With an Introduction by the Most Hon. the Marquess of Zetland . . . With 17 Illustrations. London, Hutchinson [1935] 288 p. illus.

FAIRFAX-BLAKEBOROUGH (John). Sykes of Sledmere. The Record of a Sporting Family and Famous Stud. By J. Fairfax-Blakeborough . . . London, Allan, 1929. xv [1] 263 p. front., plates, ports.

FAIRFAX-BLAKEBOROUGH (John) and St. Cloud (Rupert). A Turf Mystery. By J. Fairfax-Blakeborough and Rupert St. Cloud. [London] Allan, 1934. 214 p.

FAMOUS Horses of America. Containing Fifty-Nine Portraits of the Celebrities of the American Turf, Past and Present, With Short Biographies. Philadelphia, Porter [1877] 63 p. front. (port.), ports.

FAMOUS Sporting Prints . . . London, "The Studio, Ltd." 1927- .

> Library has: v. 2, *The Grand National* by T. Romford; v. 3, *The Derby* by George Kendall. Each plate accompanied by leaf with descriptive letterpress.

The FARRIER and Naturalist. Edited by a Member of the Zoological Society of London . . . London, Simpkin, 1828- . illus., plates. *Library has: v. 1 only.*

FAWCETT (William). Turf, Chase & Paddock. By William Fawcett. London, Hutchinson [1932] 253 p. front. (port.)

FERGUSON (William Blair Morton). Garrison's Finish. A Romance of the Race-Course. By W. B. M. Ferguson . . . Illustrations by Charles Grunwald. New York, Dillingham [1907] 282 p. front., illus.

FILLIS (James). Breaking and Riding With Military Commentaries. By James Fillis . . . Translated by M. H. Hayes . . . With Seventy Illustrations. London, Hurst, 1902. xv, 359 p. front. (port.), plates.

[FINNEY (Humphrey Stanley).] A Stud Farm Diary. By Nothing Venture . . . Lexington, Ky., The Blood-Horse, 1936. 135 p. *"Reprinted from* The Blood-Horse."

FINOT (Louis Jean). Petit-Bout, Prince des Jockeys. Roman. Paris, Michel [1926] 245 p.

FISHER (Ronald Aylmer). The Theory of Inbreeding. By Ronald A. Fisher . . . London, Oliver, 1949. viii, 120 p. tables.

FITT (J. Nevill). Hunting, Steeple-Chasing, and Racing Scenes. Illustrated by Ben. Herring. Edited by J. Nevill Fitt . . . London, Peddie [1869] 34 p. illus., plate (fold.) *"This work was published in 1869—which I learned from the reference to Blue Gown on page 26. RJT"*

FITZROY House Stable. Stud Farm and Fitzroy House Stable, Newmarket. [Compiled by British Bloodstock Agency] [London, Knapp] 1930. 156 p.

FLEITMAN (Lida Louise). Comments on Hacks and Hunters. By Lida L. Fleitman . . . New York, Scribner, 1926. xvii, 264 p. front., plates. *Full name: Mrs. John Van S. Bloodgood.*

FLETCHER (Joseph Smith). The History of the St. Leger Stakes, 1776-1901. By J. S. Fletcher . . . With Four Coloured Plates and Thirty-Two Other Illustrations. London, Hutchinson, 1902. xvi, 503 p. front., illus., tables.

FLETCHER (Joseph Smith). The History of the St. Leger Stakes, 1776-1926. By J. S. Fletcher . . . With Four Coloured Plates and Twenty-One Other Illustrations. London, Hutchinson [1926?] xv, 400 p. front., illus., tables. *Second edition.*

FLEURY (J. B.). Le Stud-Book du Sud-Ouest. Nomenclature des Produits de Pur Sang Anglais, Arabe, Anglo-Arabe Compris dans les Circonscriptions de Tarbes, Pau, Libourne, Villeneuve-sur-Lot, Perpignan & Aurillac . . . Tarbes, Prat, 1896. 568 p.

FOOTE (John Taintor). Blister Jones. By John Taintor Foote. Illustrated by Jay Hambidge. Indianapolis, Bobbs-Merrill [1913] 324 p. front., illus.

FOOTE (John Taintor). The Look of Eagles. By John Taintor Foote. Frontispiece by George Morris. New York, Appleton, 1922. 71 [1] p. front. (col.)

FOSTER (Charles James). The White Horse of Wootton. A Story of Love, Sport and Adventure in the Midland Counties of England and on the Frontier of America. By Charles J. Foster . . . Philadelphia, Porter [1878] 421 p.

FOTHERGILL (George Algernon). A Gift to the State. The National Stud. A Memorial of It Compiled, Edited, & Decorated by George A. Fothergill. With Portraits by Lynwood Palmer & the Editor. [Edinburgh, Constable] 1916. xv, 235 p. front. (port. col.), plates (col.)

FOTHERGILL (George Algernon). Twenty Sporting Designs With Selections From the Poets. By George A. Fothergill. Edinburgh, Neill, 1911. xiii, 109 p. front., plates. *Three hundred copies, no. 181.*

[FOWLER (Arthur Anderson).] The Ballad of Myra Gray and Other Sporting Verse. By Somerset [pseud.] New York, privately printed, 1927. 1 v. (unpaged) *Two hundred and fifty copies, no. 34.*

FRENTZEL (J. P.). Familientafeln des Englischen Vollbluts. (General Stud Book Vol. I-XIV.) Familienweise Zusammen-

FRENTZEL (J. P.). *Continued:*
stellung der Stuten mit Lebender Weiblicher Nachzucht
Sowie der Aus Ihnen Geborenen Hengste mit Weiblichen
zur Zucht Benutzten Nachkommen Unter Angabe Ihrer und
Ihrer Mütter Rennleistungen und Register der Hengste und
Ihrer Namhaft Gemachten Töchter. Herausgegeben vom
Landwirtschaftlichen Central-Verein für Littauen und Mas-
uren in Insterburg. Für den Druck Bearbeitet von Eberhard
von Bonin. Berlin, Parey, 1889. xxviii, 867 p. tables.
Text in German and English. Added title page in English.

"G. G." *See* HARPER (Henry George).

G. W. *See* Le STUD Book Anglais . . .

GALTREY (Albert Sidney). Memoirs of a Racing Journalist. By
Sidney Galtrey . . . With a Foreword by the Earl of Derby
. . . With 19 Illustrations. London, Hutchinson [1934]
303 p. front., illus.

GARD (T.). A Guide to the Turf. By T. Gard . . . Second
Edition With Corrections. London, Reynell, 1809. iv, 92 p.
tables.

GARD (T.). Hoyle's Guide to the Turf Containing Articles,
Rules, and Orders at Horse Races With Tables for Betting
Mathematically Calculated by T. Gard. London, Lowndes,
1814. 48 p. tables.

GASTÉ (Maurice de). Race Pure. Les Vingt Meilleures Jument-
Bases. Leur Descendance Immédiate. La Meilleure Production de Leurs Filles. Par M. de Gasté. Paris, Legoupy,
1913. 41 p.

GAYOT (Eugène Nicolas). La France Chevaline 1re Partie.
Institutions Hippiques. Par Eug. Gayot . . . Paris, au
Bureau de Journal des Haras, 1848-54. 4 v.

GAYOT (Eugène Nicolas). La France Chevaline. 2e Partie. Études Hippologiques. Par Eug. Gayot . . . Paris, au Bureau du Journal des Haras, 1850-53. 4 v.

GAYOT (Eugène Nicolas). Guide du Sportsman, ou Traité de l'Entraînement et des Courses de Chevaux. Par Eug. Gayot . . . Paris, Librairie Agricole de la Maison Rustique [1865] 576 (i. e. 376) p. illus., plates. *Third edition.*

GEE (Ernest Richard). Early American Sporting Books. 1734-1844. A Few Brief Notes. By Ernest R. Gee. With Portraits and Facsimiles. New York, Derrydale Press, 1928. [ix] 61 p. front., plates, ports., facs. *"Chronological list of early American sporting books": [vii]*

GEE (Ernest Richard). The Sportsman's Library. Being a Descriptive List of the Most Important Books on Sport. Compiled by Ernest R. Gee . . . New York, Bowker, 1940. xix, 158 p. front., plates.

GENERAL Account and Pedigree of the British Race Horse From the Earliest Times Down to the Present. By P. J. [1872] 3 v. *Handwritten. v. 3, Supplement: Daily weather tables from January 1870 through July 1872, p. 241-275.*

The GENERAL Stud Book. Containing Pedigrees of English Race Horses, etc., etc. From the Earliest Accounts to the Year 1831, Inclusive. With an Appendix . . . Three Volumes in Two . . . First American From the Second London Edition. Baltimore, Skinner, 1834. viii, 1076 p. *Bound in one volume.*

The GENERAL Stud Book. Containing Pedigrees of Race Horses, etc., etc. From the Earliest Accounts to the Year 1807, Inclusive. London, Weatherby, 1808. 1, 516 [6] p.

The GENERAL Stud Book. Containing Pedigrees of Race Horses, etc., etc. From the Earliest Accounts to the Year 1807, In-

The GENERAL Stud Book. *Continued:*
clusive. Second Edition. London, Weatherby, 1820- . *Library has: v. 1 to date. Among the earlier volumes there are ms notes, pictures and clippings laid in.*

Un GENTLEMAN. [Pseud.] Choses de Sport. Courses Militaires—Courses de Gentlemen—Rallie-Papiers—Concours Hippiques. Par un Gentleman. Saumur, Milon, 1887. 141 [2] p.

[GÉRUSEZ (Victor).] Paris à Cheval. Texte et Dessins par Crafty. Avec une Préface par Gustave Droz. Nouvelle Edition [2d ed.] Paris, Plon, 1884. 404 p. illus.

[GÉRUSEZ (Victor).] La Province à Cheval. Texte et Dessins par Crafty. Paris, Plon, 1886. 404 p. illus.

[GÉRUSEZ (Victor).] Sur le Turf. Texte et Dessins par Crafty. Courses Plates et Steeple-Chases. Paris, Plon, 1899. 404 p. illus.

GIBERT (Charles Camille Alcée) and Massa (Alexandre Phillipe Régnier, Marquis de). Historique du Jockey-Club Français, Depuis Sa Fondation Jusqu'en 1871 Inclusivement. Par Mm. A. Gibert et Ph. de Massa. Paris, Jouaust, 1893. vi, 416 [1] p. *"Cet ouvrage imprimé pour les seuls membres du Jockey-Club . . . no. 673."*

GIBSON (William). The True Method of Dieting Horses . . . The Proper Methods of Feeding . . . the Right and Proper Exercise . . . By W. Gibson. London, Taylor, 1721. viii, 236 p., vii.

GILBEY (Goeffrey) and "Consul." [Pseud.] How to Bet and Win. By Geoffrey Gilbey and "Consul." A Simple Method of Assuring a Regular Income From Betting. Indispensable to All Who Back Horses. [London] Abbey Press, 1930. 89 p. tables.

GILBEY (Quintin). Winners & Losers. By Quintin Gilbey . . .
1928. London, Welbecson Press, 1928- . illus. (part col.)
Library has: v. 1 only.

GILBEY (Sir Walter). Horses—Breeding to Colour. Thoroughbreds . . . Hackneys . . . Shirers . . . By Sir Walter Gilbey . . . Second Edition. London, Vinton, 1912. 4, 55 p.
front., illus.

GILBEY (Sir Walter). Horses Past and Present. By Sir Walter
Gilbey . . . London, Vinton, 1900. 4, 89 p. front., illus.

GILBEY (Sir Walter). Hunter Sires. Suggestions for Breeding
Hunters, Troopers and General-Purpose Horses. By I. Sir
Walter Gilbey . . . II. Charles W. Tindall . . . III. The
Right Hon. Frederick Wrench . . . IV. W. T. Trench . . .
London, Vinton, 1903. vi, 33 p. illus., plates. *"The two
articles—pages 1 to 15—were published previous to 1894 in
the* Live Stock Journal Almanac."

GILBEY (Sir Walter). Life of George Stubbs R. A. Compiled
by Sir Walter Gilbey . . . With Illustrations, the Steel Engravings by J. B. Pratt; the Wood Engravings by F. Bab-
bage. London, Vinton, 1898. xxvii, 234 p. front. (port.),
plates. *"Previous to destroying the plates, one hundred and
fifty copies of this edition have been printed . . ."*

GILBEY (Sir Walter). Racing Cups 1559 to 1850. Coursing
Cups. By Sir Walter Gilbey . . . London, Vinton, 1910.
76 p. plates.

GILBEY (Sir Walter). Thoroughbred and Other Ponies With
Remarks on the Height of Racehorses Since 1700. Being a
Revised Edition of Ponies: Past and Present. By Sir Walter
Gilbey . . . London, Vinton, 1903. 4, 156 p. illus.

GILBEY (Sir Walter). Young Race-Horses. (Suggestions for Rearing) By Sir Walter Gilbey . . . Third Edition. London, Vinton, 1898. vi, 33 p. front., illus.

GILBEY (Sir Walter) and Cuming (Edward William Dirom). George Morland. His Life and Works. By Sir Walter Gilbey . . . and E. D. Cuming. London, Black, 1907. xix, 289 [1] p. front. (col.), plates (col.)

GILMAN (Wenona). [Pseud.] *See* SCHOEFFEL (Florence Blackburn White).

GITTINGS (David Sterett). Maryland and the Thoroughbred. By D. Sterett Gittings Sponsored by the Maryland Horse Breeders Association, Inc. Baltimore, Hoffman, 1932. 148 p. front., illus.

GOBERT (Henri Joseph) and Cagny (Paul). Le Cheval de Course. Élevage, Hygiène, Entraînement, Maladies. Par H-J Gobert . . . et P. Cagny . . . Paris, Baillière, 1911. viii, 510 p. illus.

GODOLPHIN DARLEY. [Pseud.] *See* NEUHOF (Albert).

GOOCH (Thomas). The Life and Death of a Racehorse. Exemplified in His Various Stages of Existence, Till His Dissolution . . . The Whole Drawn and Engraved in Aquatinta. By Thomas Gooch . . . With an Essay, Tending to Excite a Benevolent Conduct Towards the Brute Creation, by the Late Dr. Hawkesworth. To Which Is Now Added The Song of the Race Horse, etc. London, Jeffery, 1792. 4 p. 6 mounted plates.

GOODWIN (W. J.). Pedigree of the Thorough-Bred Horse, From Three Original Sources, Comprising the Most Successful Covering Stallions for the Year 1856. London, Goodwin [1856] Folding chart mounted on cloth in backs.

GOODWIN Brothers. Goodwin's Annual Official Turf Guide
. . . Adopted and Used by All Jockey Clubs and Racing
Associations in the United States and Canada. New York,
Goodwin Brothers [1883]-1908. *Library has: 1883-1908.
Title varies slightly.*

GOODWIN Brothers. . . . How to Make or Lose Money on a
Small Capital . . . Showing the Weakness of Human Nature and Its Susceptibility to the Speculative Magnet. By
Goodwin Brothers. Fourth Edition. New York [1895] 127
p. illus.

GOODWIN Brothers. The Winning Stallions of the United States
and Canada for the Year . . . Showing the Amount Won
by Each of Their Progeny in First, Second or Third Moneys,
With Total to Each Sire, etc. Compiled From Goodwin's
Official Turf Guide. By Goodwin Brothers. New York,
18 - . *Library has: 1897-99.*

GOOS (Herman). Die Stamm-Mütter des Engl. Vollblutpferdes.
3te Ausgabe. Hamburg, Rademacher, 1897. 50 tables in
folder with alphabetical index.

GOOS (Herman). Die Stamm-Mütter des Englischen Vollblut-
pferdes. 50 Familien-Tafeln (Nach Bruce-Low Nummerirt)
Darstellend die Gerade Weibliche Abstammung, Bis auf die
Urstamm-Mütter, der Bedeutendsten in England, Frank-
reich, Deutschland, Oesterreich-Ungarn und Skandinavien
Gezogenen Renn- und Zuchtpferde des Englischen Voll-
blutes. Nebst Vorwort, Siegerlisten und Alphabetischem
Vereichniss. Vierte Ausgabe 1907. Weitergeführt von Dr.
A. de Chapeaurouge. Hamburg, Rademacher, 1907. 35 p.
50 tables and alphabetical index in folder.

GORDON (Adam Lindsay). Racing Rhymes & Other Verses. By
Adam Lindsay Gordon. Selected and Arranged by T. O.
Guen. New York, Russell, 1901. 146 p. front., illus.

GORDON (Lord Granville Armyne). The Race of To-Day. A Novel. By Lord Granville Gordon. In One Volume. London, White, 1897. 296 p.

GORDON (Lord Granville Armyne). Sporting Reminiscences. By Lord Granville Gordon. Edited by F. G. Aflalo. With Twenty-Three Illustrations in Halftone and Four in Photogravure . . . London, Richards, 1902. xii, 208 p. front. (port.), plates. *Author's photograph on cover.*

GORMAN (John Alexander). The Western Horse. Its Types and Training. By John A. Gorman . . . [Danville, Ill., Interstate Printers & Publishers] 1939. 278, 4 p. front., illus. *Index and directory paged separately.*

[GOSDEN (Thomas).] The Sportsman's Vocal Library; Containing an Extensive Collection of Songs Relative to the Sports of the Field: Including the Several Subjects of Hunting, Shooting, Racing, Coursing, Angling, Hawking, etc., etc. . . . Second Edition. London, Sherwood [1811] v, 469 p. front. (port.) *Added eng. title page. Cover stamped: Songs of the Chace, London 1810.*

GOUBAUX (Armand). The Exterior of the Horse. By Armand Goubaux, and Gustave Barrier . . . Second Edition, With 346 Figures and 34 Plates, by G. Nicolet . . . Tr. and ed. by Simon J. J. Harger . . . Philadelphia, Lippincott [etc., etc.] 1892. xxviii, 916 p. illus., plates, diagr.

GOUDIN (R.). Comment Reconnaître un Bon Cheval de Course. Préface de Charles Craste . . . Professeur Goudin. Paris, Les Éditions "Alpha" [n.d.] 70 p. illus., plates.

GOULD (Nathaniel). Charger and Chaser. By Nat Gould . . . New Edition. London, Long [1912] 126 p. *Printed in double columns.*

GOULD (Nathaniel). Fast as the Wind. A Novel by Nat Gould . . . New York, Stokes [1918] vi, 265 p.

GOULD (Nathaniel). The Lady Trainer. By Nat Gould . . . New Edition. London, Long [1908] iv, 126 p.

GOULD (Nathaniel). The Magic of Sport. Mainly Autobiographical. By Nat Gould. With Photogravure Portrait and Fifty Illustrations. London, Long [1909] x, 365 p. front. (port.), plates, ports.

GOULD (Nathaniel). On and Off the Turf in Australia. By Nat Gould (Verax) . . . London, Routledge [n.d.] 244 p.

GOULD (Nathaniel). The Rider in Khaki. A Novel by Nat Gould. New York, Stokes [1918] 279 p.

GOULD (Nathaniel). The Top Weight. By Nat Gould. New Edition. [London] Long [1908] ii, 126 p.

GOULD (Nathaniel). Warned Off. By Nat Gould . . . London, Everett [n.d.] 128 p. *Printed in double columns.*

GRAHAM (Robert Bontine Cunninghame). The Horses of the Conquest. By R. B. Cunninghame Graham . . . London, Heinemann [1930] xiv, 161 p. front., illus.

GRAHAM (Robert Bontine Cunninghame). Rodeo. A Collection of the Tales and Sketches of R. B. Cunninghame Graham. Selected and With an Introduction by A. F. Tschiffely. New York, Literary Guild, 1936. xx, 438 p.

Le GRANDI Prove Ippiche. Annuario Internazionale di Sport Ippico . . . Milano, 1922- . annual. *Library has: 1922-31.*

GREAT BRITAIN. (Parliament. House of Lords. Select Committee . . . on Horses) Report From the Select Committee of the House of Lords on Horses, Together With the Pro-

GREAT BRITAIN. *Continued:*

ceedings of the Committee, Minutes of Evidence, and Appendix. Session 1873. xvii, 405 p. *"Ordered to be printed 14th July 1873."*

GREAT BRITAIN. (Parliament. House of Lords. Select Committee to Inquire into the Laws Respecting Gaming) The Three Reports From the Select Committee of the House of Lords Appointed to Inquire into the Laws Respecting Gaming; and to Report Thereon to the House: With the Minutes of Evidence Taken Before the Committee, and an Index Thereto. (As Printed for the Lords, With the Complete Evidence; the Three Reports as One Parliamentary Paper.) . . . 1844, vii, 198 p.

"Ordered, by the House of Commons, to be printed, 9 July, 25 July, and 8 August 1844." Front fly-leaf: Ms notes indicating marked paragraphs in text. Observations on lack of testimony concerning hackneys.

GREENWOOD (Mrs. George Dean). Gloaming the Wonder Horse. By Mrs. G. D. Greenwood. Sydney, New Century Press, 1927. 140 [1] p. front., plates, tables.

GRISWOLD (Frank Gray). The Horse and Buggy Days. By F. Gray Griswold. [Norwood, Mass.] privately printed, 1936. 160 [1] p. front. (port.)

GRISWOLD (Frank Gray). Horses and Hounds. Recollections of Frank Gray Griswold. New York, Dutton, 1926. v, 275 p. front. (col.), illus. *An edition of three hundred copies.*

GRISWOLD (Frank Gray). Race Horses and Racing. Recollections of Frank Gray Griswold. [Norwood, Mass.] privately printed [Plimpton Press] 1925. vii, 216 p. front. (col.), plates.

GRISWOLD (Frank Gray). Sport on Land and Water. Recollections of Frank Gray Griswold. [Norwood, Mass.] privately printed [Plimpton Press] 1913-31. 7 v. illus. (part col.)

GRISWOLD (Frank Gray). Stolen Kisses. Recollections of Frank Gray Griswold. [Norwood, Mass.] privately printed [Plimpton Press] 1914. 143 p. illus.

GUBBINS (Nathaniel). [Pseud.] *See* MOTT (Edward Spencer).

HAGGIN (James Ben Ali). Catalogue of Stallions and Brood Mares at the Elmendorf Stud. Lexington, Kentucky. Property of James B. Haggin. 1905. iv, 406 p., iii.

HAGGIN (James Ben Ali). Catalogue of Thoroughbreds Stallions and Broodmares at Rancho del Paso, Del Paso, Calif. Property of James B. Haggin. 1903. x, 595 p., iv. *Library has the catalogue for 1905 also.*

HAILEY (Clarence). A Generation of Derby Winners. From Pictures by Clarence Hailey. This Collection Contains 28 Engravings and Can Be Obtained Nowhere Else in the World . . . Newmarket [England] 1909. 28 plates (unpaged) *Preface by Alfred E. T. Watson.*

HAINES (Frank). Turf Speculation; or 1,000 Per Cent. a Year. By Frank Haines. New York, Mentor [1905] 158 p. *First edition, 1905.*

HALBRONN (Chéri Raymond). Les Étalons de France aux XIXe Siècle. Dictionnaire des Étalons du Siècle Dernier Que l'On Retrouve les Plus Fréquemment Dans les Pedigrees Modernes. Dressé par Chéri R. Halbronn. Paris, Maulde, 1904. 123 p. (Bibliothèque de l'Établissement Chéri)

HALBRONN (Chéri Raymond). Guide de l'Éleveur. Répertoire de Sélection des Poulinières Apparentées aux "Juments-Bases." Dressé par Chéri R. Halbronn. Collaborateurs: Mm. Schillio-Halbronn, Coates et Desmares. Paris, 1910. 55 p. (Bibliothèque de l'Établissement Chéri) *Between p. 16 and 17 is the alphabetical list of "Juments-Bases" extending to 166 unnumbered pages.*

The HALF Bred Stud Book. Avon, Genesee Valley Breeders' Assn, 1925- .

> Library has: v. 1, 2, 3. "Founded in 1918 by the late Mrs. Herbert Wadworth . . . under the authority of the Jockey Club." v. 3 published by the American Remount Association, Washington, D.C., 1937.

HAMILTON (Ker Baillie). Our Saddle Horses. By Ker B. Hamilton . . . London, Smith, 1865. 39 p.

> With this is bound: On Anglican and Arabian Race-Horses. Observations and Comparisons by Practical Gentlemen, as Approved and Supported by George Holmes . . . Hull [England] Kirk [186–] 22 p. Race-Horses Past and Present. Six Letters by I. F. R. Second Edition. London, Benning, 1857. 31 p. *I. F. R.: Admiral Henry John Rous.*

HAMLIN (Cicero J.). Village Farm in the Village of East Aurora, N.Y. . . . C. J. Hamlin, prop. 1891. [Buffalo, N.Y., Wenborne-Sumner Co.] 1891. 226 p. front., illus., plates. *Standardbred stud book.*

HANCOCK (Arthur Boyd). Claiborne Farm [Compiled by Cromwell Bloodstock Agcy., Lexington, Ky., 1956] 1 v. (looseleaf unpaged) *Stallions, mares entered alphabetically.*

HANCOCK (Arthur Boyd). Ellerslie and Claiborne Studs. 1927. A. B. Hancock. Paris, Ky. 117 p.

HANCOCK (Arthur Boyd). Thoroughbred Stallions and Mares at Claiborne Stud, Paris, Ky. Ellerslie Stud, Charlottesville, Va. 1920. A. B. Hancock, Proprietor . . . [Lexington, Ky., Cromwell and Walker, 1920] 186 p.

HAND (Ninna Stanford). Hand's System of Handicapping and Turf Speculator's Guide. By Nin. S. Hand . . . A Book for Bookmakers, Owners, Trainers and Turf Speculators in General . . . New York, 1900. 1 v. (unpaged)

HANGER (George). General George Hanger to All Sportsmen, Farmers and Gamekeepers . . . Effectually to Catch All Vermin. The Ratcatching Secret . . . Embellished With a Characteristic Portrait of the Author on His Return From Shooting. A New Edition. London, Stockdale [1814] 226 p. front. (port.).

HARE (C. E.). The Language of Sport. By C. E. Hare. London, Country Life [1939] xvi, 192 p. illus. *Bibliography: p. 171-176.*

HARPER (Henry George). Horses I Have Known With Stories About Them. By "G.G." (H. G. Harper) . . . London, Long [1905] viii, 223 p.

> "These Stories appeared some years ago, serially, in *Sporting Sketches* . . . They have been carefully revised and largely rewritten, so as to make them suitable for publication in book form." On title page and cover: H. G. Harper.

[HARPER (Henry George).] New Sporting Stories. By G. G. . . . Second Edition. London, Bellairs, 1896. vii, 218 p.

[HARPER (Henry George).] Sporting Stories and Sketches. By G. G. With Frontispiece by G. Bowers. London, Paul, 1895. viii, 268 p. front. (col.) *"Some of these stories & sketches first appeared in* Illustrated Sporting and Dramatic News *and* Sporting Sketches."

HARRINGTON (George Wheaton). A Reversion of Form and Other Horse Stories. By George W. Harrington. Boston, Sherman, 1911. 226 p.

HARRIS (Norvin T.). Catalogue of the Thoroughbreds Belonging to the Hurstebourne Stud Farm. The Property of Norvin T. Harris, St. Matthews, Jefferson County, Kentucky. Compiled by John K. Stringfield, Lexington, Ky. [Louisville, Ky., Courier-Journal Job Prtg. Co., 1890] 94 p. illus.

[HARRISON (Fairfax).] The Background of the American Stud Book. Richmond, Va., privately printed, Old Dominion Press, 1933. 121 p. plates, ports., facs.

Preface signed: F. H. Typewritten notes tipped in signed F. H. and dated Feb. 7, 1928, concerning his "new friend John L. O'Connor, the equine genealogist."

[HARRISON (Fairfax).] The Belair Stud 1747-1761. Richmond, Va., privately printed, Old Dominion Press, 1929. 102 p. front., plates. *"Epistle dedicatory to William Woodward, Esq." signed Fairfax Harrison, dated December 1929. Bibliography: p. [13]-15.*

[HARRISON (Fairfax).] Early American Turf Stock. 1730-1830. Being a Critical Study of the Extant Evidence for the English, Spanish and Oriental Horses and Mares to Which Are Traced the Oldest American Turf Pedigrees . . . Richmond, Va., privately printed, Old Dominion Press, 1934-1935. 2 v. illus. *v. 1: Mares; v. 2: Horses. "The Sources": v. 1, p. [11]-19. Preface signed: F. H.*

[HARRISON (Fairfax).] The Equine F. F. Vs. A Study of the Evidence for the English Horses Imported into Virginia Before the Revolution. Richmond, Va., privately printed, Old Dominion Press, 1928. 184 p. front. (col.), illus. *Bibliography: p. [11]-24. Preface signed: F. H.*

[HARRISON (Fairfax).] The John's Island Stud (South Carolina) 1750-1788. Richmond, Va., privately printed, Old Dominion Press, 1931. 236 p. front., illus., map (fold.) *Bibliography: p. [221]-228. Preface signed: F. H.*

[HARRISON (Fairfax).] The Roanoke Stud. 1795-1833. Richmond, Va., privately printed, Old Dominion Press, 1930. 244 p. front., plates, facs. *Bibliography: p. [221]-232. Preface signed: F. H.*

HARRISON (Stanley). Gentlemen, The Horse! By Stanley Harrison. Illustrations by the Author. Lexington, Ky., Thoroughbred Press, 1951. 88 p. *Poems about the horse.*

HART (Harry S.). Swingalong Stables, Incorporated. Thoroughbreds at Tollie Young's Creekview Farm, Paris, Kentucky. Phone Paris 102. [Compiled by The Blood-Horse] [Lexington, Ky., Welsh] 1930. 80 p. illus.

HART (Harry S.). Swingalong Stud, Incorporated. Thoroughbreds, Creekview Farm, Paris, Kentucky. Office: Suite 1422, 152 West 42nd Street, New York City. [Compiled by The Blood-Horse] [Lexington, Ky., Welsh] 1931. 153 p. illus.

HAVRINCOURT (Le Comte Louis d'). Dressage en Liberté du Cheval d'Obstacles par le Cte Louis d'Havrincourt. Ouvrage Orné de Gravures d'Après les Dessins de l'Auteur et de Photographies. Paris, Legoupy, 1910. 158 p. illus., plates.

HAWK'S-EYE. [Pseud.] A Budget of Turf Notes. By Hawk's-Eye. London, Blackwood, 1871. 128 p.

HAYDON (Thomas). Sporting Reminiscences. By Thos. Haydon. London, Bliss, 1898. viii, 281 p. front. (port.), illus.

HAYES (Matthew Horace). Among Men and Horses. By M. Horace Hayes . . . Illustrated by Reproductions From Photographs. New York, Dodd, 1894. xiv, 358 p. front. (ports.), illus.

HAYES (Matthew Horace). Indian Racing Reminiscences. By M. Horace Hayes . . . Illustrated by J. K. Ferguson. London, Thacker, 1883. xvi, 291 p. front. (port.), illus.

HAYES (Matthew Horace). Points of the Horse. A Treatise on the Conformation, Movements, Breeds and Evolution of the Horse. By M. Horace Hayes . . . 666 Illustrations. Sixth (Revised) Edition. London, Hurst [1952] xxvii, 540 p. front., illus., diagr.

HAYES (Matthew Horace). Riding and Hunting. By M. Horace Hayes . . . London, Hurst, 1901. xvi, 460 p. front. (port.), illus., diagr.

HAYES (Matthew Horace). Stable Management and Exercise. A Book for Horse-Owners and Students. By M. Horace Hayes . . . Fifth edition, rev. & enl. London, Hurst [1947] 256 p. front., illus., tables.

HAYES (Matthew Horace). Training and Horse Management in India. With a Hindustanee Stable & Veterinary Vocabulary, and the Calcutta Turf Club Weights for Age and Class. By M. Horace Hayes . . . 4th ed. rev. Calcutta, Thacker, 1885. xii, 240 p., xx. tables.

HEAD (Sir Francis Bond). The Horse and His Rider. By Sir Francis B. Head . . . Second edition. London, Murray, 1861. 226 p. front., plates.

HEADLEY (Hal Price). Beaumont Stud. Lexington, Kentucky. Hal Price Headley. 1922. 61 p. *Library has also: Beaumont Stud, 1924, 64 p.*

HEADLEY (Hal Price). Beaumont Stud. Private Catalog. 1951. [Lexington, Ky., Thoroughbred Press, 1951] 63 p. *Cover title*.

HEBER (Reginald). An Historical List of Horse-Matches Run. And of Plates and Prizes Run for in Great Britain and Ireland, in . . . Containing the Names of the Owners of the Horses, That Have Run as Above, and the Names and Colours of the Horses Also. With the Winner Distinguish'd of Every Match . . . With a List Also of the Principal Cock-Matches of the Year Above, and Who Were the Winners and Loosers [*sic*] of Them, etc. By Reginald Heber. London, the author, 1752-69. *Library has: 1752-1769. Beginning with 1754 the vols. are numbered III, IV, etc.*

[HEMYNG (Bracebridge).] Out of the Ring, or Scenes of Sporting Life. By a Betting Man. London, Clarke [1876?] 152 p. (Clarke's Popular Railway Reading)

HENDERSON (Robert William). Early American Sport. A Check-List of Books by American and Foreign Authors Published in America Prior to 1860 Including Sporting Songs. Compiled by Robert W. Henderson. Second Edition, Revised and Enlarged. New York, Barnes, 1953. xxviii, 234 p. plates, facs.

HENRY (Edmond). Les Courses. Leur Utilité au Point de Vue de l'Agriculture et de l'Armée. Par M. Edmond Henry . . . Caen, Le Blanc-Hardel, 1884. 62 p.

HERBERT (Henry William). Frank Forester's Horse and Horsemanship of the United States and British Provinces of North America. By Henry William Herbert . . . With Steel-Engraved Original Portraits of Celebrated Horses. In Two Volumes. New York, Stringer, 1857. 2 v. illus. *Added eng. title page*.

HERBERT (Henry William). Hints to Horse-Keepers, a Complete Manual for Horsemen . . . and Chapters on Mules and Ponies. By the Late Henry William Herbert (Frank Forester). With Additions, Including "Baucher's System of Horsemanship;" Also Giving Directions for the Selection and Care of Carriages and Harness of Every Description, and a Memoir of the Author . . . New York, Orange [1859] 425 p. front., illus.

HERBERT (Henry William). Life and Writings of Frank Forester (Henry William Herbert). Edited by David Wright Judd . . . London, Warne [1882] 2 v. illus. *Life of the author by Col. Thomas Picton.*

HERMIT. [Pseud.] Les Chevaux de Deux Ans de . . . (Sélection sur le Stud-Book et Classement par la Valeur de l'Origine) . . . Paris, Puel, 19 - . *Library has: 1926-29.*

HERRIES (Sir William Herbert). The Successful Running and Sire Lines of the Modern Thoroughbred Horse as Shown in a Series of Tables Giving the Descent in Tail Male and Tail Female of the Principal Winners and Sires in Great Britain and Ireland and in Australia and New Zealand in Modern Times. Compiled by Sir William H. Herries . . . London, British Bloodstock Agency, 1921. xvi, 175 p. tables.

HERVEY (John Lewis). Messenger the Great Progenitor. By John Hervey . . . New York, Derrydale Press [1935] xi, 63 [1] p. front., plates.

"Five hundred copies of *Messenger* have been printed by Eugene V. Connett at the Derrydale Press of which this is number 82."

HERVEY (John Lewis). Racing in America 1665-1865 . . . Written for the Jockey Club by John Hervey. New York [1944] 2 v. plates, ports., facs.

HERVEY (John Lewis). Racing in America 1922-1936. Written for the Jockey Club by John Hervey. New York [1937] x, 293 p. plates, ports.

HIATT (James M.). The National Register of Norman Horses. With a General History of the Horse-Kind and a Thorough History of the Norman-Horse. By James M. Hiatt . . . [Bloomington, Ill.] National Norman-Horse Association, 1881. 283 [1] p. front., illus.

HICHBORN (Philip). Hoof Beats. Philip Hichborn. Boston, Badger [1912] 169 p. front., illus. *Reprinted from various periodicals.*

HIEOVER (Harry). [Pseud.] *See* BINDLEY (Charles).

HIGGINS (D. W., & Co.). Nominations to Stakes and List of Declarations. Nominations for All Stakes to Be Run During 1885, and to Those That Have Closed for 1886 and 1887, With Index . . . New York, 1885. xl, 228, 84 p. *Index paged separately.*

[HIGGINS (Francis).] Flat-Racing Explained. By Analyst. A Practical Treatise on Racing, Designed to Meet the Requirements of Owners, Breeders, Trainers, Jockeys, and the General Public. New York, Goodwin Bros., 1899. xv, 128 p.

HIGGINSON (Alexander Henry). British and American Sporting Authors. Their Writings and Biographies. By A. Henry Higginson With a Bibliography by Sydney R. Smith and Foreword by Ernest R. Gee. Berryville, Va., Blue Ridge Press, 1949. xvii, 443 p. front. (port.), ports.

HIGGINSON (Alexander Henry). Try Back. A Huntsman's Reminiscences. By A. Henry Higginson . . . With a Foreword by Henry Goodwin Vaughan . . . New York, Huntington Press, 1931. 227 p. front. (port.), illus. *"First regular edition."*

HILDRETH (Samuel Clay). The Spell of the Turf. The Story of American Racing. By Samuel C. Hildreth and James R. Crowell. With 32 Illustrations. Philadelphia, Lippincott, 1926. viii, 286 p. front., illus., ports.

HILLS (Sir John). Points of a Racehorse. By Major-General Sir John Hills. Edinburgh, Blackwood, 1903. x, 113 p. front., illus., plates. *Printed on one side of leaf.*

HINDS (John). [Pseud.] *See* BADCOCK (John).

HIRSCH (Mark D.) William C. Whitney, Modern Warwick. By Mark D. Hirsch . . . New York, Dodd, 1948. xiii, 622 p. front. (port.), illus. *Bibliography: p. 602-606.*

HIRSCH (Maximilian Justice). Dinner in Honor of Max Hirsch Given by His Friends on the Occasion of His Seventy-Sixth Birthday, July 12, 1956, Syosset, N. Y. [New York, Triangle Publications, 1956] 1 v. (unpaged) illus., ports. *Printed on one side of leaf. Mr. Hirsch's biography first appeared in* Daily Racing Form.

HISLOP (John). The Turf. With 8 Plates in Colour and 23 Illustrations in Black and White. London, Collins, 1948. 47 [1] p. illus. (Britain in Pictures)

HOBBS (Harry). The Romance of the Calcutta Sweep. By Major H. Hobbs . . . Calcutta, Thacker, 1930. 286 p.

HOBDAY (Sir Frederick Thomas George). Fifty Years a Veterinary Surgeon . . . Foreword by the Rt. Hon the Earl of Lonsdale . . . London, Hutchinson [1938] 288 p. front. (port.), illus., facs.

HODGMAN (George). Sixty Years on the Turf. The Life and Times of George Hodgman, 1840-1900. Edited by Charles R. Warren . . . London, Richards, 1903. 297 [1] p. front. (port.), plates.

HOLMES (George). On Anglican and Arabian Race-Horses. Observations and Comparisons by Practical Gentlemen, as Approved and Supported by George Holmes . . . Hull [England] Kirk [186–] 22 p. *Bound with: Hamilton, K. B. Our Saddle Horses, London, 1865.*

HONTANG (Maurice). Psychologie du Cheval. Sa Personnalité Psychologie Comparée.–Tests.–Cheval et Rat. Réactions Sensorielles.–Facultés Cérébrales.–Exploitation de l'Intelligence.–Langage Conventionnel.–Éducation: Ses Limites. –Cheval et Enfant. Préface du Général Donnio . . . Paris, Payot, 1954. 315 p. (Bibliothèque Scientifique)

HOOD (Thomas). [The Elder, 1799-1845] Epsom Races: A Poem, Comic, Punning and Racy. By Thomas Hood . . . Only 200 Copies Printed. Printed at Charles Clark's Private Press, Great Totham, Essex. London, Longman, 1836. 42 p. *Printed on one side of leaf. Title page printed in blue.*

HORE (John Philip). The History of Newmarket, and the Annals of the Turf: With Memoirs and Biographical Notices of the Habitués of Newmarket, and the Notable Turfites From the Earliest Times to the End of the Seventeenth Century. By J. P. Hore. In Three Volumes . . . London, Baily, 1886. 3 v. illus.

> v. 1: From the earliest times to the death of James I; v. 2: From the accession of Charles I to 32 Charles II A. D. 1625-1680; v. 3: History of Newmarket: From 33 Charles II (A. D. 1681) to the end of the seventeenth century; Annals of the Turf: From the Restoration (A. D. 1660) to the end of the seventeenth century.

HORE (John Philip). Sporting and Rural Records of the Cheveley Estate. Collected and Compiled by J. P. Hore, and Printed for Private Circulation Only. [London, Cox] 1899. v, 128 p. front., plates. *Cover title: The Jockey Club's New Estate, Cheveley Park, Newmarket, 1920.*

The HORSE. "The Magazine for the Horse Fancier and Breeder"
... Washington, D. C., American Remount Association,
19 - . illus. bimonthly. *Library has: v. 18 (1937), v. 19
(1938), v. 22-27 (1941-46), v. 29 (1948), v. 30 (1949)*

HORSE and Hound. A Journal for Every Sportsman. Edited by
Arthur Portman (Audax, pseud.) London, 18 - . illus.
weekly. *Library has: v. 48-55 (1930-37)*

The HORSE Review. An Illustrated Journal Devoted to Horse
Owners ... Chicago, Bauer, 18 - . illus. *Library has:
v. 39-40 (1909), v. 41-42 (1910)*

HORSE-RACING: Its History and Early Records of the Principal
and Other Race Meetings. With Anecdotes, etc. London,
Saunders, 1863. x, 446 p.

HOUËL (Ephrem Gabriel). Les Chevaux de Pur Sang en France
et en Angleterre. Par E. Houël ... Paris, Journal des
Haras, 1859. 2 pt. *Library has: Pt. 1 only. "Première
Partie (Angleterre)."*

HOUËL (Ephrem Gabriel). Les Chevaux Français en Angleterre. 1865. Par E. Houël ... Paris, Bouchard-Huzard,
1865. 32 p.

HOUSTON (Thomas). The Races: The Evils Connected With
Horse-Racing and the Steeple-Chase, and Their Demoraliz-
ing Effects. By Thomas Houston ... Paisley [England]
Gardner, 1853. 148 p.

HOWEY (M. Oldfield). The Horse in Magic and Myth. By M.
Oldfield Howey. With Five Full-Page Plates, Coloured
Frontispiece and Numerous Illustrations in the Text (In-
cluding Many Original Drawings by the Author). London,
Rider, 1923. xii, 238 p. front. (col.), plates. *Bibliography
at end of every chapter except two.*

HUGHES (G. M.). The Origin of Ascot Races: A Stray Chapter
From an Unpublished History of Sunninghill and the Forest.
By G. M. Hughes. London, Bell, 1887. 25 p.

HUMFREY (John). Horse-Breeding and Rearing in India, With
Notes on Training for the Flat and Across Country, and on
Purchase, Breaking In, and General Management. By Major
John Humfrey . . . Calcutta, Thacker, 1887. xi, ii, 147 p.

HUMFREY (John). The Steeplechase Horse: How to Select,
Train, and Ride Him. By Captain J. Humfrey. Calcutta,
Thacker, 1879. 179 p. *Alternating blank leaves for notes:
p. 150-179.*

HUMPHRIS (Edith Mary). Adam Lindsay Gordon and His
Friends in England and Australia. By Edith Humphris and
Douglas Sladen. With Sixteen Sketches by Gordon and
Numerous Other Illustrations. London, Constable, 1912.
xxxii, 464 p. front., plates, ports., facs.

HUMPHRIS (Edith Mary). The Life of Fred Archer. By E. M.
Humphris . . . Edited by Lord Arthur Grosvenor. With a
Preface by Arthur F. B. Portman. With Coloured Frontispiece and 24 Other Illustrations. London, Hutchinson,
1923. viii, 320 p. front. (port. col.), plates, ports.

HUMPHRIS (Edith Mary). The Life of Mathew Dawson With
Which Are Included Some Recollections of the Famous
Trainer by the Duke of Portland . . . and an Introduction
by Arthur Portman. By E. M. Humphris . . . With Repro-
ductions From Engravings, Paintings, and Photographs.
London, Witherby, 1928. 227 p. front. (port.), illus.

HUNT (Vere Dawson de Vere). England's Horses for Peace and
War, Their Origin, Improvement, and Scarcity. By Vere D.
de Vere Hunt . . . London, Bemrose, 1874. 170 p.

HUNT (Vere Dawson de Vere). The Horse and His Master.
With Hints on Breeding, Breaking, Stable-Management,

HUNT (Vere Dawson de Vere). *Continued:*
Training, Elementary Horsemanship, Riding to Hounds, etc. By Vere D. Hunt . . . London, Longman, 1859. x, 151 p. front.

HUNTINGTON (Randolph). History in Brief of "Leopard" and "Linden," General Grant's Arabian Stallions, Presented to Him by the Sultan of Turkey in 1879. Also Their Sons "General Beale," "Hegira," and "Islam," Bred by Randolph Huntington. Also Reference to the Celebrated Stallion "Henry Clay." [Philadelphia] Lippincott, 1885. 66 p. front. (port.), plates.

Laid in back: "Henry Clay." Pedigrees of Americus, Damascus, Clay Pilot (with description and letters), Clay Spink, Young Jack Shepard, Clay McPherson, Clay Hepburn, Clay Truth, and Clay Henry.

HUSHED Up. By A. D. L. "The Scout" of the "Daily Express." The Most Remarkable Series of True Tales of the Turf Ever Published. Every One of These Stories Is Founded on Fact. London, Raggett [n.d.] 116 p.

HUTH (Frederick Henry). Works on Horsemanship and Swordsmanship, in the Library of F. H. Huth. Bath, Seers, 1890. 258 p., xxii.

HUTH (Frederick Henry). Works on Horses and Equitation. A Bibliographical Record of Hippology. By F. H. Huth. London, Quaritch, 1887. x, 439 p.

HUZARD (Jean Baptiste). [Dit Huzard Fils, 1793-1878] Des Haras Domestiques en France; par J-B Huzard Fils . . . Paris, Huzard, 1829. viii, 452 p.

HUZARD (Jean Baptiste). [Dit Huzard Fils, 1793-1878] Notice sur les Chevaux Anglais et sur les Courses en Angleterre, Lue à la Société Royale et Centrale d'Agriculture, le 7 Mai, et à l'Académie Royale des Sciences, le 28 Juillet 1817; par J.-B. Huzard, Fils . . . Paris, Huzard, 1817. 51 p.

I. F. R. *See* ROUS (Henry John).

ILLUSTRATED Sporting News. A National Weekly Devoted to Sport and Outdoor Life. New York, Ripley, 1903-05. illus. weekly.

> Library has: v. 1, no. 1–v. 5, no. 130 (May 16, 1903–Nov. 4, 1905) Changed to: *Illustrated Outdoor News,* Sept. 30, 1905.

ILWAR (S. N.). Racing Rhymes on Turf Topics, the Thoroughbred, etc., etc., etc. By S. N. Ilwar. New York, Goodwin Brothers, 1899. 182 p.

INDENTURE of a Horse Race Betwixt the Earls of Morton and Abercorn and the Lord Boyd. Anno M.DC.XXI. [n.p., 1828?] 11 p. facs.

INGLIS (Gordon). Sport and Pastime in Australia. By Gordon Inglis. With a Preface by the Right Hon. Sir George Houstoun Reid . . . London, Methuen [1912] xix, 308 p. front., illus.

An INTRODUCTION to a General Stud-Book Containing (With Few Exceptions) the Pedigree of Every Horse, Mare, etc. of Note, That Has Appeared on the Turf for the Last Fifty Years, With Many of an Earlier Date . . . London, Weatherby, 1791. xx, 207 p.

IRELAND. (Irish Land Commission) . . . Return of Stallions Standing for Service in Ireland in Year 1896. Irish Land Commission (Agricultural Department) [Dublin, Thom, 1896] 133 p. tables. *"Confidential Copy."*

IRELAND. (Parliament. Commission on Horse Breeding) Minutes of Evidence Taken Before the Commissioners Appointed to Inquire into the Horse Breeding Industry in Ireland. With Appendices. Presented to Both Houses of Parliament by Command of Her Majesty. Dublin, Thom, 1897. vii, 523 p. tables.

IRON MASK. [Pseud.] Sportsmans Pilot. Iron Mask. 1849-50. *Library has: v. 1 (1849), v. 2 (1850) Title page lacking. No more published?*

IRONSIDE (Gilbert). A Dissertation on Horses . . . By Colonel Gilbert Ironside. London, Reynell, 1800. 30 p. *Bound with:* The Supplement to the General Stud Book, *London, 1800.*

IRVING (John Beaufain). The American Jockey Club. Official Summary of the Races at Jerome Park, Fall of 1866, With Reminiscences of the Inauguration Meeting, by John B. Irving . . . New York, Thitchener, 1866. 23 p. *Racing Calendar for Sept. 25, Oct. 1, 2, 3, 1866.*

[IRVING (John Beaufain).] The South Carolina Jockey Club. Charleston, S. C., Russell, 1857. 48 p. (pt. 1-3); 211 p. (pt. 4-9)

Binder's title: History of the Turf in S. Carolina. Stamped in gold on front cover: J. C. Cochran, Treasurer. Ms note tipped in: "Oct. 30, 1932. For an excellent note on the antecedents and life of Dr. John B. Irving see 'A Day on Cooper River' by John B. Irving and . . . 1932, pp. 187 seq. Also note the excellent location in modern terms of the former Charleston Race Courses. (signed) Robert J. Turnbull."

J., P. *See* ANNALS of the Turf; GENERAL Account & Pedigree of the British Race Horse . . .; *and* TRACES of the Turf.

JACKSON (J.). York Races: Being an Historical List of All the Plates and Prizes Run for on Clifton and Rawcliffe Ings, and Since Removed to Knavesmire, Near the Said City; Like Wise How the Mares Came in Every Year at Black Hambleton, Including the Year 1770 . . . The Sixth Edition. York, Printed and Sold by J. Jackson in Peter-gate, 1771. 1 v. (various pagings)

The JAMAICA Stud Book. *See* PALACHE (J. Thomson).

JENNINGS (Frank Clay). From Here to the Bugle. By Frank
Jennings. Illustrations Milton Menasco. Lexington, Ky.,
Thoroughbred Press, 1949. 330 p. illus. *Biography of
Arthur Boyd Hancock.*

JENNINGS (Rienzi Wilson). Taxation of Thoroughbred Racing.
By Rienzi Wilson Jennings . . . Lexington, Ky., University
of Kentucky, 1949. 126 p. (Bulletin of the Bureau of
Business Research, College of Commerce, no. 20)

The JOCKEY Club. Round Table Discussion on Matters Pertain-
ing to Racing . . . [various places] 1953- . *Library has:
1953 to date.*

The JOCKEY Club. Rules of Racing Adopted by The Jockey
Club . . . New York, Ahern, 19 - . *Library has: 1912,
1934, 1935, 1937.*

JOCKEY Club Mexicano. Registro de Caballos de Sangre Pura de
Carrera. Nacidos e Importados a México. Studbook . . .
Publicación Oficial del Jockey Club Mexicano. México,
1942- . *Library has: v. 1 (1942-47), Supp. 1947-49.*

JOCKEY-CLUB Brasileiro. Stud Book Brasileiro. Guia de Pelagem Oficial. [Rio de Janeiro] 1950. 58 p. illus. (col.)

JOCKEY-CLUB Brasilerio. Stud Book Brasileiro. Registro de
Cavalos e Eguas. Puro Sangue de Corridas Nascidos No
País e Importados. Publiçacão Oficial do Jockey Club
Brasileiro . . . [Rio de Janeiro] 1918- . *Library has: v.
1-4 (1918-43)*

The JOCKEY'S Guild. Year Book of the Jockey's Community
Fund & Guild, Inc. New York, 1945. 160 p. illus., ports.
Nelson Dunstan, ed.

JOHNSON (R.). Racing Calendar for the Year . . . Containing a Complete Account of All the Races Run in Great Britain, and Cock Mains Fought That Year; List of Stallions . . . To Which Is Added the Sweepstakes, Matches, etc. . . . By R. Johnson. To Be Continued Annually. York, Racing Calendar, 18 - . *Library has: v. 5 (1826), v. 7 (1828), v. 8 (1829), v. 20 (1841)*

JOHNSON (Thomas Burgeland). The Sportsman's Cyclopaedia; Comprising a Complete Elucidation of the Science and Practise of Hunting, Shooting, Coursing, Racing, Fishing, Hawking, Cockfighting, and Other Sports and Pastimes of Great Britain. Interspersed With Entertaining and Illustrative Anecdotes. By T. B. Johnson. Embellished With a Profusion of Highly Finished Engravings After Landseer, Ward, Cooper, Hancock, and Other Eminent Artists. London, Bohn, 1848. 2 v. illus. *Second edition.*

JOHNSTONE (Andrew). Keylock's Dams of Winners of All Flat Races in Great Britain and Ireland. 1948 to 1954. Compiled by Andrew Johnstone. The Third Edition in the Second Series. Kingston-on-Thames, Knapp, 1955. xii, 392 p.

JOHNSTONE (Andrew). Keylock's Dams of Winners of All Flat Races in Great Britain and Ireland. 1948 to 1956. Compiled by Andrew Johnstone . . . Kingston-on-Thames, Knapp, 1957. xii, 480 p. *"The definitive edition of the Second Series."*

JOURNAL des Haras, des Chasses et des Courses de Chevaux. [Paris, au Bureau du Journal, 1828-] illus. *Library has: v. 1-28 (1828-41)*

KEENE (Foxhall Parker). Full Tilt. The Sporting Memoirs of Foxhall Keene. By Alden Hatch and Foxhall Keene. New York, Derrydale Press [1938] xiii, 170 p. front. (port. col.), plates, ports.

KEIFFER (Leslie E.). Inverness Farm. Monkton, Maryland. Property of Leslie E. Keiffer. 1931. Harry Rites, Manager. [Compiled by The Blood-Horse] [Lexington, Ky., Welsh] 1931. 47 p. illus.

KELLY (Edward). The Madison Stud, Property of Edward Kelly, New York. 1893. [Compiled by F. Stevens . . .] [New York, O'Keefe] 1893. 71 p.

KENDALL (B. J.). A Treatise on the Horse and His Diseases; Containing an "Index of Diseases" . . . A Valuable Collection of Receipts, and Much Other Valuable Information. By Dr. B. J. Kendall & Co., Enosburgh Falls, Vt. Revised Edition. Boston, Gunn, 1880. 91 p. illus.

KENNARD (Mrs. Edward). The Right Sort. A Romance of the Shires. By Mrs. Edward Kennard . . . London, Ward, 1902. vi, 190 p. front., illus. *Printed in double columns. Full name: Mary E. Kennard.*

KENT (John). Racing Life of Lord George Cavendish Bentinck . . . and Other Reminiscences. By John Kent, Private Trainer to the Goodwood Stable. Edited by the Hon. Francis Lawley . . . Third Edition. Edinburgh, Blackwood, 1893. xx, 482 p. front. (port.), illus., ports., facs.

KENT (John). Records and Reminiscences of Goodwood and the Dukes of Richmond. By John Kent . . . London, Low, 1896. 232 p. front. (port.), plates, ports.

KENTUCKY. (General Assembly. Senate. Committee on Racing) Hearing Before the Senate Committee on Racing, Held in the Senate Chamber at Frankfort, Kentucky, on Friday the 27th of January, 1922.

Statements of: Helm Bruce, E. L. McCready, John A. Lee, Robert W. Bingham, George R. Hunt, Charles E. Marvin, and William Heyburn.

KENTUCKY. (State Racing Commission) . . . Biennial Report of Kentucky State Racing Commission to the General Assembly of the Commonwealth of Kentucky . . . various places, various publishers, 1908- . *Library has: 1908 to date.*

KENTUCKY. (State Racing Commission) Color Registrations. Life and . . . [Lexington, Ky., Welsh] 19 - . *Library has: 1936 to date.*

KENTUCKY. (State Racing Commission) Licenses. various places, various publishers. *Library has: 1936-39. Continued as: Licenses and Rulings. Library has: 1940 to date.*

KENTUCKY. (State Racing Commission) Rules of Racing. various places, various publishers. *Library has: 1938 to date.*

KENTUCKY Association. A Souvenir from the Kentucky Association, Inc. Lexington, Ky. Centennial Meeting Spring 1926. 10 Days Racing Saturday April 24, to Wednesday, May 5. [Lexington, Ky., 1926] 29 p. illus.

KENTUCKY Association. Stake Books. [Lexington, Ky., 1910-30] 2 v. *v. 1 (1910-26), v. 2 (1926-30) Individual stakes books bound together.*

KENTUCKY Farmer and Breeder. Lexington, Ky., 1904-08. weekly. *Library has: v. 2-5 (1905-08)*

KENTUCKY in Retrospect. Noteworthy Personages and Events in Kentucky History. 1792-1942. By Mrs. William Preston Drake, Samuel M. Wilson, Mrs. William Breckinridge Ardery. Editors: Mrs. Wm. Breckinridge Ardery, Harry V. McChesney. [Frankfort, Ky.] Sesqui-Centennial Commission, Commonwealth of Kentucky, 1942. 205 p. illus., plates (part col.)

[KENTUCKY Jockey Club (Incorporated).] Golden Anniversary of the Kentucky Derby and Churchill Downs. Fifty Years of Glorious Turf History. A Complete Story of Each Kentucky Derby; Also the Zev-In Memoriam Match Race and the Ten Broeck-Mollie McCarthy Race; With an Addendum Containing Photographs and Descriptions of the $50,000 Kentucky Special Run at Latonia and Won by Chacolet; and the $50,000 Latonia Championship Won by In Memoriam. [Louisville, Courier-Journal Job Prtg. Co., 1924] 78 p. front. (plate fold.), illus., plates.

KENTUCKY Jockey Club, Inc. Kentucky Derby Lauded by the Press of America . . . The Story Told in Photographs. With an Addendum Containing a Pictorial Glance at the $50,000 Kentucky Special, Run at Latonia June 24th, and Won by Harry Payne Whitney's Colt Whiskaway. Kentucky Jockey Club, Inc. Churchill Downs-Latonia-Lexington. n.p. [1923?] 1 v. (unpaged) illus., fold. pl., tables.

KERR (William Alexander). Practical Horsemanship. By W. A. Kerr . . . London, Bell, 1891. x, 222 p. front., illus. (The All England Series) *Extra illustrated.*

KEYLOCK (Harold Edward). Dams of Winners of All Flat Races in Great Britain and Ireland from 1915 to 1944 (Both Years Inclusive) Compiled by H. E. Keylock. London, British Bloodstock Agency, 1945. viii, 423 p.

KEYLOCK (Harold Edward). Dams of Winners of All Flat Races in Great Britain and Ireland. Compiled by Major H. E. Keylock . . . Third Edition, 1915 to 1947. Kingston-on-Thames, Knapp, 1948. xiv, 455 p.

KEYLOCK (Harold Edward). Dams of Winners of All Flat Races in Great Britain and Ireland. 1948 and 1949. Compiled by Major H. E. Keylock . . . The First Edition in a New Series. Kingston-on-Thames, Knapp, 1950. xii, 176 p.

KEYLOCK (Harold Edward). The Mating of Thoroughbred Horses. Some Conclusions and Deductions. By H. E. Keylock . . . London, British Bloodstock Agency, 1942. 95 p. tables, diagr.

KHAN (Jaffer). Racing Reminiscences and Hints on Training. By Jaffer Khan . . . Calcutta, Thacker, 1897. iv, 189 p. front. (port.)

KING (Frank M.). Longhorn Trail Drivers. Being a True Story of the Cattle Drives of Long Ago. Frank M. King . . . This First Edition Privately Published for His Friends by the Author. [Los Angeles, Haynes] 1940. xiii, 272 p. front. (port.), plates, ports., map.

KING Ranch. 100 Years of Ranching. King Ranch. Corpus Christie, Texas, Corpus Christie Caller-Times, 1953. 143 p. illus., ports.

The articles first appeared July 12, 1953, in *The Corpus Christie Caller-Times,* commemorating the King Ranch centennial.

KIPLING (Rudyard). *See* NICHOLSON (William). An Almanac of Twelve Sports.

KIRKHAM Stud. Private Stud Book of the Kirkham Stud, Kirkham, Camden, N. S. W. Compiled by T. F. Willis. September 1, 1897. Sydney, Radcliffe, 1897. 63 p.

KNIGHT (Thomas Arthur) and Greene (Nancy Lewis). Country Estates of the Blue Grass. By Thomas A. Knight and Nancy Lewis Greene. [Cleveland, Britton] 1904. 200 p. illus.

KNOWLES (G. W.). The Tale of the Turf. By G. W. Knowles . . . With Eight Illustrations. 1st Edition. London, Allan [1924] 174 p. illus.

KOONTZ (F. B.). Paulfred Farms, Tulsa, Oklahoma . . . [n. p., n.d.] 63 p. illus.

KRIK. *See* CRICKMORE (Henry G.).

L., A. D. *See* HUSHED Up. By A. D. L. . . .

LA BOYTEAUX (William Harvell). Thoroughbred Pedigree Charts. Stakes Winners 1915-1936. [n.p.] 1937. 2 v.

LAFFON (Fernand Gabriel). Le Monde des Courses. Moeurs Actuelles du Turf. L'Entraînement; les Sociétés d'Encouragement; les Propriétaires; les Entraîneurs; les Grandes Écuries; la Presse Sportive; les Gentlemen-Riders; les Jockeys; les Bookmakers; les Centres d'Élevage. Le Demi Sang et les Courses au Trot . . . Le Pari Mutuel . . . d'un Dictionnaire-Annuaire . . . Par F. Laffon (La Morlaye du "Petit Journal") Troisième Édition; Tirage Pour l'Année. 1896. Orné de 300 Illustrations et de 2 Planches en Coleurs. Paris, Rothschild, 1896. viii, 644 p. illus. (part col.) *Dictionnaire-Annuaire has separate title page; paged continuously.*

LAFFON (Fernand Gabriel). Le Monde des Courses. Par F. Laffon. Lettre-Préface de H. Escoffier. Paris, Libraire Illustrée [1887] iv, 230 p.

LAFONT-POULOTI (Esprit Paul, Chevalier de). Mémoire sur les Courses de Chevaux et de Chars en France, Envisagées Sous un Point de Vue d'Utilité Publique. Présenté à l'Assemblée Nationale, au Département & à la Municipalité de Paris, par Esprit-Paul de Lafont-Pouloti. Paris, Jussiene, 1791. xii, 32 p. front. (eng.) *From a printed catalogue tipped in: ". . . very rare and curious, as being the first book on horse racing in France . . ."*

LAFONT-POULOTI (Esprit Paul, Chevalier de). Nouveau Régime Pour les Haras, ou Exposé des Moyens Propres à Propager & à Améliorer les Races de Chevaux; Avec la

LAFONT-POULOTI (Esprit Paul, Chevalier de). *Continued:*
Notice de Tous les Ouvrages Écrits ou Traduits en François,
Relatifs à Cet Objet, par Esprit-Paul de Lafont-Pouloti . . .
Turin, la Veuve Valat-la-Chapelle, 1787. xxiv, 342 p. front.
(eng.), plates. *p. 171-342: "Quatrième partie. Notice de
tous les ouvrages écrits ou traduits en François, relatifs aux
haras."*

LA FOUCHARDIÈRE (Georges de). Petit Guide du Parfait
Parieur aux Courses. Georges de la Fouchardière. Paris,
Éditions du Siècle, 1923. 124 [1] p. (Manuels Pour
Adultes, no. 2)

LAGONDIE (Joseph Guilhen, Comte de). Le Cheval et Son
Cavalier. Hippologie–Équitation–École Pratique Pour la
Connaissance–l'Éducation–la Conservation–l'Amélioration
du Cheval de Course–de Chasse–de Guerre d'Après les
Plus Récentes Publications Anglaises sur le Turf Avec des
Tables Généalogiques et de Nombreuses Additions au Point
de Vue du Cheval Français. Par Comte J. de Lagondie . . .
Sixième Édition. Ouvrage Orné de 65 Vignettes. Paris,
Rothschild [1874?] xv, 644 p. illus.

LA GRANGE (Baroness Ernest de). Horse Racing Through the
Ages. Some Facts and Figures. By Baroness Ernest de la
Grange . . . London, "Studies" Publication [1932] 52 [1]
p. ("Studies" Useful Pocket Series)

LAMBTON (George). Men and Horses I Have Known. By the
Hon. George Lambton. London, Butterworth [1924] 320
p. front. (port.), illus. *"Second impression–October 1924."*

LA MORICIÈRE (Christophe Louis Léon Juchault de). De
l'Espèce Chevaline en France par le Général de la Moricière.
Rapport Fait au Conseil Supérieur des Haras sur les Travaux
de la Session de 1850 . . . Paris, Dusacq [1851?] 307 p.
tables, 3 maps (fold. col.)

LASTIC SAINT-JAL (Philippe Ursule Charles, Comte de). L'Ami de l'Éleveur. Réflexions Pratiques sur l'Espèce Chevaline. Ouvrage Orné de 16 Dessins et de 50 Vignettes par V. Adam. A B C du Métier par le Cte de Lastic Saint-Jal . . . Paris, Plon, 1856. 306 p. front., illus., plates. *Library copy lacks: "Portrait de l'auteur en frontispiece, par Carrière."*

LAUN (Le Dr.). [Pseud.] *See* DELAUNEY (Julien Félix).

LAWLEY (Francis Charles). Life and Times of "The Druid" (Henry Hall Dixon). By Hon. Francis Lawley. London, Vinton, 1895. xi, 336 p. front. (port.), ports.

LAWRENCE (John). The History and Delineation of the Horse, in All His Varieties . . . With a Particular Investigation of the Character of the Race-Horse, and the Business of the Turf. Illustrated by Anecdotes and Biographical Notices of Distinguished Sportsmen . . . With Instructions for Breeding, Breaking, Training, and the General Management of the Horse, Both in a State of Health and of Disease. By John Lawrence . . . London, Cundee, 1809. iv, 288 [4] p. illus., plates.

"John Lawrence of Bury St. Edmunds." Added eng. title page. Illus. after Marshall, Sartorius, Stubbs, tailpieces by Bewick.

[LAWRENCE (John).] The Sportsman's Repository; Comprising a Series of Highly Finished Engravings, Representing the Horse and the Dog, in All Their Varieties; Executed in the Line Manner, by John Scott, From Original Paintings by Marshall, Reinagle, Gilpin, Stubbs, and Cooper: Accompanied With a Comprehensive Historical and Systematic Description of the Different Species of Each, Their Appropriate Uses, Management and Improvement; Interspersed With Anecdotes of the Most Celebrated Horses and Dogs,

LAWRENCE (John). *Continued:*
and Their Proprietors; Also a Variety of Practical Information on Training and the Amusements of the Field. By the
Author of "British Field Sports." London, Sherwood, 1820.
viii, 204 [4] p. front., plates.

> Added eng. title page. Tailpieces by Thomas Bewick. "Author
> of British Field Sports": William Henry Scott, pseud. for John
> Lawrence of Bury St. Edmunds.

LAWRENCE (Richard). The Complete Farrier, and British
Sportsman: Containing a Systematic Enquiry Into the Structure and Animal Economy of the Horse . . . Canine Pathology . . . Embellished With a Series of Engravings . . .
By Richard Lawrence . . . With an Appendix . . . Together With an Abstract of the Game Act of 1831 etc., etc.
London, Kelly [1849?] iv, 518 [6] p. front., plates. *Added
eng. title page.*

The LAWS of Gaming: Comprehending the Various Statutes, Reports, and Determinations on That Extensive Subject, Particularly Relative to Horses, Racing, Cards and Frauds:
Whereunto Is Added, the Answer and Opinion of the
Learned Sir John Strange . . . for Avoiding the Penalties
Thereby Inflicted Against Gaming . . . London, Woodfall,
1764. xxiv [2] 154 p.

LAWTON (George). The Art of Winning, or How to Make Turf
Speculation Successful. In Three Parts: The Art of Handi-
capping, the Art of Playing, the Art of Odds. Including an
Explication of a New Method of Handicapping and Four
New and Original Systems of Playing. By George Lawton.
New York, Call Press, 1906. 146 p.

LAWTON (George). Number Five. A Practical System of Turf
Speculation Calculated to Win the Most for the Least. By
George Lawton . . . New York, Lawton Press [1907] 68 p.

LEACH (George Brown). The Kentucky Derby Diamond Jubilee. Compiled Under the Auspices of Churchill Downs. Written and Edited by Brownie Leach. Art Direction and Design by Louis J. Frederick. [Louisville, Gibbs-Inman, 1949] 192 p. illus., ports., map (col.) *"Distributed by Dial Press, New York."*

LECHMERE (Joscelyne). Pretty Polly. The History of Her Career on the Turf. By Joscelyne Lechmere. With a Photogravure Frontispiece and Twenty-two Other Illustrations. London, Lane, 1907. 63 p. front. (port.), illus., plates.

LECTURES Given at the . . . Annual Stud Managers Course. Sponsored Jointly by the Grayson Foundation, Inc., the American Thoroughbred Breeders Association, Inc., and the College of Agriculture of the University of Kentucky . . . Lexington, Ky., 1951- . illus. *Library has: 1951-54.*

LEE (Henry). Historique des Courses de Chevaux de l'Antiquité à ce Jour. Henry Lee. Ouvrage Illustré de Vingt-Deux Planches Hors Texte et de Soixante-Trois Gravures. Paris, Fasquelle, 1914. xx, 888 p. illus., plates. *Bibliography: xi-xvi.*

LEGOUPY (Adolphe). Le Cheval de Demi-Sang Français. Charolais, Forez, Berry et Dombes. Paris, Legoupy [1928] 95 p. plates, map (fold.) *French text followed by German, English, Spanish, and Italian translations.*

LE HELLO (Pierre Marie). Le Pur Sang Anglais et Ses Dérivés. Par P. Le Hello. Avec 28 Figures dans le Texte. Paris, Rueff, 1898. vii, 347 p. illus.

LEHNDORFF (Georg Hermann Albrecht). Horse Breeding Recollections. By G. Lehndorff. London, Cox, 1883. 124 p. tables (fold.)

Chapters taken from *A Manual for the Breeder of Horses*, 1882, by the same author and translated by him. Ms notes accompany some of the tables.

LEHNDORFF (Georg Hermann Albrecht). Horse-Breeding Recollections. By G. Lehndorff. Philadelphia, Porter, 1887. 63 p. front. (port.), illus. *The American edition without the author's introduction and tables.*

LENNOX (Lord William Pitt). Recreations of a Sportsman. By Lord William Lennox . . . In Two Volumes . . . London, Hurst, 1862. 2 vols.

LENOBLE (Henri). Les Courses de Chevaux et les Paris aux Courses. Étude Critique sur l'Organization des Courses et la Réglementation des Paris. Par Henri Lenoble . . . Paris, Larose, 1899. 5 p., v, 433 p. *First published as: "Thèse pour le Doctorat."*

LEVEY (Clarence D.). The Torrance-Clendennin Episode and the Melville Letters, on Racing, Hunting, Steeplechasing, Clubs, and Club Life, etc. . . . By Clarence D. Levey (Melville). [New York] the author, 1892. 154 p. illus.

LIBRO Genealogico (Stud Book) dei Cavalli di Puro Sangue Importati o Nati in Italia . . . Firenzi, Barbera, 18 - . *Library has: v. 2 (1886), v. 14 (1943)*

LIEBLING (Abbott Joseph). The Honest Rainmaker. The Life and Times of Colonel John R. Stingo. By A. J. Liebling. New York, Doubleday, 1953. 317 p.

LOGAN (Guy B. H.). The Classic Races of the Turf. By Guy B. H. Logan . . . With a Foreword by Sir George Thursby . . . With Twenty-Four Half-Tone Illustrations. London, Paul, 1928. 288 p. front. (port.), illus. *"Printed in Great Britain . . . 1931."*

LONDONDERRY (Edith Helen (Chaplin) Vane-Tempest-Stewart, Marchioness of). Henry Chaplin; a Memoir, Prepared by His Daughter, the Marchioness of Londonderry . . . London, Macmillan, 1926. x, 347 p. front. (port.), plates, ports. (part col.)

LONGSTREET (Stephen). [Pseud.] Stallion Road. A Novel by Stephen Longstreet . . . New York, Messner [1945] 303 p. *Real name: Philip Wiener.*

LORILLARD (Pierre). P. Lorillard's Thoroughbred Stock. Rancocas Stock Farm, Jobstown, Burlington Co., N. J. [C. Wheatly, comp.] [n.p.] 1885. 181 p. *Library has also: Studbook for 1881.*

LOTTERY. *See* VUILLIER (Jean Joseph).

LOVERS of the Horse. Brief Sketches of Men and Women of the Dominion of Canada Devoted to the Noblest of Animals. Toronto, Hunter, 1909. x, 230 p. ports.

LOW (David). Les Animaux Domestiques de l'Europe. Races de la Grande-Bretagne . . . par David Low . . . Traduit de l'Anglais et Annoté par Royer . . . Paris, Librairée Agricole de la Maison Rustique [1846?] 128 p. plates (col.)

LOW (David). The Breeds of the Domestic Animals of the British Islands Described by David Low . . . and Illustrated With Plates, From Drawings by Mr. W. Nicholson . . . Reduced From a Series of Portraits From Life, Executed for the Agricultural Museum of the University of Edinburgh, by Mr. W. Shiels . . . In Two Volumes . . . London, Longman, 1842. 2 v. in 1. *v. 1: The horse, and the ox; v. 2: The sheep, the goat, and the hog. Each part paged separately.*

LOWE (C. Bruce). Breeding Racehorses by the Figure System. Compiled by the Late C. Bruce Lowe. Edited by William Allison . . . With Numerous Illustrations of Celebrated Horses. (From Photographs by Clarence Hailey, Newmarket). London, Cox, 1895. xiv, 262 p. front., illus., plates, tables (fold.) *First edition.*

LUCKMAN (A. Dick). Sharps, Flats, Gamblers and Racehorses. By A. Dick Luckman . . . London, Richards, 1914. vii, 349 [1] p. front., illus.

LUKE (Harry). Harry Luke's Reminiscences. Forty Years on the Turf. [n.p.] the author [1911] 20 p.

Cover portrait. Tipped in: A letter from Luke to the Earl of Rosebery acknowledging the Earl's assistance in publication of the memoirs.

LUNDSFORD (Hugh). Flying Heels. By Hugh Lundsford . . . New York, Curtiss Press [1929] 271 p.

LUPTON (James Irvine). The Horse: as He Was, as He Is, and as He Ought to Be. By James Irvine Lupton . . . London, Allen, 1881. [xii] 115 [3] p. front., plates, facs.

The LURE o' the Turf. The Greatest Tales of the Turf in Prose and Poetry. Baltimore, Montee Publishing Co. [1931] 106 p.

LYALL (J. G.). The Merry Gee-Gee. How to Breed, Break, and Ride Him For'ard Away and the Noble Art of Backing Winners on the Turf. By J. G. Lyall. London, White, 1899. 232 p.

LYLE (Robert Charles). The Aga Khan's Horses. By R. C. Lyle. Illustrated by Lionel Edwards . . . London, Putnam [1938] xii, 234 [1] p. front. (col.), illus., plates (col.) "Each colored plate accompanied by guard sheet with descriptive letter press."

LYLE (Robert Charles). Brown Jack. By R. C. Lyle. Illustrated by Lionel Edwards. London, Putnam [1934] 218 [1] p. front. (col.), illus., plates.

LYND (Robert). The Sporting Life and Other Trifles. By Robert Lynd . . . New York, Scribner, 1922. 251 p.

LYON (William Edgar). The World of Horses. Edited by W. E. Lyon & G. H. S. Dixon. Illustrated From Photographs From All Over the World. Introductions by W. E. Lyon, J. A. Talbot-Ponsonby, Hiram E. Tuttle, L. D. Luard, R. S. Summerhays, G. H. S. Dixon, the Late Bertram W. Mills, G. M. Harbord, G. H. Phipps-Hornby. [London, Country Life, 1938] xi, 163 p. illus., plates.

MACEY (Alan). The Romance of the Derby Stakes. By Alan Macey. With Frontispiece & Twenty-three Other Illustrations. London, Hutchinson [1930] 287 p. front. (port.), illus.

McGEE (William Ray). Veterinary Notebook. An Elementary Guide for the Practical Horseman. By William R. McGee . . . Lexington, Ky., The Blood-Horse, 1958. vii, 179 p. illus.

MACKAY (Clarence). Thoroughbreds at Silver Brook Stud. [n.p.] 1905. 1 v. (unpaged)

McKAY (William John Stewart). The Evolution of the Endurance, Speed and Staying Power of the Racehorse. By W. J. Stewart McKay . . . With 28 Illustrations. London, Hutchinson [1937] 319 [1] p. front., illus.

McPHILLAMY (C. S.). The Thoroughbred: His Breeding and Rearing. By C. S. McPhillamy. Sydney, Brooks [1910?] xv, 111 [1] p. tables.

MADDEN (John Edward). Pedigrees of Race Horses Foaled in England, France and America at Hamburg Place Stud, Lexington, Ky. U. S. A. Property of John E. Madden. [Lexington, Ky., Welsh, 1925] 136 [2] p. illus. *Includes: Memorial to Imp. Star Shoot; Preface by Mr. Madden; excerpts from the 1913 catalog.*

MADDEN (John Edward). Thoroughbreds Property of John E. Madden. Hamburg Place Stud. Lexington, Ky. U. S. A.

MADDEN (John Edward). *Continued:*
1913. [Lexington, Ky., Treacy, 1913] 1 v. (unpaged) illus. *Includes: Bruce's Memoir of Lexington; Lord North to his grandchildren; The Auto and the Horse (poem)*

MAGNE (Jean Henry). Hygiène Vétérinaire Appliquée—Races Chevalines et Leur Amélioration. Entretien, Multiplication, Élevage, Éducation du Cheval, de l'Ane et du Mulet. Par J.-H. Magne . . . Troisième Édition Revue et Augmentée. Paris, Garnier, 1870. iv, 654 p. illus.

MAGNER (Dennis). The Art of Taming and Educating the Horse: . . . With Details of Management in the Subjection of Over Forty Representative Vicious Horses and the Story of the Author's Personal Experience; Together With Chapters on Feeding, Stabling, Shoeing, and the Practical Treatment for Sickness, Lameness, etc., With a Large Number of Recipes Heretofore Sold as Great Secrets. 944 Illustrations. By D. Magner . . . Battle Creek, Mich., Review and Herald, 1888. xxii, 1112 p. front. (port.), illus., plates.

MALBESSAN (Le Baron de). Dictionnaire des Courses Contenant la Définition des Mots Anglais et Autres Qu'On Emploie dans la Langue du Turf, la Composition des Comités de Courses de Paris et des Départements, les Noms de Gentlemen-Riders, des Éleveurs, les Couleurs des Propriétaires d'Écurie, les Noms des Jockeys et des Chevaux les Plus Fameux, Ainsi Que Chiffre des Prix Qu'Ils Ont Gagnés, etc., etc. Par le Baron de Malbessan. Paris, Sauvaitre [1888] 105 p. front.

MANCHESTER Races From Their First Commencement in the Year 1760 Carefully Handed Down to the Present Time. To Which Is Prefixed an Account of Horse-Racing From the Most Early Period. Manchester, Patrick, 1815. 76 p. *Title page lacking, handwritten title page supplied. Tipped in: 2 newspaper accounts of Manchester racing.*

MANKIEWICZ (Don M.). See How They Run. By Don M. Mankiewicz. New York, Knopf, 1951. 307 p.

MANSUY (François Charles). *See* MUSANY (François Charles).

MAPLE (Sir John Blundell). Childwick Stud, St. Albans, Herts, the Property of Sir J. Blundell Maple With Explanatory Preface . . . by William Allison . . . [London, Drewett] 1896. 1 v. (unpaged) *This appears to be a proof copy with ms notes and corrections. Library has also: 1897 ed.*

MARCHAL (Georges Henri). Les Souches des Poulinières Françaises (Volumes XIX et XX du Stud Book Français.) Paris, Les Éditions Commerciales et Agricoles [1930?] viii, 318 p.

MARKEY (Lucile Parker). Bloodstock of Calumet Farm, Lexington, Kentucky U. S. A. Spring 1955. Broodmares 57, Stallions 5 . . . Yearlings 38, Horses-in-Training 40. Mrs. Gene Markey, Owner. [Lexington, Ky., Thompson, 1955] 121 p.

MARKHAM (Gervase). Markham's Master-piece. Containing All Knowledge Belonging to the Smith, Farrier, or Horse-Leach. Touching the Curing All Diseases in Horses . . . Divided in Two Books ˙. . . 21st ed. Also the Compleat Jockey . . . London, Conyers, 1734. 318, 64 p. illus., plates. *Appendix paged separately.*

MARKHAM (Gervase). Le Nouveau et Scavant Mareschal, dans Lequel Est Traité de la Composition de la Nature, des Qualitez, Perfections, & Defauts des Chevaux . . . L'Anatomie du Corps du Cheval Avec les Figures. Un Nouveau Traité du Haras . . . un Excellent Traité Pour Bien Ferrer . . . La Representation & les Usages des Instruments, Desquels On Se Sert Dans les Operations Mentionnées en Cet Ouvrage. Traduit du Celebre Markam [*sic*] Gentil-

MARKHAM (Gervase). *Continued:*
homme Anglois. Par le Sieur de Foubert . . . Paris, Ribou, M.DC.LXVI. [xlviii] 168, 411 [3] p. front., plates (eng.) *Added eng. title page.*

MARSH (Richard). A Trainer to Two Kings. Being the Reminiscences of Richard Marsh . . . With a Foreword by the Rt. Hon. the Earl of Durham . . . With Twenty Plates. London, Cassell [1925] xvi, 336 p. front. (port.), plates, ports., facs.

MARSHALL (L. G.). The Arabian Art of Taming and Training Wild and Vicious Horses. By L. G. Marshall. [n.p.] Calhoun, 1858. 36 p.

  p. 33-34: "The Horseman's Guide and Farrier. By John J. Stutzman, West Rushville, Fairfield County, Ohio." p. 35-36: "The Secret of Subduing Wild Horses and Other Wild Animals."

MARTINENGO CESARESCO (Eugenio). The Psychology and Training of the Horse. By Count Eugenio Martinengo Cesaresco. London, Unwin, 1906. xv, 234 p. front. (eng.) *"Printed in Italy" stamped on verso of title page.*

MARTINGALE. *See* WHITE (Charles).

The MARYLAND Horse. The Official Publication of the Maryland Horse Breeders Association. Towson, Md., 1936- . illus. monthly. *Library has: 1936 to date.*

MASEFIELD (John). Right Royal. By John Masefield. London, Heinemann, 1920. 119 [1] p. Map. *Of 500 copies this is no. 229.*

MASEFIELD (John). Right Royal. By John Masefield. London, Heinemann, 1920. 119 [1] p.

MASEFIELD (John). Right Royal. By John Masefield. New York, Macmillan, 1920. 145 p. *Map on front lining paper: "Map of the Compton Course."*

MASEFIELD (John). Right Royal. By John Masefield. Illustrated by Cecil Aldin. London, Heinemann, 1922. 90 [1] p. front., plates (col.), map.

MASON (George Finch). Annals of the Horse-Shoe Club. By Finch Mason . . . With Five Illustrations by the Author. London, Chatto, 1902. 322 p. front., illus.

MASON (George Finch). Heroes and Heroines of the Grand National. By Finch Mason . . . Containing: a Complete Account of Every Race From Its Foundation in 1839 to the Present Year, Together With All Information of Interest in Connection Therewith. Embellished With Illustrations of Winners Where Procurable, Portraits of Owners, Trainers, Jockeys, etc., and Six Coloured Plates From Original Drawings by the Author. Second Edition. London, Biographical Press, 1911. xvi, 439 p. front. (col.), illus.

MASON (George Finch). Sporting Recollections. Hunting, Shooting, Cricket, Steeplechasing, Racing, etc., etc. By Finch Mason. Twenty-Four Highly-Finished Tinted Full-Page Sketches and Seventy-Eight Text Illustrations by the Author. Fifth Edition. London, Fores, 1886. 200 p. illus., plates.

MASON (George Finch). Tit Bits of the Turf. Scattered About by Finch Mason & Collected by Messrs. Fores. London, Fores, 1887. 16 plates (unpaged) *Humorous drawings by "Finch Mason."*

MASON (Richard). . . . The Gentleman's New Pocket Farrier: Comprising a General Description of the Noble and Useful Animal, the Horse . . . By Richard Mason . . . To Which Is Added, a Prize Essay on Mules; an Appendix Containing

MASON (Richard). *Continued:*
Recipes for Diseases of Horses, Oxen, Cows, etc. . . . With
Annals of the Turf, American Studbook, etc. With a Sup-
plement: Comprising an Essay on Domestic Animals, Es-
pecially the Horse . . . Pedigrees of Winning Horses . . .
With Useful Calving and Lambing Tables etc., etc. By
J. S. Skinner . . . Philadelphia, Grigg, 1848. 415, 101 p.
front., illus.

Library has also: 1863. Supplement has title page, paged separately. "Prize essay on the mule by Samuel Wyllys Pomeroy."

MASON (William Hayley). Goodwood. Its House, Park and
Grounds With a Catalogue Raisonné of the Pictures in the
Gallery of His Grace the Duke of Richmond . . . to Which
Are Added an Account of the Antient Encampment, Tumuli,
and British Village, on the Adjacent Downs: and a Detailed
Record of Goodwood Races From Their First Establish-
ment. With Six Illustrations. By William Hayley Mason
. . . London, Smith, 1839. viii, 215 p. front., plates (eng.)

MASTERS (Bat). How to Win at Racing. Explaining the
"Cycle" Method of Backing Horses. By Bat Masters . . .
London, Laurie, 1924. 111 p.

MATHEMATICIAN. [Pseud.] The Derby: a Record of Each
Race From the Earliest Period to the Present Day; the List
of Horses in Betting; Pedigree of Each Winner; Odds at
Starting. By "Mathematician" . . . London, Penny, 1869.
62 p. *Author of* Handbook of Betting *and* Betting Made
Easy.

MATTHEW (William Diller). Evolution of the Horse. In Two
Parts. Evolution of the Horse in Nature by W. D. Matthew.
The Horse Under Domestication: Its Origin and the Structure and Growth of the Teeth. By S. Harmsted Chubb. 7th
ed. [New York] American Museum of Natural History
[1929?] 74 p. illus., tables. (Guide Leaflet Series no. 36)
Bibliography: p. 70.

MEEK (C. F. U.). Winners of the Past and Their Breeding Together With Statistics Relative to the Figure System of Bruce Lowe. By C. F. U. Meek. London, International Horse Agency & Exchange, 1907. [viii] 303 [1] p. illus., tables (part fold.)

MENKE (Frank Grant). Churchill Downs and the Kentucky Derby Since 1875. By Frank G. Menke. [New York, Allied Printing] 1942. 128 p. illus., tables. *Library has also: 1943.*

MENKE (Frank Grant). Down the Stretch. The Story of Colonel Matt J. Winn As Told to Frank G. Menke . . . New York, Smith [1944] xvi, 292 [7] p. front. (col.), plates, ports. *Library has also: trade edition.*

MENKE (Frank Grant). The Story of Churchill Downs and the Kentucky Derby. By Frank G. Menke. [New York] 1940. 127 p. tables, diagr.

MENNESSIER DE LA LANCE (Gabriel René). Essai de Bibliographie Hippique Donnant la Description Détaillée des Ouvrages Publiés ou Traduits en Latin et en Français sur le Cheval et la Cavalerie Avec de Nombreuses Biographies d'Auteurs Hippiques. Par le Général Mennessier de la Lance . . . Paris, Dorbon, 1915-17. 2 v.

MENZIES (Amy Charlotte (Bewick) Stuart). Lord William Beresford . . . Some Memories of a Famous Sportsman, Soldier and Wit. By Mrs. Stuart Menzies. With Appreciations by the Earl of Cromer & Admiral Lord Beresford. 38 Illustrations, Also Reproductions of the Signatures of Those Present at the Famous Farewell Dinner at Calcutta. London, Jenkins, 1917. xiv, 336 p. front. (port.), ports., facs.

MEREDITH (George William Lewin). Training Horses for Races. A Handbook for Amateur Beginners. By Capt. G.

MEREDITH (George William Lewin). *Continued:*
W. L. Meredith. With an Introduction by Lt.-Col. Geoffrey Brooke . . . London, Constable, 1926. xiv, 63 [1] p. illus.

MERRY (Mat). The Turf: Its Humour in Anecdote & Story. By Mat Merry. London, Maclaren [1905?] vii, 191 p.

MERRY (Thomas B.). The American Thoroughbred. By Thomas B. Merry ("Hidalgo") Los Angeles, Commercial Printing, 1905. 244 [1] p. illus., tables.

MEULEMAN (Eugène Camille François Joseph). Reflexions Critiques sur l'Histoire du Pur Sang. Par le Colonel E. Meuleman. Bruxelles, Aux Éditions de Chasse et Pêche, 1926. 75 p. plates. (Bibliothèque de la Revue *Chasse & Pêche*)

MEYSEY-THOMPSON (Richard Frederick). The Horse, Its Origin and Development Combined With Stable Practice, by Colonel R. F. Meysey-Thompson . . . London, Arnold, 1911. xii, 436 p. front., illus., plates.

MEYSEY-THOMPSON (Richard Frederick). Reminiscences of the Course, the Camp, the Chase. By Colonel R. F. Meysey-Thompson. London, Arnold, 1898. 314 p.

MIHURA (Marcel Salvat Jules). L'État Bookmaker. Par Jules Mihura . . . Avec une Préface du Baron de Vaux. Paris, Rousseau [1907] xvi, 184 p. *Tailpieces by "Crafty."*

MILLS (John). Grandeur et Décadence d'un Cheval de Course. Par John Mills. Ouvrage Illustré de Planches Gravées. Paris, Goin, 1862. 212 p. plates. *"A. M. le Comte Anatole d'Alcantara. Hommage respecteux du traducteur." The translator remains unknown—Contades.*

MILLS (John). The Life of a Race Horse. By John Mills . . . [London] Office of "The Field," 1854. x, 141 p. front., illus. *First appeared weekly in* The Field.

MILLS (John). The Life of a Racehorse. By John Mills . . . London, Ward, 1854. 106 p. front. *Second edition.*

MILLS (John). The Life of a Racehorse. By John Mills . . . London, Ward, 1865. 112 p. illus. (col.)

MILLS (John). Stable Secrets; or Puffy Doddles, His Sayings and Sympathies. By John Mills . . . London, Ward, 1863. 112 p. illus.

MINIÈRE (Théodore). Ostéolymphatisme du Cheval de Course et Nouvelle Méthode d'Exercice et d'Entraînement. Par le Dr. Th. Minière . . . Paris, Baillière, 1914. 64 p.

MIRABEL (Herbert de Vigier, Comte de). Manuel des Courses. France; Angleterre; Belgique; Allemagne. Dictionnaire du Turf. Première Édition. [Paris, Dupont, 1867] 440 p. *Title page lacking. Following Table des Matières: "Renseignements Utiles et Maisons Recommandées."*

MIRANDA ROSA (F. A. de). O Puro Sangue. Estatisticas da Criação Brasileira. 1936-44. [n.p., n.d.] 351 [1] p.

Tipped in: Typewritten list of breeders, Rio—São Paulo, 1945-1948; of mères de vainqueurs classeés par étalons, Rio—São Paulo, 1945-1948; of étalons pères de vainqueurs, Rio—São Paulo, 1945-1948.

MONTI (Jerome). Pour Faire Fortune aux Courses . . . Paris, Mericaut [1910] 2 pt. *Library has: pt. 1 only, lacking pt. 2, Le Secret des Courses.*

MONTIGNY (Edmée Louis Xavier, Vicomte puis Comte de). Manuel des Piqueurs, Cochers, Grooms, et Palefreniers à

MONTIGNY (Edmée Louis Xavier). *Continued:* l'Usage des Écoles de Dressage & d'Équitation de France. Par le Comte de Montigny . . . Huitième Édition, Augmentée d'une Huitième Partie de l'Élevage et de l'Entraînement des Chevaux de Course et de Chasse, d'Après Digby Collins. Paris, Chapelot, 1905. xvi, 565 p.

MOORE (Maurice George). An Irish Gentleman, George Henry Moore . . . With a Preface by George Moore. London, Laurie [1913] xxvii, 396 p. front. (port.), plates, ports.

MOORHOUSE (Edward). The History and Romance of the Derby. Into Which Are Woven the Facts and Figures a Sportsman Requires If He Would Be Familiar With the Leading Incidents Associated With the Long Series of Contests for the Greatest Prize That Can Be Won by Votaries of the Turf. By Edward Moorhouse . . . And Containing an Appendix in Which There Is a Complete List of the Competitors in the Derby From 1780 to 1907, Together With Full Betting Returns. In Two Volumes. 2d ed . . . London, Biographical Press, 1911. 2 v. illus.

MOORHOUSE (Edward). The Racing Year. 1903. By Edward Moorhouse. Illustrated With Photographs. London, Richards [1903] 308 p. front., illus.

MORLAND (Thomas Hornby). The Genealogy of the English Race Horse; With the Natural History of His Progenitors, From the Earliest Times Down to the Period When Foreign Blood Was First Introduced Into This Kingdom . . . By T. Hornby Morland . . . London, Barfield, 1810. viii, 160 p. front. (eng.)

MORTON (Charles). My Sixty Years of the Turf. Reminiscences of the Joys and Sorrows of a Racing Life. By Charles Morton. With Frontispiece and 16 Other Illustrations. London, Hutchinson [1930] 280 p. front. (port.), plates.

[MOTT (Edward Spencer).] Dopes. A Criticism of American Arts and English Efforts. By "Nathaniel Gubbins." [pseud.] London, Everett, 1901. viii, 126 p.

[MOTT (Edward Spencer).] First Favourites. By Nathaniel Gubbins [pseud.] London, Long, 1904. 245 p.

[MOTT (Edward Spencer).] The Great Game and How It Is Played. A Treatise on the Turf, Full of Tales. By Edward Spencer [pseud.] 'Nathaniel Gubbins' . . . London, Richards, 1900. xviii, 261 p.

[MOTT (Edward Spencer).] The King's Racehorses. A History of the Connection of His Majesty King Edward VII. With the National Sport. By Edward Spencer [pseud.] London, Long, 1902. xv, 204 [1] p. front. (port.), illus., facs.

MUGGRIDGE (William). How to Train a Racehorse. Australian Horse Talk for Horse Men. By William Muggridge . . . Sydney, Brooks, 1920. xvi, 156 p. front., illus.

MUIR (J. B.). Ye Olde New-Markitt Calendar of Matches, Results, and Programs From 1619 to 1719 With the Masters, Keepers, Trainers, and Jockeys of the Royal Running Horses From Edward III. to Present Date and a Tabulated List of the Breeders, Trainers, and Training Grounds of the Winners of the Derby, Oaks, and St. Leger From Their Commencement. By J. B. Muir . . . London, the author, 1892. xii, 76 p. front.

MUIR (J. B.). Raciana or Riders' Colours of the Royal, Foreign, and Principal Patrons of the British Turf From 1762 to 1883 Arranged Alphabetically. Also an Appendix . . . With an Account of Some of the Most Interesting Sporting Matches Which Have Taken Place at Newmarket and York. Compiled by J. B. Muir . . . London, the compiler, 1890. xii, 188 p. front., illus.

MUIR (J. B.). W. T. Frampton and the "Dragon." A Refutation of the Charge Made by His Critics. Papers Are Also Included Relating to the Studs of James the First; Villiers, First Duke of Buckingham; Sir Thomas Pelham; and Sir John Pelham. Together With a List of Places Where Horse-Racing Took Place From the Roman Epoch, Through Each Reign Down to the Date of Queen Anne. With Two Illustrations. By J. B. Muir . . . London, the author, 1895. vii, 131 [1] p. front. (port.), illus.

MUNNINGS (Sir Alfred James). An Artist's Life. London, Museum Press [1950-52] 3 v. illus., ports. *"Each vol. has special t.p. only; v. 2. The second burst, v. 3. The finish."*

MUNNINGS (Sir Alfred James). . . . Pictures of Horses and English Life. With an Appreciation by Lionel Lindsay . . . London, Eyre, 1927. xii, 199 p. front. (col.), illus., plates (part col.) *"Printed on one side of leaf only after p. 27. Plates have guard sheet with letterpress."*

MUNROE (David Hoadley). The Grand National. 1839-1931. By David Hoadley Munroe. With Forewords by Lord Wavertree and A. E. C. Topham . . . London, Heinemann [1931] [xvi] 149 p. (pt. 1), pt. 2 unpaged. illus., plates, fold. chart (col.), tables.

MUSANY (François Charles). L'Élevage, l'Entraînement, et les Courses au Point de Vue de la Production et de l'Amélioration des Chevaux de Guerre. F. Musany. Avec une Étude Médicale sur l'Embonpoint et les Moyens Rationnels de le Combattre. Par le Dr. H. Libermann. Paris, Baudoin, 1890. ix, 145 p. diagr.

The author's name was Mansuy, but he used "Musany" for all his writing except his first.—Mennessier de la Lance.

The MUSEUM of Foreign Literature and Science. . . . Philadelphia, Littell, 1822-42. *Library has: v. 23 only. "The Turf" by Richard Darvill, p. 409-440.*

NATIONAL Association of State Racing Commissioners. Bulletin. Lexington, Ky., 1935- . *Library has incomplete file.*

NATIONAL Association of State Racing Commissioners. Proceedings. Lexington, Ky., 1935- . *Library has: 1935 to date.*

NATIONAL Association of State Racing Commissioners. Statistical Reports on Horses Racing in the U. S. for the year . . . Lexington, Ky., 1955- . *Library has: 1955 to date.*

NATIONAL Steeplechase and Hunt Association. Records of Hunt Meetings . . . Summary of Races Run Under Sanction of the Hunts Committee and the National Steeplechase and Hunt Association. Compiled by Frank J. Bryan and George W. Gall. New York, 19 - . *Library has: 1910-17.*

[NEUHOF (Albert).] Classements Cotés de Godolphin Darley . . . Handicap Ratings (Flat & Jumps) Plat et Obstacles. Près de 3000 Chevaux Classés d'Après Leur Valeur en Course . . . [Levallois, the author] 1950- . annual. *Library has: 1950 to date.*

NEUTER (Adolphe de). Mémoires d'un Entraîneur. La Casaque Rose. Paris, Kapp, 1925. 262 p. (Le Turf Anecdotique, v. 1, Mémoires)

NEUTER (Adolphe de). Mémoires d'un Entraîneur. Le Cinéma des Courses . . . Adolphe de Neuter. Bruxelles, Fischlin, 1930. 203 p. (Le Turf Anecdotique, v. 8)

NEUTER (Adolphe de). Mémoires d'un Entraîneur. George Stern, Jockey . . . Adolphe de Neuter. Bruxelles, Fischlin, 1929. 181 [3] p. (Le Turf Anecdotique, v. 7)

NEUTER (Adolphe de). Mémoires d'un Entraîneur. Les Guêpes Hippiques. Paris, Kapp, 1927. 268 p. (Le Turf Anecdotique, v. 5, Mémoires)

NEUTER (Adolphe de). Mémoires d'un Entraîneur. Le Magicien de Forest. (En Marge de La Casaque Rose) Lanesloot Ressuscité . . . Bruxelles, Fischlin, 1927. 236 p. (Le Turf Anecdotique, v. 4, Mémoires)

NEUTER (Adolphe de). Mémoires d'un Entraîneur. Le Roman de l'Hippodrome . . . Bruxelles, Fischlin, 1928. 177 p. (Le Turf Anecdotique, v. 6)

NEUTER (Adolphe de). Mémoires d'un Entraîneur. Le Ruban Bleu. Paris, Kapp, 1926. 310 p. (Le Turf Anecdotique, v. 3, Mémoires)

NEUTER (Adolphe de). Mémoires d'un Entraîneur au Siècle d'Épinard. (Hommes, Choses et Chevaux de Mon Temps) Adolphe de Neuter. Paris, Kapp, 1926. 220 p. (Le Turf Anecdotique, v. 2, Mémoires)

NEVILL (Ralph Henry). Light Come, Light Go. Gambling— Gamesters—Wagers—The Turf. By Ralph Nevill . . . London, Macmillan, 1909. x, 448 p. front. (col.), illus. (part col.)

Tipped in: "Dec. 15th 1915. St. James Club, Piccadilly, W. Dear sir: I have been away otherwise would have replied before. As far as I remember I got my information about 'Somerville and his old huntsman' from the Sporting Magazine. A complete set is rare but I should say a look through the early volumes (it began about 1789) might repay you. I am sorry to be of such little use. The copy of the Sporting Magazine I used is now unfortunately not available. Yours truly Ralph Nevill." Addressee unnamed.

NEVILL (Ralph Henry). Old English Sporting Prints and Their History. Ralph Nevill. Edited by Geoffrey Holme. London, The Studio, 1923. xv, 22 p. plates (part col.)

Printed on one side of leaf only after p. 22. Col. plates have guard sheets with letterpress. "The entire edition of this volume is limited to 1500 numbered copies (1000 for the British Empire and 500 for America). This copy is number 1328."

NEVILL (Ralph Henry). Old Sporting Prints. By Ralph Nevill. London, Connoisseur Magazine, 1908. 82 p. front. (col.), plates (part col.) *At head of title: "Connoisseur extra number."*

NEVILL (Ralph Henry). The Sport of Kings. By Ralph Nevill. With Sixteen Illustrations. London, Methuen [1926] 247 p. illus.

NEW YORK. (State Racing Commission) Annual Reports. State Racing Commission 1895-1906. Racing Laws of State of New York and Rules of Racing 1907. [New York, 1907] 446 p.

The NEW YORK Sportsman. New York, 18 - . weekly. *Library has: v. 15-16 (1883)*

The NEW ZEALAND Thoroughbred Breeders' Association, Inc. Register of Thoroughbred Stallions of New Zealand. Founded, Edited and Published by The New Zealand Thoroughbred Breeders' Association (Inc.) . . . Containing Tabulated Pedigrees and Turf and Stud Records of Stallions Now at the Stud in New Zealand. Together With Statistical and Other Information Which Should Be Useful to All Who Are Interested in the Derivation of Present-Day New Zealand Racehorses. [Wellington] 1951- . *Library has: v. 1 (1951)*

The NEW ZEALAND Racing Conference. The New Zealand Stud Book Containing Pedigrees of Race Horses etc., etc. Issued Under the Authority of The New Zealand Racing Conference . . . Christchurch, Christchurch Press, 1900- . *Library has: v. 1-13 (1900-38)*

NEWMAN (Neil). Famous Horses of the American Turf. By Neil Newman "Roamer." Introduction by W. S. Vosburgh

NEWMAN (Neil). *Continued:*
. . . New York, Derrydale Press, 1931-33. 3 v. illus. *v. 2
(1931): "Selected by Walter S. Vosburgh." v. 3 (1932):
"Foreword by Algernon Daingerfield."*

NEWMARKET. [Pseud.] Chapters From Turf History. By Newmarket. London, "National Review Office," 1922. 159 p.
front. (port.), illus. *Illus. have guard sheets with letterpress.*

NEW-YORK Sporting Magazine, and Annals of the American
and English Turf: a Work Entirely Dedicated to Sporting
Subjects and Fancy Pursuits . . . New-York, Colden, 1833-
34. 2 v. illus. (part col.) *Library has: v. 1, no. 1-12 (Mar.
1833-Feb. 1834)*

NICARD (Claude Édouard). L'Inbreeding et l'Outcrossing
(Consanguinité et Croisement) en Élevage de Chevaux de
Course. Par Édouard Nicard. 1er. Volume Pour Servir
d'Introduction aux Hautes Études sur l'Élevage Pur au Point
de Vue des Courses. Nevers, Mazeron Frères, 1912. *Library has: v. 1 only. v. 1 is comprised of 3 parts. Of an edition of 300 copies this is no. 147.*

NICARD (Claude Édouard). Le Langage des Éleveurs de
Chevaux de Courses. Par Édouard Nicard. Nevers, Mazeron Frères, 1902. xviii, 278 p. *Of an edition of 300 copies
this is no. 253.*

NICHOLSON (William). An Almanac of Twelve Sports. By
William Nicholson. Words by Rudyard Kipling. London,
Heinemann, 1898. 1 v. (unpaged) illus.

NIGHTINGALL (Arthur). My Racing Adventures. By Arthur
Nightingall. Edited by "G. G." (H. G. Harper) London,
Laurie [n.d.] 280 p. front. (port.), plates.

NIMROD. *See* APPERLY (Charles James).

NOISAY (Maurice de). Tableau des Courses, ou Essai sur les Courses de Chevaux en France. Par Maurice de Noisay. Illustré de Onze Lithographies en Couleurs par J. L. Boussingault. Paris, Éditions de la Nouvelle Revue Française [1921] 258 p. front., plates (col.) (Tableaux Contemporains—No. 1) *". . . Exemplaire no. 58" of an edition of 285 copies.*

NOISAY (Maurice de). Voilà les Courses! Essai sur le Sport Hippique en France Avec des Souvenirs, des Anecdotes, des Portraits, des Généralités, des Conseils et l'Histoire du Célèbre Épinard. Paris, Éditions du Siècle [1925] 254 [1] p.

NOTHING VENTURE. *See* FINNEY (Humphrey Stanley).

O'BRIEN (Richard Barry). The Life of Lord Russell of Killowen. By R. Barry O'Brien . . . With a Portrait and Facsimiles. New York, Longmans, 1901. v, 405 p. front. (port.), facs.

O'CONNOR (John Lawrence). History of the Kentucky Derby, 1875-1921. [New York, Rider Press, 1921] 141 p. *Reprinted in part from* The Thoroughbred Record.

O'CONNOR (John Lawrence). Notes on the Thoroughbred From Kentucky Newspapers. Compiled by John L. O'Connor. Privately Printed by Louis Lee Haggin. [Lexington, Transylvania Prtg. Co., 1927] 1 v. (unpaged) *Period covered: Feb. 16, 1788—Nov. 21, 1833.*

O'CONNOR (Winfield Scott). Jockeys, Crooks and Kings. The Story of Winnie O'Connor's Life as Told to Earl Chapin May. Woodcuts by Lynd Ward. New York, Cape [1930] 219 p. front. (port.)

OFFICIAL Horse Show Blue Book. New York, 1906- . annual. illus. *Library has v. 12 (1918), v. 17-28 (1923-29), v. 33-35 (1939-41), v. 37 (1943), v. 38 (1944)*

O'KELLY (Dennis). The Genuine Memoirs of Dennis O'Kelly, Esq. Commonly Called Count O'Kelly: Containing Many Curious and Interesting Anecdotes of That Celebrated Character, and His Coadjutors on the Turf and in the Field, With a Variety of Authentic, Singular, and Entertaining Militia Manoeuvres, Never Before Published. London, Stalker, 1788. 72 p.

[OLD (Walter Gorn).] The Silver Key. A Guide to Speculators. By Sepharial . . . London, Foulsham, 1919. xi, 93 [1] p.

The OLD BUSHMAN. *See* WHEELWRIGHT (Horace William).

OLIPHANT (George Henry Hewit). The Law Concerning Horses, Racing, Wagers and Gaming; With an Appendix Containing Recent Cases, Statutes etc. By George Henry Hewit Oliphant . . . London, Sweet, 1847. lxi, 322 p.

OMWAKE (John). The Conestoga Six-Horse Bell Teams of Eastern Pennsylvania. Published by John Omwake for Private Distribution. Cincinnati, the author, 1930. 163 p. front., illus. *2d edition. Appendix to 1st ed.: p. 130-136; appendix to 2d ed.: p. 137-163.*

The ORACLE of Rural Life; an Almanack for Sportsmen, Farmers, Gardeners, and Country Gentlemen, for the Year 1839. Practical Farming, by Nimrod. Gardening, etc., by Mr. Warden . . . Country Sports by Nimrod and Tom Oakleigh. Embellished With Fourteen Illustrations. London, Baily, 1839. 96 p. plates (eng.) *Added eng. title page.*

ORCHARD (Vincent R.). The Derby Stakes. A Complete History From 1900 to 1953. By Vincent Orchard. London, Hutchinson [1954] 325 [2] p. illus. *Bibliography: p. [327]*

ORCHARD (Vincent R.). Tattersalls. Two Hundred Years of Sporting History. By Vincent Orchard. London, Hutchinson [1953] 312 p. front. (col.), illus.

ORTON (John). Turf Annals of York and Doncaster, Together With Particulars of the Derby and Oaks Stakes at Epsom, From the Earliest Period Up to the Close of the Year 1843, Interspersed With Biographical Notices of Many of the Olden Jockies Who Have Earned a Notoriety on the Turf, and Other Features Connected Therewith. By John Orton . . . York, Sotheran, 1844. x, 722 p.

OSBALDESTON (George). Squire Osbaldeston: His Autobiography. Edited, With Commentary, by E. D. Cuming. Introduction by Sir Theodore Cook. With Sixteen Illustrations in Colour, and Seventy-Five in Black and White, and a Map. London, Lane [1926] lv, 260 p. front. (port. col.), illus. (part col.), map (fold.)

OSBORNE (Joseph). The Horsebreeders' Handbook: Embracing Eighty Tabulated Pedigrees With Full Particulars of the Principal Sires Advertised to Cover During the Season 1881. Edited by J. Osborne ("Beacon") London, Clegg [1881] xii, 161 p. tables.

OSBORNE (Joseph). The Horse-Breeders' Handbook: Embracing Ninety-Seven Tabulated Pedigrees, With Full Particulars of the Principal Sires Advertised to Cover During the Seasons 1889-90. Together With Full Pedigrees and Particulars of Thirty-Six of the Most Celebrated Old Sires. Embellished With Portraits of Stockwell, Ormonde, St.

OSBORNE (Joseph). *Continued:*
Simon, and Bendigo. By Joseph Osborne ("Beacon") Second Edition. (Enlarged by the Addition of Twenty More Pedigrees and an Obituary of the Celebrated Sires Since 1723.) London, Seale [1890?] lxxxix, 304 p. plates.

OSBORNE (Joseph). The Two Year Olds of 1899. Their Breeding in Full, by Whom Bred, and by Whom Trained, Alphabetically Arranged Under the Names of Their Respective Sires, With Their Principal Engagements for the Season 1899. With Introduction. By Joseph Osborne ("Beacon") . . . London, Seale, 1899. xx, 220 p.

OSMER (William). A Dissertation on Horses: Wherein It Is Demonstrated, by Matters of Fact, as Well as From the Principles of Philosophy, That Innate Qualities Do Not Exist, and That the Excellence of This Animal Is Altogether Mechanical and Not in the Blood. By William Osmer. London, Waller, 1756. 61 p.

OUTSIDER. [Pseud.] La Glorieuse Incertitude du Turf. Comment Parier et Gagner aux Courses? Étude Analytique des Méthodes de Paris. Plat—Obstacles—Trot. Par Outsider. Paris, Kapp [1926] 271 p.

P. J. *See* ANNALS of the Turf; GENERAL Account and Pedigree of the British Race Horse . . .; *and* TRACES of the Turf.

PACIFIC Coast Jockey Club. Inaugural Meeting. 1923. Tanforan Racecourse, San Bruno, California. [n.p., 1923?] 1 v. (unpaged) illus., ports.

PAGE (Harry S.). Between the Flags. The Recollections of a Gentleman Rider. By Harry S. Page. Illustrated by Edward S. Voss and From Photographs. New York, Derrydale Press, 1929. x, 313 p. front. (col.), plates (part col.)

PALACHE (J. Thomson). The Jamaica Stud Book. With Historical Sketch of the Turf. By J. Thomson Palache. Jamaica, Gardner, 1892- .

> Library has: v. 1. Cover stamped: v. 1. Inserted: Photo of "E. G. Watts (better known as John Watts)" Tipped in: Program of Barbados races, July 18, 19, 1894.

PALMER (Joseph Hill). Names in Pedigrees. Joe H. Palmer (Beadsman) Lexington, Ky., The Blood-Horse, 1939. 462 p. illus. *"Articles . . . published in the weekly issues of* The Blood-Horse [*under the pseudonym, Beadsman*]"

PALMER (Joseph Hill). This Was Racing. By Joe H. Palmer. Edited by Red Smith. Profusely Illustrated by Willard Mullin. New York, Barnes [1953] xii, 270 p. front. (port.), illus. *Library has also: trade edition.*

PARENT (Ernest Charles Louis Marie). Manuel des Courses de Chevaux. Chevaux—Entraîneurs—Jockeys—Parieurs—Hippodromes—Argot du Turf. Suivi de la Jurisprudence du Turf. Par Ernest Parent . . . Bruxelles, Parent, 1868. 140 p.

PARKER (Richard). The Whip. By Richard Parker. Novelized from Cecil Raleigh's Great Drury Lane Melodrama. Illustrated With Pictures From the Play. New York, Macaulay [1913] 314 p. front., plates.

[PARSONS (Philip).] Newmarket: or, An Essay on the Turf. Containing, Amongst Other Grave and Weighty Matters, a Parallel . . . Between Newmarket Races, and the Olympic Games; Very Proper to Be Had in All Pockets at the Next Newmarket Meeting . . . London, Baldwin, 1771. 2 v.

PATERSON (Andrew Barton). The Man From Snowy River and Other Verses. By A. B. Paterson. London, Macmillan, 1919. xvi, 184 p.

PATERSON (Andrew Barton). Rio Grande's Last Race and Other Verses. By A. B. Paterson . . . London, Macmillan, 1904. xii, 178 p. *First edition.*

PAZ (Eugène). Dictionnaire des Courses. Explication par Ordre Alphabétique de Tous les Termes Techniques Usités sur le Turf—Théorie des Paris—Mécanisme des Poules—Règlement du Jockey-Club et du Betting Room. Par Eugène Paz . . . Paris, Librairie du Petit Journal, 1867. 64 p.

PEACOCK (Thomas). The Stable Boy; a Poem. In Five Parts. By Thomas Peacock. London, Asperne, 1820. iv, 88 p. *Vignette heads each part.*

PEARCE (Charles E.). A Queen of the Paddock. A Romance of the Race Course. By Charles E. Pearce . . . New York, Brentano, 1921. 251 p.

PEARSON (Ned). [Pseud.] *See* ÉTREILLIS (Le Baron d').

PEB. [Pseud.] *See* BELLOCQ (Pierre Émile).

PEDDIE (James). Racing For Gold or, Incidents in the Life of a Turf Commissioner. With Examples of the Most Successful Systems of Speculating on the Turf and in Games of Chance. By James Peddie . . . Illustrated by A. C. Havell. London, Fores, 1891. x, 308 p. front., illus.

PETERS (J. G.). A Treatise on Equitation, or the Art of Horsemanship, Simplified Progressively for Amateurs. Forming Complete Lessons for Training Horses, and Instructions for Beginners. Illustrated With Twenty-Seven Descriptive Plates . . . By J. G. Peters . . . London, Whittaker, 1835. lv, 316 p. front., plates.

PETION (K. A.). Genealogical Lists of English Thoroughbred Horses by the Female Line. 2nd ed. Moscow, Imperial Moscow Racing Society, 1913. Charts in folder. *Russian text. Title "from the preface to the second edition."*

PHIZ. *See* BROWNE (Hablot Knight).

PICHARD ( ). Manuel des Haras, ou Système de Régénération des Races de Chevaux, Applicable à Toutes les Parties de l'Empire Français; à l'Usage de Ceux Qui, par Goût ou par Spéculation, se Livrent à l'Élève des Chevaux. Suivi de la Manière de Purger les Chevaux à l'Anglaise. Par Pichard . . . Paris, Delacour, 1812. xiv, 325 (i.e. 423) p. front. (eng.)

PICK (William). An Authentic Historical Racing Calendar of All Plates, Sweepstakes, Matches, etc. Run for at York, From the First Commencement of the Races There in the Year 1709, to the Year 1785 Inclusive . . . With an Account of the Cock-Matches Fought at York in Each Race-Week for Upwards of Forty Years . . . The Whole Carefully Compiled From Authentic Materials by W. Pick . . . York, Blanchard [1786?] viii, 198 p.

With this is bound: Pedigrees and Performances of the Most Celebrated Race-Horses, That Have Appeared Upon the English Turf, Since the Time of Basto . . . In Three Parts. 132 p. Paged separately.

PICK (William). An Historical Account of All the Plates, Matches, and Sweepstakes, Run for at Newmarket, From the Year 1728. From the Volumes of Cheney, etc. With Corrections by W. Pick of York. [York, Pick, 1770] 254 p.

Ms notes: "The contents have the same pagination and the same paper as the *Vade Mecums.* I think that the publisher intended to publish a calendar solely dealing with Newmarket

PICK (William). *Continued:*

and then found it would not pay and never completed it. (signed) R. J. T." Ms note: "The contents of this volume first appeared in the *Sportsmans and Breeders Vade Mecum* in serial form, continued throughout the issues of 1789-90-91-92-93-94-95. The account was run under the table of contents as 'Account of the Races at New Market in the year 1728 to the second spring meeting 1773.' The complete series has pages numbered to 350. This binding is the same as that used on the *Annual* 'Blue boards, paper back.' (signed) J. L. O'C." Following in the same hand: "This volume is possibly a 'one book edition.' Perhaps the printers own copy." Typewritten note: "I have tested a number of pages by collating them with Cheny, Heber, etc., and also (for the entries before 1750) with Weatherby's *Abridgment* (1829). I find that Pick added a number of annotations, but as to 'corrections' I do not find anything which is not in Weatherby's *Abridgment* and later in Baily. As to the provenience of the volume, I have made a note of an hypothesis, which is in the book with the card of bibliographic notes by O'Connor and yourself. It seems to me that there may well be in country houses in Yorkshire other such volumes, similarly made up from the files of the *Vade Mecums,* but probably bound in other styles. In any event, it seems that it is misleading to call the book, as the binder did with your copy, *Pick's Newmarket Calendar of 1770.* (signed) F. H. May 26, 1933." Typewritten note: "It is suggested that the Raymond-O'Connor-Turnbull volume was made up for an individual, not necessarily the publisher, by binding separately an incomplete collection of sheets extracted from the *Vade Mecums.* As the pagination is continuous it was apparently the publisher's intention that the subscribers for the *Vade Mecums* might do this, and others may, therefore, have done so. If so, the book is not necessarily unique. (signed) F. H. May, 1933."

PICK (William). Pedigrees and Performances of the Most Celebrated Race-Horses, That Have Appeared on the English Turf Since the Time of Basto, Flying Childers, etc. With an Historical Account of the Most Favourite Arabians, Turks, Barbs, English Stallions, and Brood-Mares: Alphabetically Digested. In Three Parts. York, the author [1786?] 132 p. *Bound with the author's* An Authentic Historical Racing Calendar, *York [1786?]*

PICK (William). Racing Calendar Containing an Account of the Plates, Sweepstakes, & Matches, Run for in . . . an Alphabetical List of the Winning Horses, and a Complete Index, With Their Pedigrees. Also a List of Stallions . . . To Which Is Added, an Account of All the Great Coursing Meetings in the Kingdom . . . and the Cockings for . . . By W. Pick . . . York, Bartholoman, 17 - . *Library has: v. 17-41 (1802-27)*

PICK (William). The Sportsman and Breeder's Vade Mecum; or, An Historical Account of All the Races in Great Britain, for . . . With an Alphabetical List of the Winning Horses, etc., etc. . . . An Abstract of the Cock-Matches Fought in . . . To Which Is Likewise Given the Races at Newmarket, in 1728 to the October Meeting 1744 . . . Compiled by W. Pick . . . York, 1786- . *Library has: 1789, 1791-98, 1800.*

PICK (William). The Turf Register, and Sportsman & Breeder's Stud-Book. Containing the Pedigrees & Performances of All the Horses, Mares, and Geldings That Have Appeared Upon the British and Irish Turfs as Racers; Likewise of Such as Have Been Kept in the Stud as Stallions and for Breeding . . . With an Account of the Most Favourite Arabians, Turks, and Barbs, Brought Into England, and From Whom Has Descended the Most Valuable Blood in the United Kingdoms. The Whole Calculated for the Information and Use of Sportsmen and Breeders; and the Lovers of That Noble Animal the Horse. By William Pick . . . York, Bartholoman, 1803- . *Library has: v. 1, 1803 (to 1763); v. 2, 1805 (to 1772); v. 3, 1822 (to 1782); v. 4, 1867 (to 1792) v. 3, 4 were pub. by R. Johnson, York.*

PIERCE (Emmons Sylvester). Poems of the Turf and Other Ballads. By Em. Pierce. Buffalo, N. Y., Wenborne-Sumner, 1890. 135 p. front. (port.) *Head- and tail-pieces signed "Sumner."*

PINEL (Honoré Philippe). A. B. C. du Sportsman. Par Honoré Pinel . . . Paris, Ducrocq, 1869. 3 v. illus. (col.) *"1re series, no. 1: Robes et Marques; no. 2: Conformations; no. 3: Les Races."*

"PITTSBURG PHIL." [Pseud. for George E. Smith] *See* COLE (Edward W.).

PLATT (James Edward). Bruntwood Stud, Cheadle, Cheshire, the Property of Mr. James E. Platt . . . Stud Groom, J. C. Corston. Cheadle, Marsh, 1898. 58 p.

PLATT (James Edward). The Thoroughbred Race-Horse. Its Breeding & Early Management. By Major James Edward Platt. London, Tavistock Press [1927] 110 p. front. (port.)

Mr. Turnbull's note, tipped in: "See for serious errors on p. 50 *The Bloodstock Breeders Review* of 1927 in which there is a review of this book."

POLAND. Society for Promoting Horsebreeding in Poland. Tabulated Pedigrees of Thoroughbred Horses. Warsaw, 1932. tables (unpaged)

POND (John). The Sporting Kalendar. Containing a Distinct Account of What Plates and Matches Have Been Run for in . . . an Article for Making a Newmarket Match, a Description of a Post and Handy-Cap Match, a Table Shewing What Weight Horses Are to Carry for the Give and Take Plates; and of What Matches Have Been Run for at Newmarket, from October the 1st, 1718, to October 1751, etc. By John Pond. London, Woodfall, 1751-57. 7 v. *Library has: v. 1-7 (1751-57)*

PONIATOWSKI (André). The Burlingame Stock Farm. Burlingame, Cal. Prince A. Poniatowski. [San Francisco, Hicks-Judd, 1893] 128 p.

PONS (Adolphe). Season of 1930. Mereworth Stud Stallions. Apply to Adolphe Pons . . . or R. Kenneth Kane . . . [n.p., 1930?] 1 v. (unpaged)

PONTET (Th.). Dictionnaire Généalogique des Chevaux de Pur Sang Importés ou Nés en France et Livrés à le Reproduction Depuis 1800 Jusqu'en 1865. Par Th. Pontet . . . Paris, Dupont, 1869. xi, 260 p.

PONTET (Th.). Répertoire Historique des Chevaux de Race Pure en France. Publié Avec l'Autorisation de Son Excellence le Ministre de l'Agriculture, du Commerce et des Travaux Publics sur les Documents Réunis. Par M. Pontet . . . 1re Partie—Reproduction. (1801 à 1853) Paris, Dupont, 1856. xxiv, 288 p. *Library has: pt. 1 only.*

POORE (Benjamin Perley). Biographical Sketch of John Stuart Skinner. By Ben. Perley Poore. Reprinted from "The Plough, the Loom and the Anvil" 1854. By John L. O'Connor. [New York, J. L. O'Connor, 1924] 34 p.

PORTEFIN (J.). Le Cheval de Courses. Par un Entraîneur. Paris, Legoupy [1916] 119 p. illus., plates. *Cover title.*

PORTER (John). John Porter of Kingsclere. An Autobiography Written in Collaboration With Edward Moorhouse. London, Richards, 1919. x, 505 p. front. (port.)

PORTER (John). Kingsclere. By John Porter. Edited by Byron Webber. With 19 Full-Page Illustrations and Others. London, Chatto, 1896. xviii, 369 p. front. (port.), plates, ports.

Tipped in: Two letters from John Porter and newspaper clippings relating to his wedding in 1905, retirement in 1906, and death at 82 in 1922.

PORTER (William Trotter). A Quarter Race in Kentucky, and Other Sketches, Illustrative of Scenes, Characters, and Incidents, Throughout "The Universal Yankee Nation." Edited by William T. Porter . . . With Illustrations by Darley. Philadelphia, Peterson [1854] 203 p. front., illus. (Library of Humorous American Works) *Added title page.*

PORTER'S Spirit of the Times. A Chronicle of the Turf, Field Sports, Literature and the Stage. New York, 1856-61. 11 v. illus. weekly. *Editor: William Trotter Porter. Library has: v. 1-6.*

PORTLAND (William John Arthur Charles James Cavendish-Bentinck, Sixth Duke of). Memories of Racing and Hunting. By the Duke of Portland. New York, Scribner, 1935. xvi, 364 p. front. (port.), illus., facs.

PORTRAITS of Broodmares Belonging to the Royal Stud at Hampton Court. By C. W. London, Sams, 1837. 3 v. (unpaged) plates. *3 v. bound together, numbered 1, 2, 3; no. 1 only dated.*

PORTRAITURE of the Most Famous Racehorses in the Reign of Queen Anne, Geo. I & II. [London, Butler, 1753] 25 plates. *24 numbered plates with descriptive text surrounding portrait. 1st plate unnumbered, dated 1751.*

POWELL (Willis J.). Tachyhippodamia; or, The New Secret of Taming Horses. Giving Full Directions How to Break and Ride Colts . . . With Numerous Valuable Receipts for Diseases of Horses . . . By Willis J. Powell. To Which Is Added The Breaking, Training, and Taming Horses, by J. S. Rarey . . . Philadelphia, Hubbard, 1877. xvi, 161 p. front., illus.

[POWNALL (Henry).] Some Particulars Relating to the History of Epsom, Compiled From the Best Authorities; Containing a Succinct and Interesting Description of the Origin of Horse Racing, and of Epsom Races, With an Account of the Mineral Waters, and the Two Celebrated Palaces of Durdans and Nonsuch, etc., etc. To Which Is Added, an Appendix, Containing a Botanical Survey of the Neighbourhood. With Six Plates. By an Inhabitant . . . Epsom, Dorling, 1825. xiv, 208 p. front. (col.), illus.

PRIAM. *See* COLLINS (Charles James).

PRIOR (Charles Mathew). Early Records of the Thoroughbred Horse Containing Reproductions of Some Original Stud-Books, and Other Papers of the Eighteenth Century. Collected and Edited by C. M. Prior . . . London, The Sportsman Office, 1924. 171 p. illus., plates.

PRIOR (Charles Mathew). The History of the Racing Calendar and Stud-Book From Their Inception in the Eighteenth Century, With Observations on Some of the Occurrences Noted Therein. By C. M. Prior . . . London, The "Sporting Life," 1926. 271 p., ix. *Index paged separately.*

PRIOR (Charles Mathew). The Royal Studs of the Sixteenth and Seventeenth Centuries, Together With a Reproduction of the Second Earl of Godolphin's Stud-book, and Sundry Other Papers Relating to the Thoroughbred Horse. By C. M. Prior . . . With 11 Illustrations. London, "Horse and Hound," 1935. xi, 213 p., xiii-xx. illus., plates, facs. *Index paged separately.*

[PRIOR (Florence Mary).] Prior's "H.-B." Stud-Book. An Attempt to Register the Pedigrees and Performances of the Best Known of Our Native Families of Racehorses, That

PRIOR (Florence Mary). *Continued:*
Are Ineligible for Entry in the General Stud-Book . . . By the Compiler of "The Register of Thoroughbred Stallions." London, Cox, 1914- . illus. *Library has: v. 1 (1914); v. 2 (1922); v. 3 (1928)*

PROCTOR (Richard Wright). Our Turf, Our Stage, and Our Ring. By Richard Wright Proctor . . . With Illustrations by William Morton . . . Manchester [England] Dinham, 1862. vi, 91 p. front., illus.

"Notices of the Press" (works by the author and artist): p. 92-100. Tipped in: Letter from author telling of choice of title and publication details.

QUEENSLAND Turf Club. The Queensland Racing Calendar . . . By the Authority of the Queensland Turf Club. Brisbane, Diddams, 19 - . *Library has: v. 17 (1903); v. 18 (1904)*

A RACE in Four Cantos. The Eve, Morning, Noon, and Night. Bath, Crutwell [n.d.] 35 p. *Binding stamped: "Litchfield Races." Laid in: "Lancelot & Maroon first & second for the great St. Leger 1840."*

RACING and Breeding. European Review. Paris, 1947- . illus. (part col.) 3 no. a year. *Library has: 1947-50. Cover illus. (col.) notable.*

RACING and Steeplechasing. Racing by the Earl of Suffolk and Berkshire, and W. G. Craven With a Contribution by the Hon. F. Lawley. Steeple-Chasing by Arthur Coventry and Alfred E. T. Watson. Numerous Illustrations by J. Sturgess. Third Edition. London, Longmans, 1889. 419 p. front. (col.), illus. (Badminton Library of Sports and Pastimes) *Library has also: No. 128 of 250 copies of the large paper edition, 1886.*

The RACING Handbook and Horses in Training. . . . London, "The Sportsman," 19 - . *Library has: 1901.*

RACING Illustrated. . . . Edited by Henry Smurthwaite (Vigilant of The Sportsman) . . . London, 1895- . illus. weekly. *Library has: v. 1-3 (July 2, 1895–Dec. 30, 1896)*

RACING in America. [1665-1936] Written for the Jockey Club . . . New York [1922-37] 4 v. illus., plates. *v. 1-2 (1665-1865), v. 4 (1922-36) by John Lewis Hervey; v. 3 (1866-1921) by Walter Spencer Vosburgh.*

RACING in France. Paris, 1950. 96 p. illus. (part col.) *The parts by various authors. Caricatures by Peb.*

RADCLIFFE (John B.). Amongst the Yorkshire Trainers: or Four Days at Malton & Middleham. By J. B. Radcliffe ("Saxon") . . . Newcastle, Daily Journal, 1899. 135 p. *"Reprinted from the* Newcastle Daily Journal."

RADCLIFFE (John B.). Ashgill; or The Life and Times of John Osborne. Written and Compiled by J. B. Radcliffe "Saxon." London, Sands, 1900. xxii, 500 p. front. (port.), plates, ports.

Tipped in: Two letters from John Osborne, newspaper clippings telling of Osborne's training successes in 1913 at the age of 80, and his death in 1922.

RAE-BROWN (Campbell). Goneaway's Race, and Other Sporting Ballads for Recitation, etc. (Including Three Dramatic Duologues.) By Campbell Rae-Brown . . . London, Everett [1907] 48 p.

RANCK (George Washington). Guide to Lexington, Kentucky, With Notices Historical and Descriptive of Places and Objects of Interest, and a Summary of the Advantages and

RANCK (George Washington). *Continued:*
Resources of the City and Vicinity, by G. W. Ranck . . .
Lexington, Ky., Transylvania Printing & Publishing Co.,
1883. 86 p. front., illus.

RANSOM (James Harley). Who's Who and Where in Horsedom
. . . Compiled by J. H. Ransom. Lexington, Ky., 1948- .
illus., ports. annual. *Library has: v. 1 to date. v. 8 title:*
"Who's Who in Horsedom." Separate index to v. 1-5.

RAPIER. *See* WATSON (Alfred Edward Thomas).

RAREY (John Solomon). The Art of Taming Horses by J. S.
Rarey. A New Edition, Revised, With Important Additions
and Illustrations, Including Chapters on Riding & Hunting,
for the Invalid and Timid. By the Secretary . . . London,
Routledge, 1858. 233 p. front., illus.

RAREY (John Solomon). The Modern Art of Taming Wild
Horses. By J. S. Rarey. Columbus, Follett, 1858. 59 p.

The RASP. Mounted Service School, U. S. Army, Fort Riley,
Kansas, 19 - . illus. *Library has: 1913, 1914.*

RAYMOND (George B.). Catalogue of Books on Angling, Shooting, Field Sports, Natural History, the Dog, Gun, Horse,
Racing and Kindred Subjects Belonging to George B. Raymond . . . New York, printed for private distribution,
1904. 46 [4] p. *"No. 51 of 100 copies printed." Ms notes:*
"Addenda," p. [47]

RECORD of Hunt Race Meetings in America, Comprising Complete Charts of All Races in . . . as Published Exclusively
in the Magazine Polo . . . [New York, 1932-] illus. annual. *Library has: v. 1-10 (1932-41)*

REEVES (Boleyne). Colburn's Kalendar of Amusements in Town and Country for 1840. Comprising London Seasons and Sights . . . Races, Hunts, and Steeplechaces . . . With Twelve Illustrations by R. Cruikshank. Edited by Boleyne Reeves . . . London, Colburn, 1840. 356 p. illus.

REEVES (J. H.). The Orange County Stud Book Giving a History of All Noted Stallions Bred and Raised in Orange County; Together With Symptoms and Treatment of the Diseases of the Horse, by J. H. Reeves . . . Unionville, N. Y., the author, 1872. 159 p.

REGISTER of Thoroughbred Stallions Containing the Tabulated Pedigrees and Racing Performances of . . . Sires at the Stud . . . London, Turf Newspapers, 1910- . *Library has: v. 1-14, 18 to date. Begun by Florence Mary Prior.*

RENDEL (John). The Horse Book. By John Rendel. New York, Fawcett, 1953. 144 p. illus. (Fawcett Book 183) *"Published by Fawcett for Sterling Publishing Co., Inc."*

REVUE des Éleveurs de Chevaux de Pur Sang. Volume Annuel Illustré Consacré à l'Élevage et aux Courses en France . . . Paris, 1919- . illus. annual. (Bibliothèque du "Tattersall Français")

Library has: v. 1-13 (1919-31) Publisher varies. Preface, v. 1: "Voici venue au monde la 'Revue des Éleveurs de Chevaux de Pur Sang,' soeur Française de la 'Bloodstock Breeder's Review.'" After the first issue it more and more resembled the British publication.

REYNOLDS (James). A World of Horses. By James Reynolds. A Conversation Piece Devoted to All Aspects of the Subject, Horse. The Way a Human Regards a Horse and the Way a Horse Regards a Human. Illustrated With Photographs and Drawings in Black and White by the Author. New York, Creative Age Press [1947] x, 259 p. front., illus.

RICE (James). History of the British Turf, From the Earliest Times to the Present Day. By James Rice . . . London, Low, 1879. 2 v. illus.

RICHARDS (Franklin Thomas Grant). Double Life. A Novel. By Grant Richards . . . London, Richards, 1920. 318 p.

RICHARDS (Sir Gordon). My Story. Sir Gordon Richards. London, Hodder [1955] 256 p. front., illus., ports.

RICHARDSON (Charles). The English Turf. A Record of Horses and Courses by Charles Richardson. Edited by E. T. Sachs. With Forty-Nine Illustrations and Eight Plans. New York, Dodd, 1901. xvi, 350 p. front., plates, plans.

RICHARDSON (Charles). The New Book of the Horse. By Charles Richardson . . . With Twenty-Nine Coloured Plates and Numerous Photographic Illustrations and an Extensive Veterinary Section . . . London, Cassell, 1911. 2 v. (paged continuously) illus. (part col.) *Various contributing authors.*

RICHARDSON (Charles). Racing at Home and Abroad . . . By Charles Richardson. London, 1923-31. 3 v. illus.

v. 1 (1923), v. 2 (1927), v. 3 (1931) v. 3: *Racing & Breeding in America and the Colonies* by John Hervey and others.

RICHARDSON (John Maunsell). Gentlemen Riders Past and Present. By John Maunsell Richardson and Finch Mason. London, Vinton, 1909. xxi, 487 [1] p. front. (port.), ports.

RICHARDSON (Mary E.). The Life of a Great Sportsman (John Maunsell Richardson) by His Sister Mary E. Richardson. With an Introduction by Victoria, Countess of Yarborough. "Racing Career" and "As an Owner" by the Late Finch Mason. Over 100 Full Page Illustrations Including Six Original Sketches by Finch Mason. London, Vinton, 1919. xxiii, 281 [1] p. front. (port.), plates, ports.

RICKETTS (Percy Edward). The Modern Racehorse. Conformation, Breeding and Heredity. By Lieut.-Col. P. E. Ricketts . . . Illustrated by Drawings and Photographs of Celebrated Horses. London, Constable [1923] xiii, 161 [1] p. front., illus., plates, diagr.

RICKETTS (Percy Edward). The Racehorse. Conformation and Action. By Lt.-Col. P. E. Ricketts . . . London, Constable, 1927. vii, 54 p. front., diagr.

RICKMAN (Eric). On and Off the Racecourse. With an Introduction by the Earl of Derby . . . London, Routledge, 1937. 283 p. front., illus.

RIDGEWAY (William). The Origin and Influence of the Thoroughbred Horse. By William Ridgeway . . . With Numerous Illustrations. Cambridge, University Press, 1905. xvi, 538 p. illus. (Cambridge Biological Series)

RIGGS (Elmer Samuel). The Geological History and Evolution of the Horse. By Elmer S. Riggs . . . Chicago, Field Museum, 1932. 54 p. illus. (Field Museum of Natural History, Chicago, Geology Leaflet 13) *Bibliography: p. 54. "xix pl. on 10 leaves."*

RIMINGTON (Michael Frederic). The Reforming of Dangerous and Useless Horses. By Lieutenant Mike Rimington . . . Aldershot, Gale, 1948. 75 p. front. (port.), illus. *"First impression, 1925; second impression, 1948."*

ROBERTS (James). The Sportsman's Pocket Companion: Being a Striking Likeness or Portraiture of the Most Eminent Race Horses & Stallions, That Ever Were in This Kingdom, Represented in Variety of Attitudes. To Which Is Added Their Genuine, Complete, but Concise Pedigrees & Per-

ROBERTS (James). *Continued:*
formances. Interspersed With Variety of Tail-Pieces & Em-
bellishments Alluding to the Sport. The Whole Calculated
for the Utility and Entertainment of the Nobility and Gen-
try, as Well as Breeders & Lovers of That Noble and Useful
Animal. Drawn by James Roberts & Engraved by Henry
Roberts . . . This Work Is so Contrived That It May Be
Framed & Glazed in Various Sizes, & Will Make Most
Elegant and Pleasing Furniture . . . [London] Roberts
[1760?] 40 plates (eng.)

ROBERTSON (J. B.). The Principles of Heredity Applied to
the Racehorse. By J. B. Robertson . . . Originally Published Weekly in "The Winning Post," November 20, 1909,
to January 22, 1910. London [1910?] 43 p.

ROBINSON (John Robert). 'Old Q' A Memoir of William
Douglas Fourth Duke of Queensberry . . . By John Robert
Robinson . . . London, Low, 1895. xvii, 362 p. front.
(port. col.), illus. *No. 71 of an edition of 125 copies.*

ROCHE (Arthur Somers). The Sport of Kings. By Arthur
Somers Roche . . . Illustrated by Arthur I. Keller. Indianapolis, Bobbs-Merrill [1917] 324 p. front., plates.

ROE (Frederic Gordon). Sporting Prints of the Eighteenth and
Early Nineteenth Centuries. By F. Gordon Roe . . . With
an Introduction by C. Reginald Grundy. 48 Plates in
Colour, 2 in Monochrome. London, The Connoisseur
[1927] xiv, 50 p. front. (col.), plates (col.) (The Connoisseur Series of Books for Collectors) *Unpaged after
p. 50.*

ROMER (Frank). Tit for Tat. A Story of the Race Gangs. By
Frank Romer. London, Duckworth [1925] 208 p.

ROSE (John Baillie). Four Short Chapters on Horses, Hunting, and the Turf. By the Late Major Rose . . . Edinburgh, Constable, 1855. vii, 50 p.

ROSE (Stuart). The Maryland Hunt Cup. By Stuart Rose. With a Foreword by Jacob A. Ulman and a Chart of the Course by Gordon Ross. New York, Huntington Press, 1931. 171 p. plates, ports., map (fold.), facs. *"First regular edition."*

ROSS (James Kenneth Matthews). Boots and Saddles. The Story of the Fabulous Ross Stable in the Golden Days of Racing. By J. K. M. Ross. Illustrated With Photographs. New York, Dutton [1956] 272 p. front. (col.), illus., ports.

ROSSMORE (Derrick Warner William Westenra, Fifth Baron). Things I Can Tell. By Lord Rossmore. London, Nash, 1912. xiii, 270 p. front. (port.), plates, ports.

ROUDAUD (Élie). Études sur le Cheval Pur Sang et sur les Courses des Notre Époque. Par Élie Roudaud. Paris, Sagnier, 1877. 227 p.

ROUS (Henry John). On the Laws and Practise of Horse Racing, etc., etc. By the Hon'ble Admiral Rous. London, Baily, 1866. xvi, 164 [2] p.

Ms letter laid in: "13 Berkeley Square, June 7, 1869. Dear Sir— The Hunt stakes over ten flights of Hurdles is *nil* simply because there were only nine—jumping a 10th hurdle beyond the wg post will not square the account—I give great credit to C—if he does not flourish in whatever business he is engaged I am much mistaken. He must recollect that after a horse has passed the the winning chair, the judge has no business to look at him—I am dear sir Yours truly H J Rous. To Charles Williams Esq."

[ROUS (Henry John).] Race-Horses Past and Present. Six Letters by I. F. R. Second Edition. London, Benning, 1857. 31 p. *Bound with: Hamilton, K. B. Our Saddle Horses, London, 1865.*

ROUSE (Rolla). Turf Betting Simplified, Introducing With Explanatory Rules and Examples, Tables on an Entirely New Plan, by Which on Any Number of Independent Events, the Odds May Be Compared and Valued in a Few Seconds, and Without Trouble; and Except in Very Complicated Cases, in a Moment and by the Memory. With Rules for Calculating the Odds in Any Number of Dependant Events, Finding the Value of a Bet, etc. etc. etc. By Rolla Rouse . . . London, Sherwood, 1844. 34 p.

ROUSUCK (Emanuel Jay). The Mighty Lexington at 7 Years of Age. Portrait of "Lexington" by Thomas J. Scott. [Baltimore, n.p., n.d.] 1 v. (unpaged) front. *Entirely hand-lettered and designed by Paul Hessemer.*

ROYAL Dublin Society. Register of Thorough-Bred Stallions Certified to Be Free From Hereditary Disease and Suitable for Improving the Breed of Horses. . . . Dublin, Thom, 18 - . illus. *Library has: v. 3 (1897)*

RUFF'S Guide to the Turf . . . London, 18 - .

Library has: 1901, 1921-24, 1926-41, 1950 to date. Begun in 1842 as *Guide to the Turf, or, Pocket Racing Companion* by W. Ruff.

RULES and Regulations for the Government of Racing, Trotting, and Betting, as Adopted by the Principal Turf Associations Throughout the United States and Canada. Compiled at the Office of "Wilkes' Spirit of the Times." New York, Brown [1866] 272 p.

With this is bound: The Turfman's Referee; Containing Numerous Decisions on Disputed Points on Racing, Trotting, and Betting. Compiled From the "Answers to Correspondents," as Given in "Wilkes' Spirit of the Times . . ." [New York, Brown, 1867] 65 p.

RUSSELL (Campbell). Miracles of the Turf. By Campbell Russell . . . London, Long [192–] xiv, 220 p. front. (port.), ports.

RUSSELL (Campbell). Triumphs & Tragedies of the Turf. By Campbell Russell . . . Second Edition. London, Long [n. d.] xi, 222 p. front. (port.), ports.

RUSSELL (Fox). In Scarlet and Silk; or Recollections of Hunting and Steeplechase Riding. By Fox Russell . . . With Two Drawings in Colour by Finch Mason. Second Edition. London, Bellairs, 1896. 295 p. front. (col.), plate (col.)

RUSSELL (Fox). Sporting Society, or Sporting Chat and Sporting Memories. Stories Humorous and Curious; Wrinkles of the Field and the Race-Course; Anecdotes of the Stable and the Kennel; With Numerous Practical Notes on Shooting and Fishing From the Pen of Various Sporting Celebrities and Well-Known Writers of the Turf and the Chase. Edited by Fox Russell. Illustrations by Randolph Caldecott. In Two Volumes . . . London, Bellairs, 1897. 2 vols. illus.

RUTHERFORD (Susan B.) The Derby Dixienary. Lawrence-burg, Ky., the author, 1941. 1 v. (unpaged) illus.

"SABTRETACHE." See BARROW (Albert Stewart).

SAINT ALBIN (Albert Huot de Longchamp de). Les Courses de Chevaux en France. Par A. de Saint-Albin (Robert Milton [pseud.]) Ouvrage Contenant 19 Gravures sur Bois, 36 Photogravures et 66 Vignettes par Crafty. Paris, Hachette, 1890. iv, 475 p. illus. (Bibliothèque du Sport)

SAINT GEORGES. [Pseud.] See CATERS (Baron Louis de).

SAINT SAUVEUR (   ). Les Grands Étalons de Pur Sang de France. Paris, 1922 1 v. (unpaged) plates. Title page lacking.

SANDERS (James Harvey). Horse-Breeding; Being the General Principles of Heredity Applied to the Business of Breeding

SANDERS (James Harvey). *Continued:*
Horses, With Instructions for the Management of Stallions, Broodmares and Young Foals, and the Selection of Breeding Stock. By J. H. Sanders . . . Chicago, the author, 1885. 249 p.

SANFORD (John). Pedigrees and Family Histories of Broodmares and Foals in England and France. Also the Stallion "Archaic." The Property of Mr. John Sanford, Amsterdam, New York. All Communications to Mr. H. Hughes, Amsterdam, New York, U. S. A. [London, Knapp, 1921] 112 p. *"Compiled by The British Bloodstock Agency, ltd."*

SANFORD Stud Farms. 1923 Yearlings (Foals of 1922) at Sanford Stud Farms (Incorporated) . . . Compiled by Fasig-Tipton Co. [n.p., n.d.] 1 v. (unpaged)

SARL (Arthur J.). Horses, Jockeys & Crooks. Reminiscences of Thirty Years' Racing. By Arthur J. Sarl. A Foreword by the Right Hon. the Earl of Lonsdale . . . With 19 Illustrations. New York, Dutton [1936] 288 p. front. (port.), plates, ports.

[SCHARF (Emily Ellen).] Famous Saddle Horses. Stories About the Most Important Horses in the Early Days of the American Saddle Horse . . . Compiled by Susanne [pseud.] A Reference Book for Breeder and Exhibiter. Illustrated by 93 Authoritative Photographs. Louisville, Farmers Home Journal, 1932. 2 v. *Library has: v. 1 only.*

[SCHOEFFEL (Florence Blackburn White).] Saddle and Sentiment. By Wenona Gilman [pseud.] New York, Outing Co. [1892] 284 p. front., illus. *"Mrs. G. J. Schoeffel."*

SCHREIBER (Barney). Catalogue of Thoroughbreds. Stallions and Broodmares at Woodlands Stock Farm, Bridgeton, Missouri. Property of B. Schreiber. [n.p.] 1907. [vi] 193 p., ii. illus.

SCHREIBER & Sons. Portraits of Noted Horses of America . . . [Philadelphia, 1874?] *Library has: v. 1 only. No more published?*

SCOTT (Alexander). Turf Memories of Sixty Years. By Alexander Scott (Edited by W. J. Collins) With Sixteen Illustrations. London, Hutchinson [1925] xiii, 320 p. front. (port.), plates.

SCOTT (W. L.). Algeria Stud Farm, Property of W. L. Scott, Erie, Pa. . . . Tabulated and Compiled by F. B. Whipple. [Erie, Herald Printing & Publishing Co.] 1885. 171 [2] p.

SÉGUIN (Armand). Observations sur les Courses du Champ-de-Mars, et sur Quelques Nouvelles Dispositions du Réglement de 1822 Relatif à Ces Courses; par Armand Séguin . . . Paris, LeBlanc, 1822. 51 p.

SÉGUIN (Armand). Le Régulateur des Classemens de Vitesse des Chevaux de Course, par Armand Séguin. Paris [Everat] 1829. vi, 176 [2] p.

> Undated ms note by R. J. T.: "Memo. J'ai pensé hier au sujet de livre de Armand Séguin. Je crois que le mien est le vrai édition première; quand on a aperçu l'erreur dans le titre ou a réimprimé, et quand on a réprimé on a fait un nouveau erreur dans le table de matières. L'exemplaire que le Général Mennessier a vu, c'est le deuxième imprimerie." Mennessier gives the title as: "Le Régulateur des Classements de Vitesse des Chevaux de Course . . ." He points out an error in pagination in the table of contents to which the ms note refers.

SENEX. [Pseud.] Observations on Horses, Horsemanship, and Hunting. By Senex. Brighton, Curtis, 1851. 61 p. *This appears to be a proof copy.*

SEPHARIAL. *See* OLD (Walter Gorn).

SÉVY (L. de). [Pseud.] *See* TURQUET DE BEAUREGARD
(Yves Louis Marie).

SHAFFER (Charles Benjamin). Coldstream Stud. Lexington,
Ky. Dr. John Baird, Manager. [Lexington, Ky., Welsh
Printing Co.] 1930. 97 p. *"Compiled by The Blood-Horse."*

SHAFFER (Charles Benjamin). Coldstream Stud. Lexington,
Ky. Stallions. Mares. [n.p., 1928] 1 v. (unpaged) illus.
Library has also: 1929.

SHARKEY (P.). Irish Racing Calendar; Containing an Account
of the Plates, Matches, and Sweepstakes, Run for in Ireland
in the Year . . . Together With an Abstract for All the
Matches, Sweepstakes, etc. Now Made, to Be Run at the
Curragh . . . With Other Articles of Intelligence. By P.
Sharkey . . . Dublin, Whitworth, 17 - . *Library has: v.
11 (1800); v. 14 (1804)*

SHARP (J. F. Mainwaring). The Thoroughbred Mares' Record
Showing the Female Ascendancy and Giving the Racing
Performances of the Progeny of 2,670 Mares, Tracing Back
to Eclipse, Herod, and Matchem. Also the Pedigrees and
Winnings of Principal Sires Since 1850. Compiled by J. F.
Mainwaring Sharp . . . London, Galopin Press [1929]
xx, 566 p. front., illus.

SHARPE (Harry). The Practical Stud Groom. By Harry Sharpe
. . . Second Edition. London, British Bloodstock Agency,
1930. 154 p., vii. illus. *Appendix: vii.*

SHEARDOWN (William). Doncaster Races. Historical Notices, etc. . . . By William Sheardown . . . Second Edition. Doncaster, Brooke [1861-76] *Three issues of* Historical Notices *bound together, 1861, 1866, 1876.*

SHERER (John). Rural Life Described and Illustrated, in the Management of Horses, Dogs, Cattle, Sheep, Pigs, Poultry, etc., etc.: Their Treatment in Health and Disease; With Authentic Information on All That Relates to Modern Farming, Gardening, Shooting, Angling, etc., etc. By John Sherer . . . and a Complete System of Modern Veterinary Practise. Illustrated With Upwards of One Hundred Steel Engravings. London, London Printing & Publishing Co. [1860] 2 v. (paged continuously) *Title page lacking, v. 1; added eng. title page lacking, v. 2.*

SHIPMAN (Evan). The Racing Memoirs of John Hertz as Told to Evan Shipman. Chicago [Scribner] 1954. xviii, 156 p. front. (ports.), plates (part col.)

SIDNEY (Samuel). The Book of the Horse: (Thorough-bred, Half-bred, Cart-bred), Saddle and Harness, British and Foreign, With Hints on Horsemanship; the Management of the Stable; Breeding, Breaking, and Training for the Road, the Park, and the Field. By S. Sidney . . . With Full-Page Coloured Illustrations and Numerous Wood Engravings. London, Cassell [1881?] 604 p. front. (col.), illus. (part col.)

SIEVIER (Robert Standish). The Autobiography of Robert Standish Sievier . . . London, Winning Post, 1906. ii, 363 p. front. (port.)

SILTZER (Frank). Newmarket: Its Sport and Personalities. By Frank Siltzer. A Foreword by the Earl of Durham . . . With Thirty-Two Illustrations in Colour and Half-Tone. London, Cassell, 1923. xiv, 279 p. front. (col.), plates (part col.), ports. (part col.), plans. *"Each colored plate accompanied by guard sheet with descriptive letterpress."*

SILTZER (Frank). The Story of British Sporting Prints. By Captain Frank Siltzer . . . With Four Coloured and Sixteen Black-and-White Illustrations. New York, Scribner,

SILTZER (Frank). *Continued:*
    1925. xiii, 409 p. front., plates (part col.), ports. *Bibliography: p. 380-81. Library has also: "New edition, revised and enlarged, 1929."*

SIMMS (Edward Francis). Thoroughbred Yearlings of Xalapa Farm, Bourbon County Kentucky. E. F. Simms. Lexington, Byrnes, 1920. 65 p. *"Edited by Thos. B. Cromwell."*

SIMMS (Edward Francis). Thoroughbreds of Xalapa Farm, Bourbon County, Kentucky. E. F. Simms. [Lexington, 1920] 175 p. illus. *"Edited by Thos. B. Cromwell."*

[SINCLAIR (Harry F.).] Rancocas Stock Farm. Jobstown Burlington County New Jersey. Address All Communications to Samuel C. Hildreth . . . [Lexington, Ky., Welsh, 1925] 1 v. (unpaged)

SLATER (John Herbert). Illustrated Sporting Books. A Descriptive Survey of a Collection of English Illustrated Works of a Sporting and Racy Character, With an Appendix of Prints Relating to Sports of the Field. By J. Herbert Slater . . . London, Gill, 1899. viii, 203 p. *Arranged alphabetically by title.*

SLOAN (James Forman). Tod Sloan. By Himself. Edited by A. Dick Luckman. With Thirty-Two Illustrations. New York, Brentano, 1915. xvi, 310 p. front. (port.), illus.

SMART (Henry Hawley). Long Odds. A Novel. By Hawley Smart . . . In Three Volumes. London, White, 1889. 3 v.

SMITH (Charles Hamilton). The Natural History of Horses. The Equidae or Genus Equus of Authors. By Lieut.-Col. Chas. Hamilton Smith . . . Illustrated by Thirty-Five Coloured Plates, With Portrait and Memoir of Gesner. Edinburgh, Lizars, 1841. xv, 352 p. front. (port.), plates. (The Naturalist's Library. Mammalia. Vol. XII) *Added eng. title page. Extra-illustrated.*

SMITH (George E., "Pittsburg Phil"). *See* COLE (Edward W.).

SMITH (Harry Worcester). Life and Sport in Aiken and Those Who Made It. By Harry Worcester Smith . . . New York, Derrydale Press [1935] xi, 237 p. front. (port. col.), illus.

SMITH (Harry Worcester). A Sporting Family of the Old South. By Harry Worcester Smith With Which Is Included Reminiscences of an Old Sportsman by Frederick Gustavus Skinner. Albany, Lyon, 1936. xvii, 477 p. front. (port.), plates, ports., facs. *Added title page.*

SMITH (Harry Worcester). A Sporting Tour Through Ireland, England, Wales and France, in the Years 1912-1913: Including a Concise Description of the Packs of Foxhounds, Mode of Hunting, Types of Horses and the Crack Riders. General Observations on the History of the Counties of Ireland, the Castles and Cabins: A View of the Customs and Manners of the Irish People; Together With a Story of Fox Hunting in England and France. And a Chapter on the Welsh and Mr. Curre's Hounds, Concluding With a Word Picture of the Grand National Steeplechase of 1913. By Harry Worcester Smith . . . Illustrated With Photogravures and Over Sixty Photographs From Life Illuminating the Text. [Columbia, S. C., State Co.] 1925. 2 v. (paged continuously) illus. *Added eng. title page.*

SMITH (Nicholas Hanckey). Observations on Breeding for the Turf, Containing Also Remarks on the Comparative Excellence of the English Race Horse of the Present Day and Former Times: With an Account of the Foreign Stallions and Mares Imported Into England, and the Performances of Their Produce on the Turf, etc. etc. By Nic.s Hanckey Smith. London, Whittaker, 1825. vii, 303 p.

SMITS (Alfred Eugène Marie). A Propos du Raid Bruxelles-Ostende. Notes et Rapports, 27 Août 1902. Bruxelles, Bulens, 1903. 110 p. plates, map (fold.), diagr.

SNOWY (J.). The Stanley of the Turf. By J. Snowy. London, Chapman, 1896. vi [1] 248 p. Cover port.

SOCIÉTÉ d'Encouragement Pour l'Amélioration des Races de Chevaux et le Développement des Courses en Belgique.

> Bound together: Rapport Annuel du Président, 1835, et Liste Nominative des Membres, 1836, 35 p.; Réglement des Courses de Chevaux Données par la Société d'Encouragement . . . 24 et 26 Septembre 1836, 8 [1] p.; du Toict, Emmanuel C., Vicomte, Opuscule sur les Chevaux de Cours; par le Vicomte E. du Toict . . . Luxembourg, Lamort, 1825, 24 p.; Statuts et Réglement de Chasse à Courre, 1836, 36 p. Includes classified membership list; Société d'Encouragement Pour l'Amélioration des Races de Chevaux et le Développement des Courses en Belgique. Réglement des Courses, 1837, 17 [1] p.; ms letter in French to M. Van De Weyr (?); Report of the President, 1836, and a list of membership for 1837, 80 p.

SOLLEYSEL (Jacques de). The Compleat Horseman: Discovering the Surest Marks of the Beauty, Goodness, Faults, and Imperfections of Horses . . . Also the Art of Shoeing . . . Together With the Best Method of Breeding Colts . . . By the Sieur de Solleysell [sic] . . . To Which Is Added, a Most Excellent Supplement of Riding . . . Made English From the Eighth Edition of the Original. By Sir William Hope . . . The Whole Illustrated With Copper Cuts Curiously Engrav'd. The Second Edition Corrected From Many Errors in the Former Edition. London, Bonwick, 1717. 2 v. in 1. illus., plates (part fold.)

SOMERSET. See FOWLER (Arthur Anderson).

SOUTH CAROLINA Jockey Club. Rules of the South-Carolina Jockey Club, Adopted February, 1824. Revised January 1st, 1847. Charleston, S. C., Miller, 1847. 14 p., xvii.

SPARROW (C. Edward). The Maryland Jockey Club of Baltimore City. Preakness Day, May 12, 1924 . . . Compiled and Edited by C. Edward Sparrow . . . [Baltimore, Sun, 1924] 72 p. illus.

SPARROW (Walter Shaw). British Sporting Artists From Barlow to Herring. By Walter Shaw Sparrow. With a Foreword by Sir Theodore Cook and Twenty-Seven Illustrations in Colour and Seventy-Six in Black & White. London, Lane; New York, Scribner [1922] xvii, 249 p. front. (col.), plates (part col.)

SPEED (John Gilmer). The Horse in America. A Practical Treatise on the Various Types Common in the United States, With Something of Their History and Varying Characteristics. By John Gilmer Speed . . . New York, McClure, 1905. xii, 287 p. front. (col.), plates (part col.)

SPENCER (Edward). [Pseud.] See MOTT (Edward Spencer).

SPIRIT of the Times. New York, 1831-61. 31 v. illus. weekly.

Title varies slightly. Editor varies. Library has: v. 5-31 (no. 1-17) See also PORTER'S Spirit of the Times, and WILKES' Spirit of the Times.

SPLAN (John). Life With the Trotters. By John Splan, With a Chapter on How Goldsmith Maid and Dexter Were Trained. (From Information Furnished by Mr. Budd Doble) . . . Chicago, White, 1889. vi, 450 p. front. (port.)

Le SPORT Algérien. Chronique du Turf de l'Algérie et de la Tunisie de 1894 (Courses Plates, à Obstacles et au Trot) Publiée par Le Sport Algérien . . . Alger, Baldachino, 1895. lvi, 248 p.

SPORTING Anecdotes; Original and Select; Including Characteristic Sketches of Eminent Persons Who Have Appeared on the Turf: With an Interesting Selection of the Most Extraordinary Events Which Have Transpired in the Sporting World; a Correct Description of the Animals of Chase; and of Every Other Subject Connected With the Various Diversions of the Field. By an Amateur Sportsman. [London] Cundee [1807] xv, 579 p. front.

The SPORTING Life. The British Turf and the Men Who Have Made It. Being an Historical and Contemporary Work on Racing in the British Isles From Its Earliest Inception to the Present Day. With Numerous Engravings and Halftone Illustrations Including All Derby Winners From the Year 1860 to the Present Year Together With an International Section Containing Articles, etc., on Racing in All Parts of the World. Compiled by The Sporting Life. London, Biographical Press, 1906. x [1] 502 p. illus., plates. *"A History of Racing by Edward Moorhouse," p. 1-45.*

The SPORTING Life. Racing Map of Gt. Britain. [London, Geographia] 1924. 17 p. map (fold.) *Contains list of trainers and courses with key to location on the map.*

SPORTING Life Turf Handbook. 1915 . . . London, The Sporting Life, 1915. 208 p.

> Cover: "Containing 140 Tabulated Pedigrees of Winners of Principal Races, and General Statistics of Racing Under Jockey Club Rules for the Year 1914."

The SPORTING Magazine; or, Monthly Calendar of the Transactions of the Turf, the Chace, and Every Other Diversion Interesting to the Man of Pleasure, Enterprize, and Spirit . . . London, 1792-1870. 156 v. illus. *Publisher varies.*

The SPORTING Mirror. Edited by "Diomed." Celebrities, Votaries, Portraits, Biographies, Doings . . . [London] Etherington, 1881-86. 10 v. *Library has: v. 1-8. v. 1, no. 1 (Jan.-Feb. 1881) lacking.*

The SPORTING Review. A Monthly Chronicle of the Turf, the Chase, and Rural Sports in All Their Varieties. Edited by "Craven" . . . London, Ackermann, 1839-70. 64 v. illus.

> Library has: v. 1-8. 8 v. bound in 4. Each vol. has a separate title page, and is paged separately. Maps of British Race Courses by George Tattersall in v. 3-4.

SPORTING Sketches. An Illustrated Record of the World of Sport . . . Literary & Artistic, Original & Up to Date . . . Founded & Edited by T. H. Roberts. London, Lucas, 18 - . illus. weekly.

Library has: v. 4-5 (Feb.-Aug. 1896) Cover: "Presentation Copy of Sporting Sketches." Instantaneous photographs of races.

The SPORTSMAN. British Sports and Sportsmen. Past & Present. Compiled and Edited by "The Sportsman." . . . London, "British Sports and Sportsmen," 1908. 2 v. illus. *Cover title: British Sports and Sportsmen.*

The SPORTSMAN. British Sports and Sportsmen. Racing, Coursing and Steeplechasing. Compiled and Edited by "The Sportsman." London, 1911. 2 v. illus.

The SPORTSMAN'S Dictionary; or, The Gentleman's Companion: for Town and Country. Containing Full and Particular Instructions for Riding, Hunting, Fowling, Setting, Fishing, Racing, Farriery, Cocking, Hawking, etc. With the Various Methods to Be Observed in Breeding and Dieting of Horses Both for the Road and Turf . . . and the Manner of Curing Their Various Diseases and Accidents . . . Illustrated With Copper-Plates, Representing All the Different Kinds of Nets, Snares, and Traps, That Are Now Made Use of. London, Fielding, 1778. 1 v. (unpaged) illus. *Printed in double columns.*

SPRINGFIELD (Rollo). The Horse and His Rider; or, Sketches and Anecdotes of the Noble Quadruped, and of Equestrian Nations. By Rollo Springfield. New York, Wiley, 1847. iv, 203 p. front., illus.

STAINFORTH (Martin). Racehorses in Australia With Paintings by Martin Stainforth. Edited by Dr. W. H. Lang, Ken

STAINFORTH (Martin). *Continued:*
Austin and Dr. Stewart McKay. Sydney, Art in Australia, 1922. 184 p. illus., plates (col.) *Artist's copy with ms notes.*

STANFORD (Leland). Tenth Annual Catalogue of Trotting and Thoroughbred Stock Owned at Palo Alto Stock Farm. Leland Stanford, Proprietor. Menlo Park, Santa Clara County, California. [San Francisco, Hicks-Judd] 1892. 576 p.

The STEEPLE Chase Calendar. A Consecutive Chronicle of the Sport in Great Britain, From the Great Match Over Leicestershire in 1826 to the Close of 1844. To Which Is Added, the Irish Sport From the Autumn of 1842. The Whole Properly Arranged, and Furnished With Copious Index, List of Winning Horses, Rules, Colours of the Riders, etc., etc. London, Wright, 1845. xxiv, 269 p. *"By Henry Corbet."*

STERN (Jean). Les Courses de Chantilly Sous la Monarchie de Juillet. Jean Stern. Paris, Lévy [1913] vii, 420 p. plates, facs., plans.

STILLMAN (Jacob Davis Babcock). The Horse in Motion as Shown by Instantaneous Photography With a Study on Animal Mechanics Founded on Anatomy and the Revelations of the Camera in Which Is Demonstrated the Theory of Quadrupedal Locomotion. By J. D. B. Stillman . . . Executed and Published Under the Auspices of Leland Stanford. Boston, Osgood, 1882. viii, 127 p. front., illus., plates (part col.)

Preface by Leland Stanford. "The original photographs that served as the basis of the analysis of the paces, were executed by E. J. Muybridge."

[STODDART (Joseph).] The Turf. Sportsmen of Today. By
The Admiral (Editor of "Sporting Luck") . . . London
[n.p., 1891?] 104 p. illus.

STOKES (William E. D.). The Right to Be Well Born or Horse
Breeding in Its Relation to Eugenics. By W. E. D. Stokes
. . . New York, the author [1917] 256 p. front. (port.),
illus.

STONEHENGE. See WALSH (John Henry).

STONG (Philip Duffield). Horses and Americans. By Phil Stong.
With a Frontispiece in Color and One Hundred and Three
Illustrations From Old Prints and Photographs. End Paper
and Chapter Heads by Kurt Wiese. New York, Stokes,
1939. xx, 333 p. front. (col.), illus. *Bibliography: p.
317-328.*

A STRAIGHT and Unmistakeable "Tip" for the Million, at "Long
Odds;" or, Revelations Touching Race-Horses, Jockeys, Bet-
ting-Men, Professional "Tipsters," "Touters," and Other
Sporting Characters, Practising on Public Gullibility. By
an Ex-Jockey . . . London, Vickers, 1867. iv, 123 p.

STREETT (William B.). Gentlemen Up. By William B. Streett.
With Illustrations by Paul Brown. New York, Derrydale
Press, 1930. 60 p. front. (col.), illus. (part col.)

STRUTT (Joseph). . . . On the Sports and Pastimes of the
People of England. Including the Rural and Domestic Rec-
reations, May-Games, Mummeries, Pageants, Processions,
and Pompous Spectacles, From the Earliest Period to the
Present Time. Illustrated by Engravings Selected From
Ancient Paintings; in Which Are Represented Most of the
Popular Diversions. By Joseph Strutt. Second Edition.
London, Bensley, 1810. xlix, 357 p. front., illus.

STUBBS (George) and Stubbs (George Townley). Review of the Turf, From the Year 1750, to the Completion of the Work; Comprising the History of Every Horse of Note, With Pedigree and Performances. Embellished With Prints, From Pictures Painted, and Plates Engraved, by Messrs. G. & G. T. Stubbs. London, Stubbs, 1794. 2 v. front. (col.), illus.

Le STUD Book Anglais. Par G. W. . . . Paris, Société Française E. I. P., 1923. 18 p. *"Traduction de M. L. R. Paris, Janvier, 1923." (Signed) G. W., Milan, Novembre 1922.*

SUMMERHAYS (Reginald S.). The Problem Horse. By R. S. Summerhays. Illustrated by John Board. London, Winchester [1949] 104 p. illus.

The SUPPLEMENT to the General Stud-Book. Being the Produce of Mares, Continued to 1799, Inclusive: by the Same Author. To Which Is Added, A Short Dissertation on Horses, by Colonel Gilbert Ironside. London, Weatherby, 1800. xvi, 132, 30 p.

SUSANNE. *See* SCHARF (Emily Ellen).

SUTCLIFFE (Leonard Stansfield). Photographs of Thoroughbred Mares by L. S. Sutcliffe. Lexington, Ky. [1929?] *Library has: v. 2. Mounted photographs alphabetically arranged of 106 mares in America.*

SUTCLIFFE (Leonard Stansfield). Photographs of 205 Thoroughbred Sires by L. S. Sutcliffe. Lexington, Ky. [1929] *Library has: v. 1. Mounted photographs alphabetically arranged.*

SUTHERLAND (E. G.). The New Zealand Turf Historical Review. Racing, Trotting and Breeding as an Industry. Auckland, 1945. 304 p. illus., ports. *Tipped in: Supplement, Dec. 8, 1945.*

SYLVANUS. *See* COLTON (Robert).

TAPLIN (William). The Sporting Dictionary, and Rural Repository of General Information Upon Every Subject Appertaining to the Sports of the Field. Inscribed to the Right Honorable the Earl of Sandwich . . . By William Taplin . . . In Two Volumes . . . London, Vernor, 1803. 2 v. illus.

[TATTERSALL (George).] The Cracks of the Day. Edited by Wildrake. [London] Ackermann [1844] iv, 271 p. front., illus.

[TATTERSALL (George).] The New Sporting Almanack, a Manual of Instruction and Amusement. Edited by "Wildrake." 1845. London, Ackermann, 1845. 80 p. illus., plates (eng.) *Added title page.*

TATTERSALL (George). The Pictorial Gallery of English Race Horses; Containing Portraits of All the Winners of the Derby, Oaks, and St. Leger Stakes, During the Last Twenty Years; and a History of the Principal Operations of the Turf. By George Tattersall. Illustrated by Ninety Engravings, Chiefly on Steel, After Paintings by Cooper, Herring, Hancock, Alken, Hall, and Others. London, Bohn, 1850. viii, 336 p. front., illus. *Half-title: The Royal Gallery of English Race Horses.*

[TATTERSALL (George).] The Pictorial Gallery of English Race Horses; Including Portraits of All the Winning Horses of the Derby, Oaks, and St. Leger Stakes, During the Last Thirteen Years; and a History of the Principal Operations of the Turf; With Sketches of Some of Its Most Distinguished Members. By Wildrake. Illustrated by Seventy-Five Engravings, Chiefly on Steel by Cooper, Herring, Hancock, and Others. London, Bohn, 1844. iv, 312 p. front., illus. *Added title page.*

TATTERSALL (George). Sporting Architecture. By George Tattersall, Surveyor. London, Bohn [1850?] vi, 97 p. front., plates, plans. *Eng. title page with vignette.*

TAUNTON (Theodore). Famous Horses With Portraits, Pedigrees, Principal Performances, Descriptions of Races, and Various Interesting Items Extending Over a Period of Nearly Two Centuries. By Theo. Taunton. London, Low [1895] viii, 396 [3] p. illus., tables.

TAUNTON (Thomas Henry). Portraits of Celebrated Racehorses of the Present and Past Centuries in Strictly Chronological Order, Commencing in 1702 and Ending in 1870 Together With Their Respective Pedigrees and Performances Recorded in Full. By Thomas Henry Taunton . . . In Four Volumes . . . London, Low, 1887-88. 4 v. illus., plates. *v. 1, 1887 (1702-96); v. 2, 1887 (1797-1824); v. 3, 1888 (1824-42); v. 4, 1888 (1842-70)*

The TECHNIQUE of Betting. London, Simpkin [n.d.] iii [3] 42 p., vii-xxx. *p. vii-xxx, account of Totalisator with illus.*

TEMPLER (Richard C.). Sires of Winners. The Stallion Side of Breeding and Racing. Edited by Richard C. Templer. Foreword by the Duke of Norfolk . . . London, Batchworth Press, 1949. 2 v. in 1 illus. *v. 3 (1949-56), London, Pedigree Press, 1957.*

TESIO (Federico). Puro-Sangue. Animale da Esperimento. Milano, Editoriale Sportiva e Societa Editrice Ippica [1947] 229 [2] p. illus., diagr. (col.)

[TEYSSIER DES FARGES (George Aimé).] Les Courses en France et à l'Etranger. Tome Premier. Historique et Organisation Avec Dix-Huit Planches Imprimées Hors Texte et de Nombreuses Vignettes. S.-F. Touchstone [pseud.] Paris, Lahure [1894] x, 389 p. front., plates. *No more published?*

[TEYSSIER DES FARGES (George Aimé).] L'Élevage du Pur Sang en France. Guide Pratique de l'Éleveur Donnant les Performances, les Pedigrees et le Prix de Saillie des Étalons Appartenant à l'État et aux Particuliers. Avec Quatre Planches. Paris, Rothschild, 1893. 254 p. illus. *Library has: 1893, 1894.*

[TEYSSIER DES FARGES (George Aimé).] Historique des Étalons Pur-Sang Anglais et Français et des Juments Françaises les Plus Célèbres Ayant Paru sur le Turf de 1764 à 1887. Ouvrage Précédé d'une Lettre-Préface de M. le Duc de Beaufort. Paris, Rothschild, 1889. xxv, 165 p. illus., plates (col.)

Facing title page: S.-F. Touchstone [pseud.] . . . Les Chevaux de Course. Pedigree-Description-Historique. 60 Portraits en Couleur par V.-J. Cotlison, L. Pénicaut et Le Nail. Texte Orné de 182 Vignettes par Crafty, Cotlison, Le Nail, Arsenius, Pénicaut, Cousturier, etc. Paris, Rothschild, 1889.

[TEYSSIER DES FARGES (George Aimé).] History of Celebrated English and French Thorough-Bred Stallions and French Mares Which Appeared on the Turf From 1764 to 1887. Preceded by a Preface From the Duke of Beaufort. Translated From the French by C. B. Pitman. London, Nimmo, 1890. xxv, 165 p. illus., plates (col.)

Facing title page: S.-F. Touchstone [pseud.] Race Horses. Pedigree-Description-History. Translated From the French by C. B. Pitman. Sixty Coloured Plates by V. J. Cotlison, L. Pénicaut, and Le Nail. Also One Hundred and Thirty-Four Vignettes in the Text by Crafty, Cotlison, Le Nail, Arsenius, Pénicaut, Cousturier, etc. Coloured by Hand. London, Nimmo, 1890.

[TEYSSIER DES FARGES (George Aimé).] La Race Pure en France Classement par Étalons. Des Poulinières Inscrites au Stud-Book Français (1818-1894) Précédée d'une Étude sur la Formation de la Race Pure en France le Choix et le Role des Poulinières. Avec Trois Planches. S.-F. Touchstone [pseud.] Paris, Legoupy, 1895. 374 p. front. (col.), plates.

THAYER (Bert Clark). August in Saratoga. A Sentimental Journey to Horse Haven, Oklahoma, and the Back Stage of America's Grandest Horse Drama With 109 Photographs by the Author. Dedicated to His Majesty the Thoroughbred Horse. By Bert Clark Thayer. New York, Sagamore Press [1937] 79 [1] p. front., illus.

THAYER (Bert Clark). Beautiful Hialeah. Being the Second in a Series of Sentimental Journeys to America's Leading Race Courses. By Bert Clark Thayer and George F. T. Ryall. [New York, Thayer, 1938] 79 p. front. (col.), illus.

THAYER (Bert Clark). Horses in the Blue Grass. By Bert Clark Thayer, Joe H. Palmer, John Hervey, W. Jefferson Harris. New York, Duell [1940] 78 p. illus. *"With 149 photographs by Bert Clark Thayer."*

THÉTARD (Henry). Histoire et Secrets du Turf. 13th Edition. Paris, Laffont, 1947. 369 p. illus.

THOMPSON (Charles). Rules for Bad Horsemen; Hints to Inexpert Travellers; and Maxims Worth Remembering by the Most Experienced Equestrians. By Charles Thompson . . . A New Edition, With Modern Additions, by John Hinds [pseud.] London, the author, 1830. viii, 87 p. front., plate.

THORMANBY. *See* WILLMOTT-DIXON (Willmott).

THOROUGHBRED Horse Association. Lexington, Ky., 1917-23. *Typed stenographic reports of meetings in 1917-23.*

THOROUGHBRED Racing Associations of the United States. Two-Year-Olds of . . . New York, 1944- . annual. *Library has: 1944 to date. Title varies: 1950-53, "American Champions and Two Year Olds of . . . "*

The THOROUGHBRED Record. Lexington, Ky., 1875- . illus. weekly.

> Library has: v. 1-45, 47-52, 55 to date. Title varies: *Kentucky Livestock Record,* 1875-85; *Livestock Record,* 1886-95; *Thoroughbred Record,* 1896 to date. Editor varies.

The THOROUGHBRED Record. Annual Statistical Review . . . Lexington, Ky., 1948- . annual. *Library has: 1948 to date.*

THOROUGHBRED Sales Catalogs. Bound volumes: 1917-39. Saratoga, New York City, Lexington, Ky.

TIMEFORM. Race Horses of . . . The Annual Edition of . . . Timeform . . . London, Portway [1949-] illus. annual. *Begun as:* Best Horses of . . . *By Phil Bull . . . London, Portway, 1944-48. Library has: 1944 to date.*

TINKER (Edward Larocque). . . . The Horsemen of the Americas and the Literature They Inspired. New York, Hastings House, 1953. 149 p. front. (col.), illus. (part col.) (Books of the Americas, 1) *Bibliography: p. 119-149.*

[TONGUE (Cornelius).] Stable Practise; or, Hints on Training for the Turf, the Chase, and the Road: With Observations Addressed to All Who Are Concerned in Racing, Steeple-Chasing, and Fox-Hunting. By Cecil [pseud.] . . . London, Longman, 1852. xv, 240 p. front.

[TONGUE (Cornelius).] The Stud Farm or Hints on Breeding for the Turf, the Chase and the Road. Addressed to Breeders of Race Horses and Hunters, to Landed Proprietors and Especially to Tenant Farmers. By Cecil [pseud.] . . . London, Routledge, 1873. xii, 244 p. front., illus., plans. *"A new edition—thoroughly revised."*

TOUCHSTONE (S. F.). [Pseud.] *See* TEYSSIER DES FARGES (George Aimé).

TOZER (Basil). The Horse in History. By Basil Tozer . . . With Twenty-Five Illustrations. London, Methuen [1908] xx, 304 p. front., illus., plates. *"Some works consulted":* *xvii-xx.*

TRACES of the Turf. By P. J. [1870?] 2 v. *Handwritten.*

TRARIEUX (Jean). Si les Chevaux Pouvaient Parler, ou Quelques Vérités sur les Courses. Jean Trarieux. Paris, Delamain [1926] 166 p. *"Cinquième édition."*

TREACY (William) and Walker (Kenner). American Thoroughbred Stallion Register . . . Containing Tabulated Pedigrees, Performances and Other Family Data of . . . Stallions Doing Service in the United States and Canada; Tabulated Pedigrees of . . . Stallions, the Property of the Breeding Bureau of the Jockey Club . . . Information Anent the Bruce-Lowe Figure System and Other Matters Pertinent to Turf History. Compiled by Treacy & Walker. Lexington, Ky., the compilers, 1921-25. 2 v.

TREVATHAN (Charles E.) The American Thoroughbred. By Charles E. Trevathan. New York, Macmillan, 1905. ix, 495 p. front., illus., plates, ports. (American Sportsman's Library) *"Of this book one hundred (100) copies have been printed on large paper, of which this is no. 44."*

The TRIAL of Mr. Samuel Emden, of Turf Celebrity, on the 24th February, 1808, Before Sir James Mansfield and a Special Jury, for Maliciously Arresting George Witherden, Esq. for £1880, on a False Affidavit. Taken in Short Hand by Mr. Farquharson. To Which Is Added, A Short Sketch of a Trial Which Took Place at the Last Middlesex Sessions, on the Prosecution of the Said Emden Against Mr. Joseph Hills . . . on a Malicious and Ill Founded Charge of Perjury. [n.p.] 1808. 67 p.

TRIANGLE Publications. Daily Racing Form Chart Book . . . Containing Official Result Charts, Fully Indexed, of All Races Run at Recognised North American Tracks . . . New York [1925-] *Library has: 1925 to date.*

[TROYE (Edward).] The Race Horses of America. First Number. [New York, the author, 1867] 12 p. front., port.

No more published. Bound in: "Notes by Harry Worcester Smith Lordvale Library, 1930 to Accompany the Race Horses of America. First Number. By Edward Troye (1808-1874) 1867."

The TURF. A Satirical Novel . . . In Two Volumes. London, Colburn, 1831. 2 v.

TURF and Sport Digest. Handicapping Horses to Win. Factors to Consider in Making Race Selections. Compiled by Turf and Sport Digest. Baltimore, Montee Publishing Company, 1937. vii, 139 p.

TURF Argentino. Publicacion oficial de la Asociacion de Criadores S. P. C. Buenos Aires, 1940- . annual. illus. *Library has: 1940-44.*

TURF Characters. [London, 1875?] vi, 128 p. *Title page lacking. Bound with:* Won By A Neck, *London, 1875.*

The TURF Companion for . . . Containing the Principal Engagements Made to Be Run in Great Britain During That Year: Including the Sweepstakes etc. Which Closed on . . . To Which Are Added, the Derby and Oaks' Stakes for . . . Also, the Winners of the Derby, the Oaks, and St. Leger Stakes From Their Commencement. York, Johnson, 18 - . *Library has: 1826-27, 1830-31, 1833-35, 1840-41.*

TURF Facts & Wrinkles Specially Written for the Uninitiated, by an Eminent Sportsman . . . London, Smith [1886] ii [2] 65 p.

TURF, Field and Farm. New York, 1865-1903. weekly. *Library has: v. 1-29, 32-57, 59, 61, 63-66, 68-69, 71-72.*

The TURF Herald. Or Annual Racing Calendar. [London] 1824- . *Library has: 1824-26. "Annals of Sporting: a Magazine Entirely Appropriated to Field Amusements."*

The TURFMAN'S Referee; Containing Numerous Decisions on Disputed Points on Racing, Trotting, and Betting. Compiled From the "Answers to Correspondents," as Given in "Wilkes' Spirit of the Times . . ." [New York, Brown, 1867] 65 p. *Bound with:* Rules and Regulations for the Government of Racing . . . *New York, 1866.*

TURNER (Joseph). Records of the Turf, Containing a Faithful and Correct Account of All the Principal Races Run for Throughout the Country, From Their Commencement; With the Betting, Description of the Races, Horses That Started, Weights, and Jockeys That Rode; Also, the Pedigrees and Performances of Most of the Celebrated Horses and Mares, With Their Produce, etc., and a Variety of Sporting Anecdotes, and Memoirs of Celebrated Turf Men. Compiled by Joseph Turner. London, Ackerman [1843] viii, 232 p.

[TURQUET DE BEAUREGARD (Yves Louis Marie).] Saut d'Obstacles et Galop de Course. Étude Cinématographique. Troisième Édition Revue et Augmentée. Préface de M. le Dr. Weiss . . . L. de Sévy [pseud.] Paris, Legoupy [1918] 248 p. illus., plates, diagr.

TUTING (William) and Fawconer (Thomas). The Sporting Calendar: Containing an Account of the Plates, Matches, and Sweepstakes, That Have Been Run in Great-Britain and Ireland in the Year . . . By William Tuting and Thomas Fawconer . . . London, Miller, 1769-76. 8 v. *Library has: v. 1-8. v. 2 includes racing in North America.*

TWEEDIE (William). The Arabian Horse, His Country and People With Portraits of Typical or Famous Arabians and Other Illustrations. Also a Map of the Country of the Arabian Horse, and a Descriptive Glossary of Arabic Words and Proper Names. By Major-General W. Tweedie . . . London, Blackwood, 1894. xix, 411 p. front. (col.), illus., map (fold.)

> Bibliography: p. xi-xiii. Of 100 copies, no. 28. "H A J" gold stamped on cover. "Ex Libris Henry Arthur Johnstone, 1899" blind stamped on leather fly-leaf.

[UNDERWOOD (Thomas Rust).] Thoroughbred Racing & Breeding. The Story of the Sport and Background of the Horse Industry. [Baltimore] Privately Printed for Thoroughbred Racing Associations of the U. S. [Dulany-Vernay Co., 1945] 239 p. illus. *End Papers: The Life of a Thoroughbred, Skeleton, and Parts of the Horse.*

UNDERWOOD (Thomas Rust) and Day (John Isaac, Jr.). Call Me Horse. Interesting, Humorous, and Informative Notes and Anecdotes About Horse Racing and Breeding. Edited by Tom R. Underwood and John I. Day. Illustrated by Leonard Romagna. New York, Coward [1946] viii, 120 p. illus.

UNITED Hunts Racing Association. Spring Meeting . . . Autumn Meeting, 1926 . . . Belmont Park Terminal. New York, 1926. 36 p. illus., ports.

UNITED STATES (Department of Agriculture) Yearbook of Agriculture . . . Washington, Government Printing Office, 1895- . illus. *Library has: 1942,* Keeping Livestock Healthy; *1948,* Grass.

UNITED STATES (Department of Agriculture. Bureau of Animal Industry) Special Report on Diseases of the Horse.

UNITED STATES. *Continued:*
Prepared Under the Direction of Dr. D. E. Salmon . . . by Drs. Michener, Law, Harbaugh, Trumbower, Liautard, Holcombe, Huidekoper, and Dickson . . . Washington, Government Printing Office, 1890. 560 p. illus. *Library has: 1890, rev. ed. 1903, 1916, 1942.*

UNITED States Trotting Association. Annual Yearbook. Trotting and Pacing in . . . Hartford, Conn., 1885- . annual. *Library has: 1940 to date.*

UPTON (Roger D.). Newmarket & Arabia. An Examination of the Descent of Racers and Coursers. By Roger D. Upton . . . London, King, 1873. xi, 211 p. charts (fold.)

VAN LOAN (Charles Emmett). Old Man Curry. By Charles E. Van Loan. New York, Doran [1917] 276 p. front.

VAN RENSSELAER (Stephen). Points on Buying a Horse. Showing the Means by Which Unsoundness May Be Discovered. Also the Tricks and Methods Frequently Used to Effect Sales. Together With an Elaborate Resumé of the Horses Qualities Fitting Him for Special Purposes. By Stephen Van Rensselaer. [Elizabeth, N. J., Times Pub. Co., 1904] viii, 60 p.

VAN STOCKUM (C. M.). Sport. Attempt at a Bibliography of Books and Periodicals Published During 1890-1912 in Great Britain, the United States of America, France, Germany, Austria, Holland, Belgium and Switzerland Systematically Arranged and According to the Languages by C. M. Van Stockum. Together With a Supplement of Laws and Regulations Concerning: Game—Fishery—Motor-Cars and Cycling—Aeronautics—Patents and an Extensive Index to Authors and Matters. New York, Dodd, 1914. 289 p. *Printed in double columns.*

VENANCOURT (Daniel de). La Vie Fiévreuse au Champ de Course. En Plein Roman—Un Favori—Les Tuyaux—Pur Sang et Demi-Sang—La Carrière d'un Cheval—Patron d'Écurie—Les Crocodiles—Les Trois Commissaires—Pari Mutuel et Pari Libre—Une Grande Journée—Le Logogriphe —Jeux sur les Chevaux—Jeux sur les Hommes—La Veine et le Guignon. Paris, Ningler [1907] 300 [1] p.

VET. *See* ANDERSON (Jesse Sylvester).

VIAL DE SAINBEL (Charles). Elements of the Veterinary Art, Containing an Essay on the Proportions of the Celebrated Eclipse; Six Lectures on Farriery, or the Art of Horse-Shoeing, and on the Diseases of the Foot. An Essay on the Grease . . . An Essay on the Glanders . . . The Whole Illustrated With Nine Anatomical, Geometrical and Mechanical Engravings. By Charles Vial de Sainbel . . . To Which Is Prefixed a Short Account of His Life. The Third Edition. London, Wright, 1797. *Sections paged separately. "Published for benefit of widow."*

VIAL DE SAINBEL (Charles). Essai sur les Proportions Geometrales de l'Eclipse. Par M. Charles Vial de Saintbel [*sic*] . . . London, Couchman, 1791. viii, 67 p. plates (fold.) *Text in English and French.*

VIAL DE SAINBEL (Charles). The Posthumous Works of Charles Vial de Sainbel . . . Translated From the Original French. London, Martin, 1795. 83, 127 [1] p. front. (port.), plates (fold.) *Eclipse essay included and paged separately.*

Un VIEUX SPORTSMAN. [Pseud.] Guide du Parieur aux Courses. Contenant les Combinaisons les Plus Favorables. Les Règlements du Jockey-Club et du Salon des Courses.

Un VIEUX SPORTSMAN. *Continued:*

Ainsi que les Tables de Proportions Nécessaires à Tous les Paris. Par Un Vieux Sportsman. Paris, Goin, 1863. 212 p. front. (col.)

VIGILANT. *See* VOSBURGH (Walter Spencer).

VILLEROY (Félix Ambroise). Manuel de l'Éleveur de Chevaux. Par Félix Villeroy . . . Paris, Librairie Agricole de la Maison Rustique, 1856-57. 2 v. in 1. illus. *Bound together, paged separately.*

VOIGT (Charles Adolph). Famous Gentlemen Riders at Home and Abroad. By Charles Adolph Voigt. With 24 Illustrations. London, Hutchinson [1925] 420 p. front., ports.

VON OETTINGEN (Burchard). Horse Breeding in Theory and Practise. By Burchard von Oettingen . . . Translated From German. London, Low, 1909. viii, 469 p. tables.

VOSBURGH (Walter Spencer). Cherished Portraits of Thoroughbred Horses From the Collection of William Woodward. With Notes by W. S. Vosburgh. [New York] privately printed [Derrydale Press] Ernest R. Gee, 1929. vii, 297 p. illus., plates. *Foreword by Mr. Woodward.*

VOSBURGH (Walter Spencer). "Cherry and Black." The Career of Mr. Pierre Lorillard on the Turf. By W. S. Vosburgh. [New York] printed for P. Lorillard, 1916. viii, 158 p.

[VOSBURGH (Walter Spencer).] Famous American Jockeys. Compiled by Vigilant, Racing Editor, "The Spirit of the Times." New York, Saalfield [1883?] 66 p. *Cover title, title page lacking.*

VOSBURGH (Walter Spencer). Racing in America. 1866-1921. Written for the Jockey Club by W. S. Vosburgh. New York, privately printed, the Jockey Club [1922] x, 249 p. front., plates, diagr.

VOSBURGH (Walter Spencer). Thoroughbred Types. 1900-1925. Photographic Portraits of Notable Race Horses, Steeplechase and Cross-Country Horses, Hunters and Polo Ponies. With Descriptive Texts by W. S. Vosburgh, Charles D. Lanier, Frank J. Bryan and James C. Cooley. New York, privately printed, 1926. 277 p. illus.

"The committee certifies that of this edition seventy-five copies have been printed, on Strathmore Old Stratford paper in the Aquatone process, of which this is no. 29. (signed) Walter S. Vosburgh." Library has also: no. 78 of the edition of 250 copies.

VUILLIER (Jean Joseph). Les Croisements Rationnels Dans la Race Pure. Par le Lt.-Colonel Vuillier (Lottery). Traité Technique d'Élevage. Étude des Principaux Étalons du Monde Entier. [Paris, Maulde, 1928] 325 p. tables.

VUILLIER (Jean Joseph). Les Croisements Rationnels Dans la Race Pure. Traité Technique d'Élevage. Études des Principaux Étalons Européens par J. Vuillier (Lottery) Paris, Legoupy, 1902-06. 2 v. illus.

[VUILLIER (Jean Joseph).] Deuxièmes Tables de Dosages. Lottery. [Paris, Maulde] 1928. v, 124 [1] p. tables. *Introduction in English and French. Published simultaneously with* Les Croisements Rationnels . . .

[VUILLIER (Jean Joseph).] Registre des Dosages du Haras. [Lottery] [Paris, Maulde] 1928. 7 p. tables.

[VUILLIER (Jean Joseph).] Tables de Dosages. Lottery. [Besançon, Jacquin, 1906] 47 [1] p. tables.

W., C. *See* PORTRAITS of Broodmares . . .

W., G. *See* Le STUD Book Anglais . . .

WACKEROW (Charles). Tables of Pedigrees of Thorough-Bred Horses From the Earliest Accounts to the Year . . . Inclusive. Elaborated and Published by Charles Wackerow . . . Hamburg, Rademacher, 1900-18. 4 v. tables. *v. 1 (1900)*, Tata; *v. 2 (1904)*, Vienna; *v. 3 (1911)*, Vienna; *v. 4 (1918)*, Unter Retzbach N.-Ö.

WALKER (B.). An Historical List of Horse-Matches, Plates and Prizes, Run for in Great-Britain and Ireland, in the Year . . . Containing I. The Names of the Owners of the Horses That Have Run . . . II. The Winner Distinguished of Every Match . . . III. The Conditions of Running . . . IV. A Table of Weights . . . V. A List of Stallions Who Covered in . . . VI. A List of Stallions to Cover in . . . VII. A List of the Principal Cock-Matches . . . Winners and Losers of Them. With an Index to the Whole. By B. Walker . . . London, the author, 1770-71. 2 v. *No more published.*

WALKER (William Hall). The Sire and Family Number (Bruce Lowe,) of Each Mare Contained in the General Stud Book, Volume XVIII. 100 Copies Only. No. 35. Edited by and Printed Privately for Wm. Hall Walker. Gateacre, Lancashire, 1898 . . . 248 p. *"Corrected copy, 1901."*

WALKER (William Hall). Stallion Register Containing Tabulated Pedigrees and Family Numbers, Performances, Fees, and Other Information of . . . Horses at the Stud in England and Ireland. Compiled and Edited for Private Circulation by William Hall Walker. [Liverpool] 1900-04. 2 v.

WALKER (Woods). Walker Foxhounds. Their Origin and Development. By Woods Walker. Illustrations by Becky White and Mayme Walter. Cynthiana, Ky., Hobson, 1945. ix, 101 p. front., illus., ports.

WALL (John Furman). Practical Light Horse Breeding. Third
Edition (Revised). By John F. Wall . . . With Foreword
by Mr. E. R. Bradley . . . [Baltimore, Monumental Printing Co.] 1936. 146 p. illus.

WALL (John Furman). Thoroughbred Bloodlines. An Elementary Study. In Two Volumes. Revised. By John F. Wall
. . . Baltimore, Monumental Printing Co., 1939. 2 v.
illus., plates, tables. *Introduction to first edition includes
bibliography, v. 1; charts I-IX, sire lines, X-XIX, mares,
v. 2.*

WALL (John Furman) and Jennings (Frank Clay). Judging the
Horse—For Racing, Riding and Recreation. By John F. Wall
. . . and Frank Jennings. [Lexington, Ky.] Thoroughbred
Press, 1955. 208 p. illus.

WALL (Richard). A Dissertation on Breeding of Horses, Upon Philosophical and Experimental Principles; Being
an Attempt to Promote Thereby an Improvement in
the Present Manner of Breeding Racers, and Horses
in General. Also Some Material Observations Upon
Those Sorts of Foreign Horses Which Are Adapted to
Racing; Particularly Those of the Kingdom of Yem-
ine, in Arabia Faelix, or South Arabia. Also Those
of Arabia Petrea, or North Arabia. And Likewise Those
of Barbary, Turky, and Ethiopia. In a Letter to a
Friend. By Richard Wall. London, Woodfall [1758]
92 p.

WALLACE (Edgar). The Calendar. By Edgar Wallace . . .
London, Collins [1930] 288 p.

WALLACE (Edgar). Educated Evans. By Edgar Wallace . . .
London, Collins [1929] 251 p.

WALLACE (Edgar). The Green Ribbon. By Edgar Wallace. Garden City, N. Y., Doubleday, 1930. 311 p. *"Published for The Crime Club, Inc."*

WALLACE (John Hankins). American Stud Book, Being a Compilation of the Pedigrees of American and Imported Blood Horses, With an Appendix of All Animals Without Extended Pedigrees Prior to 1840. And a Supplement Containing All Horses and Mares That Have Trotted in Public in 2m.40s., and Geldings That Have Trotted in 2m.35s., and Many of Their Progenitors and Descendants, With All That Is Known of Their Blood, From the Earliest Trotting Races Till the Close of 1866. By J. H. Wallace. Vol. 1. New York, Townsend, 1867. 1 v. illus. *No more published.*

WALLACE (John Hankins). The Horse of America in His Derivation, History, and Development. Tracing His Ancestors . . . Including the Horses of the Colonial Period . . . Showing How the Trotting Horse Is Bred . . . With Maps and Illustrations. By John H. Wallace . . . New York, the author, 1897. xiii [2] 575 p. front. (port.), plates, maps.

"Received by Cyrus Lukens from his friend John H. Wallace Nov. 3, 1897." Tipped in: Letter from Wallace to Lukens, Aug. 17, 1870; "The American Trotting Register Association" (signed) Cyrus Lukens, March 1896. Marginal notes, 1906.

WALLACE (John Hankins). Wallace's American Trotting Register Containing the Pedigrees of Trotting Horses, Their Ancestors and Descendants . . . New York, Wallace's Monthly, 18 - . *Library has: v. 3-22 (1879-1921)*

WALLACE (John Hankins). Wallace's Year-Book of Trotting and Pacing in . . . New York, Wallace's Monthly, 18 - . *Library has: v. 2-36 (1887-1920)*

[WALSH (John Henry).] British Rural Sports; Comprising Shooting, Hunting, Coursing, Fishing, Hawking, Racing, Boating, and Pedestrianism, With All Rural Games and Amusements. By Stonehenge. Illustrated. 17th Edition Revised Throughout With Numerous Additions by "The Field" Staff. [London, Warne, 1888] 1039 p. illus., plates. *Library copy imperfect: title page lacking, supplied from Library of Congress.*

[WALSH (John Henry).] Le Cheval Anglais. Extrait du Manuel du Sport, Publié à Londres en 1856 par Stonehenge. Avec Tables Généalogiques. Traduit de l'Anglais par le Comte J. de Lagondie . . . Paris, Dentu, 1860. viii, 392 p. illus. *Illustrations printed in black and red.*

WALSH (John Henry). The Horse in the Stable and the Field; His Management in Health and Disease. By J. H. Walsh . . . ("Stonehenge") . . . From the Last London Edition. With Copious Notes and Additions, by Robert McClure . . . And an Essay on the American Trotting Horse, and Suggestions on the Breeding and Training of Trotters. By Ellwood Harvey . . . Illustrated With Over Eighty Engravings. Philadelphia, Porter [1869] xii, 540 p. illus., plates, tables.

WALSH (John Henry). The Horse, in the Stable and the Field: His Varieties, Management in Health and Disease, Anatomy, Physiology, etc. etc. By J. H. Walsh . . . (Stonehenge) . . . With One Hundred and Seventy Illustratons [sic] . . . London, Routledge, 1883. x, 622 p. front., illus.

WANKLYN (W. H. E.). The Australasian Racehorse. A Record of Successful Racehorses and Sires in Australia and New Zealand From the Earliest Period. Compiled by W. H. E. Wanklyn . . . Christchurch, Christchurch Press Co., 1908. vi, 322 p.

WANKLYN (W. H. E.). The Australasian Racehorse. Supplement Which Includes the Brood Mares Added to Vol. IX Australian Stud Book and Vol. IV New Zealand Stud Book, and the Sires and Brood Mares Imported Since the Original Work Was Published. Compiled by W. H. E. Wanklyn . . . Christchurch, Christchurch Press Co., 1910. 76 p.

WANKLYN (W. H. E.). The Great Sire Lines. Tables Showing Their Successes and Failures. Edited and Compiled by W. H. E. Wanklyn . . . London, Cox [n.d.] 1 v. (unpaged) tables.

WARBURTON (Frederick Tynte). The Race Horse. How to Buy, Train, and Run Him. By Lieut.-Col. Warburton . . . London, Low, 1892. xii, 270 p. front.

WARE (Francis Morgan). First-Hand Bits of Stable Lore. By Francis M. Ware . . . Boston, Little, 1903. x, 297 p. front., illus., plates. *"Published December, 1902."*

WARE (Francis Morgan). Our Noblest Friend the Horse. By Francis M. Ware . . . Boston, Page, 1903. vi [3] 368 p. front., illus., plates. *"Published November, 1902."*

WASHINGTON. (State College, Pullman. College of Agriculture. Department of Animal Husbandry) Stockmen's Handbook. Stockmen's Short Course. December 1956. Institute of Agricultural Sciences, State College of Washington, Pullman. [iv] 266 p. tables. *Section II: Stud Managers Short Course: p. 160-222.*

WATSON (Alfred Edward Thomas). Galicia. Her Forbears and Her Offspring. By Alfred E. T. Watson . . . With 30 Illustrations. Privately Printed for Mr. A. W. Cox ("Mr. Fairie") London, Longmans, 1915. viii, 178 p. front., illus., tables.

WATSON (Alfred Edward Thomas). A Great Year. Lord
Glanely's Horses. By Alfred E. T. Watson . . . With Illustrations. London, Longmans, 1921. viii, 216 [1] p. front.
(port.), illus., plates.

WATSON (Alfred Edward Thomas). Green; Yellow Sleeves,
Belt and Cap. By Alfred E. T. Watson . . . Privately
Printed for Mr. Frank Bibby of Hardwicke Grange, Shrews-
bury . . . London, Longmans, 1919. 221 p. front., plates,
plan.

WATSON (Alfred Edward Thomas). King Edward VII. as a
Sportsman. By Alfred E. T. Watson. With an Introduction
and a Chapter on "Yachting" by Captain the Hon. Sir Sey-
mour Fortescue . . . Contributions by the Marquess of
Ripon . . . and Others. With 1 Photogravure Plate, 10
Plates in Colour, 12 Rembrandt-Gravure Plates, and 79 Half-
Tone Illustrations. London, Longmans, 1911. xxx, 380
[1] p. front. (port.), plates. *Of 255 copies, no. 121.*

WATSON (Alfred Edward Thomas). Prince Palatine. His Pedigree & Performances. By Alfred E. T. Watson . . . Printed
for Private Circulation. London, Longmans, 1917. 91
[1] p. front., illus., table.

WATSON (Alfred Edward Thomas). Racecourse and Covert
Side. By A. E. T. Watson . . . With Illustrations by John
Sturgess. London, Bentley, 1883. 325 p. front., illus.

WATSON (Alfred Edward Thomas). Racing and 'Chasing. A
Collection of Sporting Stories by Alfred E. T. Watson . . .
With Illustrations by Charles E. Brock, H. M. Brock, G. H.
Jalland, Harrington Bird, & G. D. Giles. London, Long-
mans, 1897. xii, 344 p. front., illus. *Binding stamped:
"Vancroft Stud."*

WATSON (Alfred Edward Thomas). The Racing World and Its Inhabitants. Edited by Alfred E. T. Watson. London, Macmillan, 1904. vii, 309 p. front. (col.), plates (col.)

WATSON (Alfred Edward Thomas). A Sporting and Dramatic Career. By Alfred E. T. Watson . . . London, Macmillan, 1918. vi, 390 [1] p. facs.

WATSON (Alfred Edward Thomas). The Turf. By Alfred E. T. Watson. Illustrated. London, Lawrence, 1898. vii, 272 p. front., illus.

[WATSON (Alfred Edward Thomas).] Types of the Turf: Anecdotes and Incidents From the Course and the Stable. By "Rapier." London, Illustrated Sporting and Dramatic News, 1883. 115 p. ports.

WATSON (Alfred Edward Thomas). The Year's Sport: A Review of British Sports and Pastimes for the Year 1885. Edited by Alfred E. T. Watson . . . London, Longmans, 1886. vi, 549 p.

WATSON (James). Watson's Racing Guide, for . . . October Edition, Containing a Record of All Meetings Past, and Full Programmes, With Nominations, for Meetings to Come; With an Index to Both Racing and Nominations. New York, Watson's Turf Guides, 18 - . *Library has: 1875.*

WATSON (James). Watson's Racing Guide. Annual Edition . . . Containing a Record of All Race-Meetings During . . . New York, 18 - . *Library has: 1875-77.*

WEATHERBY (Charles). The Racing Calendar Abridged . . . From the Earliest Accounts to the Year 1750 Inclusive. London, the author, 1829. *Library has: v. 1 only. No more published?*

WEATHERBY & Sons. The Racing Calendar for the Year . . .
Races Past. Published for the Jockey Club by Weatherby &
Sons . . . London, 1773- .

Library has: 1773 to date. Since 1846 2 v. appear each year:
Races Past, Races to Come. The Library has *Races Past* only.

WEBBER (Byron). Pigskin and Willow. With Other Sporting
Stories. By Byron Webber. In One Volume. London,
Hogg, 1883. 4, 363 p.

WECTER (Dixon). The Saga of American Society. A Record
of Social Aspiration. 1607-1937. By Dixon Wecter. New
York, Scribner, 1937. xiii, 504 p. front. (port.), plates,
ports.

[WEEKS (Lyman Horace).] The American Turf. An Historical
Account of Racing in the United States With Biographical
Sketches of Turf Celebrities. New York, Historical Co.,
1898. 484 [1] p. illus., ports.

WELCH (Ned). Who's Who in Thoroughbred Racing. By Ned
Welch . . . Washington, 1946-47. 2 v. ports., facs. *v. 1,
1st ed., 1946; v. 2, 2d ed., 1947.*

WENTWORTH (Judith Anne Dorothea Blunt-Lytton, Baroness).
Horses in the Making. By Lady Wentworth. London, Allen [1951] xviii, 155 p. illus. (part col.)

WENTWORTH (Judith Anne Dorothea Blunt-Lytton, Baroness).
Thoroughbred Racing Stock and Its Ancestors. The Authentic Origin of Pure Blood . . . With Additional Chapters From the Notes of the Late Lady Anne Blunt . . .
and Wilfred Scawen Blunt, on the Arabian Breed . . . by
Lady Wentworth. With 388 Plates in Half-Tone and 21
Plates in Colour, and Many Diagrams in the Text. New
York, Scribner, 1938. 475 p. front. (col.), illus., plates
(part col.) *Illustration supplement unpaged.*

WESTCHESTER Racing Association. Belmont Park. 1947. New York, 1947. 120 [1] p. illus.

On lining paper: Plan of Belmont Park, Long Island, N. Y. and list of owners whose horses were stabled and raced at Belmont in 1947.

The WESTERN Agriculturist and Practical Farmer's Guide. Prepared Under the Superintendence of the Hamilton County Agricultural Society. Cincinnati, Robinson, 1830. xii, 367 p. front., illus.

[WHEELWRIGHT (Horace William).] Sporting Sketches Home & Abroad. By The Old Bushman . . . With Original Illustrations by G. Bowers. Printed in Colours. London, Warne [1865?] xii, 434 p. front. (col.), illus. (col.)

[WHITE (Alfred).] Kelvington. A Tale for the Turf and the Table. By "Whitebelt." With Frontispiece. London, Wyman, 1883. xii, 234 p. front.

[WHITE (Charles).] Turf Characters: the Officials, and the Subalterns. By Martingale . . . London, Bentley, 1852. xvi, 128 p.

"WHITEBELT." *See* WHITE (Alfred).

WHITNEY (Cornelius Vanderbilt). Reference Catalogue of C. V. Whitney Thoroughbreds. Cornelius V. Whitney, Owner; Ivor Balding, Manager; Sylvester E. Veitch, Trainer; W. A. Harris, Farm Superintendent. [n.p., 1950] 1 v. (looseleaf unpaged)

WHITNEY (Harry Payne). The Thoroughbred Stud of H. P. Whitney, esq. 1928. [Lexington, Ky., privately published, 1928] 284 p. front. (col.)

WHITNEY (William Collins). The Whitney Stud. 1902. New York [Styles, 1903] xliv, 594 p.

WHO'S Who and Where in Horsedom. *See* RANSOM (James Harley).

WHYTE (James Christie). History of the British Turf, From the Earliest Period to the Present Day. By James Christie Whyte . . . In Two Volumes. London, Colburn, 1840. 2 v. illus.

WIDENER (Joseph Early). Elmendorf Stud. 1926. Mr. J. E. Widener. [London, British Bloodstock Agency, 1926] 154 p. *For added pedigrees: p. 142-154.*

WIDENER (Joseph Early) and Widener (Peter Arrell Brown). The Renowned Collections of Sporting and Colored Plate Books . . . Belonging to the Estates of the Late Peter A. B. Widener and Joseph E. Widener . . . New York, Parke-Bernet Galleries, 1944. 148 p. front., plates.

WIDENER (Peter Arrell Brown). Without Drums. By P. A. B. Widener . . . New York, Putnam [1940] 279 p. front. (port.), illus., ports.

WIENER (Philip). *See* LONGSTREET (Stephen). [Pseud.]

WILDRAKE. *See* TATTERSALL (George).

WILKES' Spirit of the Times. A Chronicle of the Turf, Field Sports, Literature and the Stage. New York, 1859-1902. 144 v. illus. weekly. *Title varies. Editor varies. Library has: v. 1-104 (v. 30-86 omitted in numbering), 106-122, 125, 126.*

WILLIAMS (Roger D.). The Foxhound. By Roger D. Williams . . . New York, Macmillan, 1923. 140 p. port., diagr.

[WILLMOTT-DIXON (Willmott).] Famous Racing Men With Anecdotes and Portraits. By "Thormanby" . . . London, Hogg, 1882. 128 p. front. (port.), ports.

[WILLMOTT-DIXON (Willmott).] Kings of the Turf. Memoirs and Anecdotes of Distinguished Owners, Backers, Trainers, and Jockeys Who Have Figured on the British Turf With Memorable Achievements of Famous Horses. By "Thormanby" . . . With Thirty-Two Portraits. London, Hutchinson, 1898. viii, 378 p. front. (port.), ports.

[WILLMOTT-DIXON (Willmott).] Sporting Stories. By "Thormanby." London, Mills [190–] 384 p. front. (col.), illus. (part col.)

WILSON (Edward). Stories About Horses Illustrative of the Intelligence, Fidelity, and Docility of That Noble Animal. By Edward Wilson. Embellished With Eight Engravings. Paterson, N. J., Burnett, 1851. 64 p. front., illus.

WINTER (George Simon). . . . Bellerophon, Sive Eques Peritus. Hoc Est Artis Equestris Accuratissima Institutio, Opere Bipartito, Seu Duobus Libris, Absoluta: Quorum Prior Modum Explicat . . . Posterior Autem Quomodo Indomitus, Intractatus . . . Norimbergae, Sumtibus Wolfgangi Mauritii Endteri, & Haeredum Johannis Andreae Endteri, Anno M DC LXXVIII. [xvii] 191 p. illus., plates. *Bound with the author's* Hippiater Expertus . . . *Norimbergae, 1678.*

WINTER (George Simon). . . . Hippiater Expertus, Seu Medicina Equorum Absolutissima, Tribus Libris Comprehensa: Quorum I. Agit de Equorum Temperamentis . . . II. De Affectibus Internis Thoracis . . . III. De Omnis Generis Unguentis . . . in Gratiam Exterarum Quoque Gentium ex Vernacula in Latinam Translata, Nuncq. Primum Typis Exscripta. Norimbergae, Sumtibus Wolfgangi Mauritii Endteri, & Haeredum Johannis Andreae Endteri, Anno M DC LXXVIII. [xxi] 490 p. [ix] plates.

With this is bound the author's *Bellerophon* . . . Norimbergae, 1678, and *Tractatio Nova de Re Equaria Complectens Partes Tres* . . . Nürnberg, 1672.

WINTER (George Simon). . . . Tractatio Nova de Re Equaria Complectens Partes Tres. Quarum Prima. Agit de Rei Equariae Commodis & Utilitate . . . Secunda. De Natione, Defectibus, Forma, Coloribus, Signis . . . Tertia. De Persona & Officio Perorigae, Hippocomi, Supremi Stabularii . . . et in Usum Quoq. Exterarum Nationum è Germanico in Latinum, Italicum et Gallicum Translata . . . à M.C. L.M. . . . Nürnberg, In Verlegung Johann Andreae und Wolfgang Endtern dess Jüngern Sel. Erben, Anno M DC LXXII. [xix] 169 p. illus., plates (part fold.) *Bound with the author's* Hippiater Expertus . . . *Norimbergae, 1678.*

WON by a Neck. A Sporting Novel. To Which Is Added Turf Characters. London, Ward, 1875. 175 p. *With this is bound:* Turf Characters [*London, 1875?*]

WOOD (John George). The Uncivilized Races of Men in All Countries of the World; Being a Comprehensive Account of Their Manners and Customs, and of Their Physical, Social, Mental, Moral and Religious Characteristics. By Rev. J. G. Wood . . . With New Designs by Angas, Danby, Wolf, Zwecker etc., etc. In Two Volumes. London, Brainard, 1873. 2 v. illus.

WOOD (R. W.). How to Become a Bookmaker. With a Supplement on the Subject of Tic-Tac. By R. W. Wood. London, Postlib Publications [n.d.] 39 p. illus.

WOOD Park Stud. Wood Park Stud Co. Meath, Ireland. 10 Miles From Dublin and 10 Hours From London. For Further Particulars Apply Mr. F. Dillon . . . [London, British Bloodstock Agency, 1924?] 56 p.

WOODBURN Sales Catalogues. For 1860, 1863-64, 1866-76.

   15 catalogues bound together. Cover label hand-lettered; ms notes throughout. Library copy belonged to Mr. Lucas Broadhead listed as agent for Woodburn Farm in the catalogues.

WOODHOUSE (Frederick). A Record of the Melbourne Cup: Giving a Full Account of Every Race for the Cup, With Portraits of All the Winners, Drawn Under the Supervision of Fred. Woodhouse, Senr. Melbourne, Woodhouse, 1889. xii, 40 p. illus., plates (col.)

WOODRUFF (Hiram Washington). The Trotting Horse of America; How to Train and Drive Him. With Reminiscences of the Trotting Turf. By Hiram Woodruff. Edited by Charles J. Foster . . . Including an Introductory Notice by George Wilkes, and a Biographical Sketch by the Editor. New York, Ford, 1868. xxxvi, 412 p. front. (port.)

WOODWARD (William). A Memoir of Andrew Jackson Africanus. By William Woodward in Affectionate Memory of a Long and Faithful Service. [n.p.] privately printed [Derrydale Press] 1938. x [1] 54 p. front. (port.), illus.

"One hundred and fifty copies of A Memoir of Andrew Jackson have been printed by Eugene V. Connett at the Derrydale Press. This copy is no. 147."

WRANGEL (C. G.). Das Buch vom Pferde. Ein Handbuch für Jeden Besitzer und Liebhaber von Pferden von Graf C. G. Wrangel . . . Dritte Vermehrte und Verbesserte Auflage. Mit 608 Abbildungen in Holzschnitt, 11 Kunstbeilagen und dem Portrait des Verfassers. Stuttgart, Schickhardt, 1895. 2 v. illus., plates.

WRAXALL (Sir Henry). [Pseud.] and Hemyng (Bracebridge). The Nobleman on the Turf; or, In Bad Hands. By Sir Henry Wraxall . . . and Bracebridge Hemyng. New Edition. London, Clarke [n.d.] 155 p. (Clarke's Popular Railway Reading)

WYNDHAM (Hugh Archibald). The Early History of the Thoroughbred Horse in South Africa. By the Hon. H. A. Wyndham. London, Milford, 1924. 275 p. illus., tables.

YATES (Arthur). Arthur Yates, Trainer and Gentleman Rider. An Autobiography Written in Collaboration With Bruce Blunt. London, Richards, 1924. 278 p. front. (port.), plates, ports.

YATES (L. B.). The Autobiography of a Race Horse. By L. B. Yates. New York, Doran [1920] 234 p.

YATES (L. B.). Picking Winners With Major Miles. By L. B. Yates . . . Indianapolis, Bobbs-Merrill [1922] 331 p.

YATES (Norris Wilson). William T. Porter and the Spirit of the Times. A Study of the Big Bear School of Humor. By Norris W. Yates. Baton Rouge, La., Louisiana State University Press [1957] xi, 222 p. illus.

YOUATT (William). The Horse, by William Youatt. A New Edition With Numerous Illustrations. Together With a General History of the Horse; a Dissertation on the American Trotting Horse, How Trained and Jockeyed, an Account of His Remarkable Performances; and an Essay on the Ass and the Mule, by J. S. Skinner . . . Philadelphia, Lea, 1846. xvi, 448 p. illus.

YOUATT (William). The Structure, and the Diseases of the Horse, With Their Remedies; Also Practical Rules to Buyers, Breeders, Breakers, Smiths, etc. Being the Most Important Parts of the English Edition of "Youatt on the Horse," Somewhat Simplified. Brought Down to 1849 by W. C. Spooner . . . To Which Is Prefixed an Account of the Breeds in the United States Compiled by Henry S. Randall . . . Auburn and Buffalo, Miller, 1854. xvi, 483 p. front., illus.

YOUNG (John Richard). The Schooling of the Western Horse. By John Richard Young. Norman, University of Oklahoma Press [1954] xiv, 322 p. illus. *"With drawings by Randy Steffen and diagrams by Larry Kumferman."*

YOURELL (Marty). Memoirs of a Jockey. By Marty Yourell. Louisville, Ky., Dorian Press, 1925. 108 p. front. (port.), plates, ports.

ZITO (Anthony). *See* BETTS (Tony). [Pseud.]

Bibliography

American Library Directory. 20th ed. New York: Bowker, 1954.

The American Racing Manual. Chicago: Triangle Publications, 1953, 1958.

Contades, Gérard, Comte de. *Bibliographie Sportive. Les Courses de Chevaux en France (1651-1890)*. Paris: Rouquette, 1892.

Cushing, William. *Initials and Pseudonyms: a Dictionary of Literary Disguises*. New York: Crowell, 1885.

Downs, Robert Bingham. *American Library Resources*. Chicago: A.L.A., 1951.

Gee, Ernest Richard. *Early American Sporting Books, 1734-1844*. New York: Derrydale, 1928.

Gee, Ernest Richard. *The Sportsman's Library*. New York: Bowker, 1940.

Halkett, Samuel, and Laing, John. *Dictionary of Anonymous and Pseudonymous English Literature*. Edinburgh: Oliver & Boyd, 1928-56.

Henderson, Robert William. *Early American Sport*. 2d ed., rev. & enl. New York: Bowker, 1953.

Higginson, Alexander Henry. *British and American Sporting Authors. Their Writings and Biographies . . . With a Bibliography by Sydney R. Smith and Foreword by Ernest R. Gee*. Berryville, Va.: Blue Ridge Press, 1949.

Huth, Frederick Henry. *Works on Horses and Equitation*. London: Quaritch, 1887.

Mennessier de la Lance, Gabriel René. *Essai de Bibliographie Hippique*. Paris: Dorbon, 1915-17.

Peddie, Robert Alexander. *Subject Index of Books Published Before 1880*. London: Grafton, 1933-48.

Prior, Charles Mathew. *The History of the Racing Calendar.* London: "Sporting Life," 1926.

Slater, John Herbert. *Illustrated Sporting Books.* London: Gill, 1899.

The Sporting Library of the Late George B. Raymond. New York: American Art Association [1926].

Stonehill, Charles Archibald. *Anonyma and Pseudonyma.* London: C. A. Stonehill, Jr., 1927.

Thoroughbred Record. Lexington, Ky.

Subject Index

MANY TITLES in the following subject index could be placed as suitably under any one of several subject headings as the one selected. The author's emphasis in his work rather than the range of subject matter he may have covered has been the determining factor in placing the title. As the guide has been arranged alphabetically by author, the subject index has followed that form also.

ANATOMY, CONFORMATION

ANECDOTES

ARAB *see* BREEDS AND TYPES

ARCHITECTURE
> Birch, J. Examples of Stables . . .
> Tattersall, G. Sporting Architecture.

ARTISTS
> Fothergill, G. A. Twenty Sporting Designs.
> Gilbey, W. Life of George Stubbs.
> Gilbey, W., and Cuming, E. W. D. George Morland.
> Munnings, A. J. . . . Pictures of Horses . . .
> Nevill, R. H. Old English Sporting Prints . . .
> Nevill, R. H. Old Sporting Prints.
> Nicholson, W. An Almanac of Twelve Sports.
> Roe, F. G. Sporting Prints . . .
> Siltzer, F. The Story of British Sporting Prints.
> Sparrow, W. S. British Sporting Artists . . .
> Stainforth, M. Racehorses in Australia . . .
> Stubbs, G., and Stubbs, G. T. Review of the Turf . . .
> Troye, E. The Racehorse of America.

BETTING, GAMBLING, PARIMUTUELS
> Albigny, G. d'. Les Paris aux Courses . . .
> Ariel [Pseud.] Astronomy Applied to Horse Racing . . .
> Bellingham, C. Confessions of a Turf Crook . . .
> Brolaski, H. Easy Money . . .
> Brown, C. F. The Turf Expositor . . .
> Buck, F. S. Horse Race Betting . . .
> Cavailhon, E. . . . Les Courses et les Paris.
> Churchill, S. Betting and Gambling.
> Cole, E. W. Racing Maxims . . .
> Comstock, A. Gambling Outrages . . .
> Delauney, J. F. Les Courses . . .
> Delisser, G. P. How to Win at the Races . . .
> Denman, J. . . . Betting Systematized.
> Dey, T. H. Leaves From a Bookmaker's Book.
> Dey, T. H. . . . Opinions of a Betting Man . . .
> Gard, T. A Guide to the Turf.
> Gard, T. Hoyle's Guide . . .
> Gilbey, G., and "Consul" [Pseud.] How to Bet and Win.
> Goodwin Bros. How to Make or Lose Money . . .
> Haines, F. Turf Speculation . . .
> Hobbs, H. The Romance of the Calcutta Sweep.
> La Fouchardière, G. de. Petit Guide . . .
> Lawton, G. Art of Winning . . .
> Lawton, G. Number Five . . .
> Lenoble, H. Les Courses de Chevaux . . .

BETTING, GAMBLING, PARIMUTUELS. *Continued:*
Lyall, J. G. The Merry Gee Gee . . .
Masters, B. How to Win at Racing.
Mihura, M. S. J. L'État Bookmaker.
Monti, J. Pour Faire Fortune aux Courses . . .
Nevill, R. H. Light Come, Light Go.
[Old, W. G.] The Silver Key.
Oliphant, G. H. H. The Law Concerning Horses, Racing . . .
Outsider [Pseud.] La Glorieuse Incertitude du Turf.
Peddie, J. Racing for Gold . . .
Rickman, E. On and Off the Racecourse.
Rouse, R. Turf Betting Simplified . . .
Straight and Unmistakable "Tip" . . .
Technique of Betting, The.
Vieux Sportsman, Un [Pseud.] Guide du Parieux aux Courses.
Wood, R. W. How to Become a Bookmaker.

BIBLIOGRAPHY
[Banks, F. S.] Index of Engravings . . .
Comminges, M. A. Les Races Chevalines . . .
Contades, G. Bibliographie Sportive . . .
Gee, E. R. Early American Sporting Books . . .
Gee, E. R. The Sportsman's Library . . .
Harrison, F. The Background of the American Stud Book.
Henderson, R. W. Early American Sport . . .
Higginson, A. H. British and American Sporting Authors . . .
Huth, F. H. Works on Horsemanship . . .
Huth, F. H. Works on Horses and Equitation . . .
Lafont-Puloti, E. P. Nouveau Régime . . .
Mennessier de la Lance, G. R. Essai de Bibliographie
    Hippique . . .
Raymond, G. B. Catalogue of Books . . .
Slater, J. H. Illustrated Sporting Books.
Van Stockum, C. M. Sport: An Attempt at a Bibliography . . .
Widener, J. E., and Widener, P. A. B. The Renowned
    Collections . . .

BIOGRAPHY, MEMOIRS
Allison, W. Memories of Men and Horses.
Allison, W. "My Kingdom for a Horse!"
Apperly, C. J. My Life and Times.
Apperly, C. J. Nimrod Abroad.
[Apperly, C. J.] The Turf.
Arcaro, G. E. I Ride to Win!
Astley, J. D. Fifty Years of My Life . . .
Betts, T. Across the Board.
Bird, T. H. Admiral Rous and the English Turf.

BIOGRAPHY, MEMOIRS. *Continued:*

Bovill, M. 'Roddy Owen' . . .
Brinley, F. Life of William T. Porter.
Brolaski, H. Easy Money . . .
Brown, S. L. Rarey, the Horse's Master and Friend.
Buckman-Linard, S. My Horse; My Love.
Champion de Crespigny, C. Forty Years of a Sportsman's Life.
Champion de Crespigny, C. Memoirs.
Cheltonian, A [Pseud.] Autobiographies of the Archers . . .
Cobbett, M. R. Racing Life . . .
Cobbett, M. R. Wayfaring Notions . . .
Custance, H. Riding Recollections . . .
Darling, S. Reminiscences.
Davis, J. H. The American Turf.
Day, W. Reminiscences . . .
Day, W. Turf Celebrities I Have Known.
Dodds, E. K. Canadian Turf Recollections . . .
Donoghue, S. "Just My Story."
Fairfax-Blakeborough, J. Northern Sport . . .
Fairfax-Blakeborough, J. Paddock Personalities . . .
Fairfax-Blakeborough, J. Sykes of Sledmere . . .
Gilbey, W. Life of George Stubbs.
Gilbey, W., and Cuming, E. W. D. George Morland.
Gould, N. The Magic of Sport . . .
Hayes, M. H. Among Men and Horses.
Herbert, H. W. Life and Writings.
Higginson, A. H. British and American Sporting Authors . . .
Higginson, A. H. Try Back . . .
Hildreth, S. C. The Spell of the Turf . . .
Hirsch, M. D. William C. Whitney . . .
Hirsch, M. J. Dinner in Honor of . . .
Hodgman, G. Sixty Years on the Turf . . .
Humphris, E. M. Adam Lindsay Gordon . . .
Humphris, E. M. The Life of Fred Archer.
Humphris, E. M. The Life of Mathew Dawson . . .
Jennings, F. C. From Here to the Bugle.
Keene, F., and Hatch, A. Full Tilt . . .
Kent, J. Racing Life of Lord George Cavendish Bentinck . . .
Kent, J. Records and Reminiscences of Goodwood . . .
Khan, J. Racing Reminiscences . . .
King, F. M. Longhorn Trail Drivers . . .
Lawley, F. C. Life and Times of "The Druid" . . .
Londonderry, E. H. V.-T.-S. Henry Chaplin; A Memoir . . .
Lovers of the Horse . . .
Luke, H. Harry Luke's Reminiscences . . .
Marsh, R. A Trainer to Two Kings . . .
Menke. F. G. Down the Stretch.

BIOGRAPHY, MEMOIRS. *Continued:*
    Menzies, A. C. (B.) S. Lord William Beresford . . .
    Moore, M. G. An Irish Gentleman . . .
    Morton, C. My Sixty Years of the Turf.
    Munnings, A. J. Autobiography.
    Nightingall, A. My Racing Adventures.
    O'Brien, R. B. The Life of Lord Russell of Killowen.
    O'Connor, W. S. Jockeys, Crooks and Kings.
    O'Kelly, D. The Genuine Memoirs of . . .
    Orchard, V. R. Tattersalls.
    Osbaldeston, G. Squire Osbaldeston, His Autobiography . . .
    Poore, B. P. Biographical Sketch of John Stuart Skinner . . .
    Porter, J. John Porter of Kingsclere.
    Porter, J. Kingsclere.
    Portland, W. J. A. C. J. C.-B. Memoirs of Racing . . .
    Radcliffe, J. B. Ashgill; or the Life and Times of John Osborne.
    Richards, G. My Story.
    Richardson, J. M. Gentlemen Riders Past and Present.
    Richardson, M. E. The Life of a Great Sportsman (John Maunsell Richardson).
    Robinson, J. R. 'Old Q' a Memoir . . .
    Rossmore, D. W. W. W. Things I Can Tell.
    Russell, C. Triumphs & Tragedies of the Turf.
    Sarl, A. J. Horses, Jockeys & Crooks.
    Scott, A. Turf Memories of Sixty Years.
    Shipman, E. The Racing Memoirs of John Hertz . . .
    Sievier, R. S. The Autobiography of . . .
    Sloan, J. F. Tod Sloan.
    Smith, H. W. Life and Sport in Aiken . . .
    Smith, H. W. A Sporting Family of the Old South.
    Snowy, J. The Stanley of the Turf.
    Sporting Life, The. The British Turf . . .
    Sportsman, The. British Sports and Sportsmen. Past & Present.
    [Stoddart, J.] The Turf. Sportsmen of Today.
    Watson, A. E. T. King Edward VII as a Sportsman.
    Watson, A. E. T. A Sporting and Dramatic Career.
    [Weeks, L. H.] The American Turf.
    Welch, N. Who's Who in Thoroughbred Racing.
    Widener, P. A. B. Without Drums.
    Willmott-Dixon, W. Famous Racing Men . . .
    Willmott-Dixon, W. Kings of the Turf . . .
    Woodward, W. A Memoir of Andrew Jackson Africanus.
    Yates, A. Arthur Yates, Trainer and Gentleman Rider.
    Yates, N. W. William T. Porter . . .

BLACKSMITH *see* FARRIERY

BOOKMAKING *see* BETTING

BREEDING—HISTORY
Allison, W. The British Thoroughbred Horse . . .
Anderson, J. D. Making the American Thoroughbred . . .
Buffard, P. J. V. L'Élevage . . .
Busby, H. Recollections of Men & Horses.
Canti, E. Nel Mondo de Galoppo . . .
Cavailhon, E. . . . Les Haras de France . . .
Clark, B. A Short History of the Horse . . .
Copperthwaite, R. H. The Turf and the Racehorse . . .
Dimon, J. American Horses and Horse Breeding . . .
Easby Abbey Breeding Stud.
Estes, J. A., and Palmer, J. H. An Introduction . . .
Gayot, E. N. La France Chevaline . . .
General Account and Pedigree of the British Race Horse . . .
Gilbey, W. Horses Past and Present.
Great Britain. Parliament. House of Lords. Select Committee
   . . . on Horses.
[Harrison, F.] The Belair Stud.
[Harrison, F.] Early American Turf Stock . . .
[Harrison, F.] The Equine F.F.Vs.
[Harrison, F.] The John's Island Stud.
[Harrison, F.] The Roanoke Stud.
Herbert, H. W. Frank Forester's Horse and Horsemanship.
Hunt, V. D. de V. The Horse and His Master . . .
Huzard, J. B. Des Haras Domestiques . . .
Ireland. Parliament. Commission on Horse Breeding . . .
La Moricière, C. L. J. de. De l'Espèce Chevaline en France.
Lupton, J. I. The Horse: as He Was . . .
[Mott, E. S.] The King's Racehorses . . .
O'Connor, J. L. Notes on the Thoroughbred . . .
Prior, C. M. The Royal Studs . . .
Roudaud, E. Études sur le Cheval . . .
Speed, J. G. The Horse in America.
Stong, P. D. Horses and Americans.
[Teyssier des Farges, G. A.] La Race Pure en France . . .
Tozer, B. The Horse in History.
Wallace, J. H. The Horse of America . . .
Western Agriculturist, The.
Winter, G. S. . . . Tractatio Nova de Re Equaria . . .

BREEDING—THEORIES
Allison, W. The British Thoroughbred Horse . . .
Apperly, C. J. Nemrod ou l'Amateur des Chevaux de
   Courses . . .

BREEDING—THEORIES. *Continued:*

    Becker, F. S. The Breed of the Racehorse . . .
    Bedout, L. Notes sur la Méthode . . .
    Bruce, S. D. The Thoroughbred Horse . . .
    Curot, E., and Fournier, P. Le Pur Sang . . .
    Dawkins, G. H. Present Day Sires . . .
    Day, W. The Horse. How to Breed . . .
    Fisher, R. A. The Theory of Inbreeding.
    Gilbey, W. Horses—Breeding to Colour . . .
    Gilbey, W. Hunter Sires . . .
    Gilbey, W. . . . Young Race-Horses . . .
    Hunt, V. D. de V. The Horse and His Master . . .
    Keylock, H. E. The Mating of Thoroughbred Horses . . .
    King Ranch. 100 Years of Ranching.
    Lafont-Pouloti, E. P. Nouveau Régime . . .
    Lehndorf, G. H. A. Horse Breeding Recollections.
    Lowe, C. B. Breeding Racehorses by the Figure System.
    McPhillamy, C. S. The Thoroughbred, His Breeding . . .
    Magne, J. H. Hygiène Vétérinaire Appliquée . . .
    Meek, C. F. U. Winners of the Past . . .
    Morland, T. H. The Genealogy of the English Race Horse . . .
    Musany, F. C. M. L'Élevage, l'Entraînement . . .
    Nicard, C. E. L'Inbreeding et l'Outcrossing . . .
    Nicard, C. E. Le Langage des Éleveurs . . .
    Osmer, W. Dissertation on Horses.
    Pichard, . Manuel des Haras . . .
    Platt, J. E. The Thoroughbred Race-Horse.
    Ricketts, P. E. The Modern Racehorse.
    Robertson, J. B. The Principles of Heredity . . .
    Sanders, J. H. Horse-Breeding . . .
    Smith, N. H. Observations on Breeding . . .
    Stokes, W. E. D. The Right to Be Well Born . . .
    Tesio, F. Puro-Sangue.
    [Tongue, C.] The Stud Farm . . .
    Von Oettingen, B. Horse Breeding in Theory . . .
    Vuillier, J. J. Les Croisements Rationnels . . . (1902-06, 1928)
    Vuillier, J. J. Deuxièmes Tables des Dosages . . .
    Vuillier, J. J. Registre des Dosages du Haras.
    Wall, R. A Dissertation on Breeding Horses . . .
    [Walsh, J. H.] Le Cheval Anglais.
    Wentworth, J. A. D. W. B.-L. Thoroughbred Racing Stock . . .
    Winter, G. S. . . . Tractatio Nova de Re Equaria . . .

BREEDS AND TYPES

    Abbildungen Königlich Württembergischer Gestütts Pferde von Orientalischen Racen.

BREEDS AND TYPES. *Continued:*
  Abou Bekr Ibn Bedr. Le Nâcérî.
  Blunt, Lady Anne. Bedouin Tribes . . .
  Borden, S. The Arab Horse.
  Boucaut, J. P. The Arab, the Horse of the Future . . .
  Boucaut, J. P. The Arab, the Thoroughbred . . .
  Brown, G. Biographical Sketches . . .
  Carter, W. G. H. The Horses of the World . . .
  Craven, W. G. The Royal Commission . . .
  Curr, E. M. Pure Saddle-Horses . . .
  Daumas, M. J. E. Les Chevaux du Sahara . . .
  Daumas, M. J. E. Principes Généraux . . .
  Denhardt, R. M. The Horse of the Americas.
  de Trafford, H. F. The Horses of the British Empire.
  Dimon, J. American Horses & Horse Breeding . . .
  Dixon, H. H. Saddle and Sirloin.
  Durand, E. Ponies' Progress.
  Gilbey, W. Thoroughbred and Other Ponies . . .
  Gorman, J. A. The Western Horse . . .
  Hamilton, K. B. Our Saddle Horses.
  Houël, E. G. Les Chevaux de Pur Sang . . .
  Houël, E. G. Les Chevaux Français . . .
  Huntington, R. History in Brief of "Leopard" and "Linden" . . .
  Huzard, J. B. Notice sur les Chevaux Anglais . . .
  Lawrence, J. The History and Delineation of the Horse . . .
  [Lawrence, J.] The Sportsman's Repository . . .
  Le Hello, P. M. Le Pur Sang Anglais et Ses Dérivés.
  Low, D. Les Animaux Domestiques de l'Europe.
  Low, D. The Breeds of the Domestic Animals of the British
    Islands.
  Magne, J. H. Hygiène Vétérinaire Appliquée . . .
  Merry, T. B. The American Thoroughbred.
  Meuleman, E. C. F. J. Reflexions Critiques . . .
  Meysey-Thompson, R. F. The Horse, Its Origin . . .
  Morland, T. H. The Genealogy of the English Race Horse . . .
  Pinel, H. P. A. B. C. du Sportsman.
  Rendel, J. The Horse Book.
  Reynolds, J. A World of Horses.
  Richardson, C. The New Book of the Horse.
  Ridgeway, W. The Origin & Influence of the Thoroughbred
    Horse.
  Roudaud, E. Études sur le Cheval . . .
  [Scharf, E. E.] Famous Saddle Horses.
  Sidney, S. The Book of the Horse . . .
  Smith, C. H. The Natural History of Horses.
  Speed, J. G. The Horse in America.

BREEDS AND TYPES. *Continued:*
  Springfield, R., The Horse and His Rider . . .
  Thayer, B. C. Horses in the Blue Grass.
  Tweedie, W. The Arabian Horse . . .
  Upton, R. D. Newmarket & Arabia.
  Vosburgh, W. S. Thoroughbred Types.
  Walsh, J. H. Le Cheval Anglais.
  Walsh, J. H. The Horse in the Stable . . .
  Wentworth, J. A. D. W. B.-L. Horses in the Making.
  Wentworth, J. A. D. W. B.-L. Thoroughbred Racing Stock . . .
  Wrangel, C. G. Das Buch vom Pferde.
  Wyndham, H. A. The Early History of the Thoroughbred Horse
    in South Africa.
  Youatt, W. The Horse . . .

CONFORMATION *see* ANATOMY, CONFORMATION

COLORS (Racing)
  Blake, C. W. Caps and Jackets . . .
  . . . Colours at a Glance . . .
  Kentucky. State Racing Commission. Color Registrations.
  Muir, J. B. Raciana, or Riders' Colours . . .

COACHING *see* HORSEMANSHIP

DICTIONARIES
  Baranowski, Z. The International Horseman's Dictionary.
  Blaine, D. P. An Encyclopaedia of Rural Sports . . .
  Boardman, S. L. Handbook of the Turf . . .
  Day, J. I., Jr., and Barber, R. . . . Racing Almanac.
  Étreillis, . Dictionnaire du Sport Français . . .
  Hare, C. E. The Language of Sport . . .
  Johnson, T. B. The Sportsman's Cyclopaedia . . .
  Malbessan, . Dictionnaire des Courses . . .
  Mirabel, H. de V. Manuel des Courses.
  Paz, E. Dictionnaire des Courses.
  Sportsman's Dictionary, The.
  Taplin, W. The Sporting Dictionary . . .

DISEASES *see* VETERINARY MEDICINE

ESSAYS
  Cler, A. La Comédie à Cheval.
  Crosland, T. W. H. Who Goes Racing.
  Doyle, J. A. Essays . . .

ESSAYS. *Continued:*
>Houston, T. The Races . . .
>Knowles, G. W. The Tale of the Turf.
>[Mott, E. S.] Dopes.
>Rose, J. B. Four Short Chapters on Horses . . .
>Trarieux, J. Si les Chevaux Pouvaient Parler . . .
>[White, C.] Turf Characters . . .

. EVOLUTION
>Carter, W. G. H. The Horses of the World . . .
>Matthew, W. D. Evolution of the Horse.
>Ridgeway, W. The Origin and Influence of the Thoroughbred Horse.
>Riggs, E. S. The Geological History and Evolution of the Horse.

. FARRIERY
>[Badcock, J.] . . . Farriery . . .
>[Badcock, J.] The Veterinary Surgeon . . .
>Carver, W. Practical Horse Farrier . . .
>Curot, E. La Ferrure . . .
>Curot, E. Galopeurs et Trotteurs . . .
>Magner, D. Art of Taming and Educating . . .
>Markham, G. Markham's Masterpiece . . .
>Solleysel, J. de. The Compleat Horseman . . .

FEEDING AND FEEDSTUFFS
>Curot, E., and Fournier, P. Comment Nourrir . . .
>U.S. Department of Agriculture. Yearbook of Agriculture. Grass. (1948)

FICTION
>[Allison, W.] "Blairmount?"
>[Apperly, C. J.] The Life of a Sportsman.
>Ball, R. Penny Farthing.
>[Barrow, A. S.] Between the Flags.
>Beaumont, G. Riders Up!
>Beery, J. The Thoroughbreds.
>Bellairs, A. The God of the Turf.
>Blossom, H. M. Checkers.
>Buck, C. N. Sandollar.
>[Clark, C.] The Flying Scud.
>Clay, Mrs. J. M. The Sport of Kings . . .
>Collins, C. J. Dick Diminy . . .
>Collins, G. E. Tales of Pink and Silk.
>Cooper, E. H. The Monk Wins.

FICTION. *Continued:*
    Cooper, P. Great Horse Stories.
    Cox, H. E. de F. The Amateur's Derby . . .
    Cullen, C. L. Taking Chances.
    Derby Day, The . . .
    Fairfax-Blakeborough, J. The Disappearance of Cropton.
    Fairfax-Blakeborough, J. A Turf Mystery.
    Ferguson, W. B. M. Garrison's Finish . . .
    Finot, L. J. . . . Petit-Bout . . .
    Foote, J. T. Blister Jones.
    Foote, J. T. The Look of Eagles.
    Foster, C. J. The White Horse of Wootton.
    Graham, R. B. C. Rodeo.
    Gould, N. Charger and Chaser.
    Gould, N. Fast as the Wind.
    Gould, N. The Lady Trainer.
    Gould, N. The Rider in Khaki.
    Gould, N. The Top Weight.
    Gould, N. Warned Off.
    Harper, H. G. New Sporting Stories.
    Harper, H. G. Sporting Stories and Sketches.
    Harrington, G. W. A Reversion of Form . . .
    Hichborn, P. Hoof Beats.
    Hushed Up. A. D. L.
    Kennard, Mrs. E. The Right Sort . . .
    Liebling, A. J. The Honest Rainmaker . . .
    Longstreet, S. [Pseud.] Stallion Road.
    Luckman, A. D. Sharps, Flats, Gamblers . . .
    Lundsford, H. Flying Heels.
    Mankiewicz, D. M. See How They Run.
    Mills, J. Grandeur et Décadence d'un Cheval de Course.
    Mills, J. The Life of a Racehorse. (1854, 1865)
    Parker, R. The Whip.
    Pearce, C. E. A Queen of the Paddock . . .
    Porter, W. T. A Quarter Race in Kentucky . . .
    Richards, F. T. G. Double Life.
    Roche, A. S. The Sport of Kings.
    Romer, F. Tit for Tat.
    [Schoeffel, F. B. W.] Saddle & Sentiment.
    Smart, H. H. Long Odds.
    Turf, The.
    Van Loan, C. E. Old Man Curry.
    Wallace, E. The Calendar.
    Wallace, E. Educated Evans.
    Wallace, E. The Green Ribbon.

FICTION. *Continued:*
　Webber, B. Pigskin and Willow.
　[White, A.] Kelvington.
　Wilson, E. Stories About Horses.
　Won by a Neck.
　Wraxall, H. [Pseud.] and Hemyng, B. The Nobleman on the
　　Turf . . .
　Yates, L. B. Picking Winners With Major Miles.

FOLKLORE, LEGEND, MAGIC
　Hare, C. E. The Language of Sport.
　Howey, M. O. The Horse in Magic and Myth.

FOX HUNTING *see* HUNTING

GAMBLING *see* BETTING, etc.

GENETICS
　Bateson, W. Mendel's Principles . . .

HANDICAPPING
　Chetwyne, G. Racing Reminiscences . . .
　Dowst, R. S., and Craig, J. Playing the Races.
　Hand, N. S. Hand's System of Handicapping . . .
　[Neuhof, A.] Classements Cotés . . .
　Turf and Sport Digest, comp. Handicapping Horses to Win.

HORSEMANSHIP
　Adams, J. An Analysis of Horsemanship . . .
　Allen, J. Principles of Modern Riding . . .
　Arcaro, G. E. The Art of Race Riding.
　Aubry, C. Histoire Pittoresque . . .
　Berenger, R. The History and Art of Horsemanship.
　Berterèche de Menditte, P. J. B. E. Les Courses de Résistance.
　Chamberlin, H. D. Riding and Schooling Horses.
　Dixon, H. H. Scott and Sebright.
　Dodge, T. A. Riders of Many Lands.
　Fillis, J. Breaking and Riding . . .
　Fleitman, L. L. Comments on Hacks . . .
　[Gérusez, V.] Paris à Cheval.
　[Gérusez, V.] La Province à Cheval.
　Hayes, M. H. Riding and Hunting.
　Head, F. B. The Horse and His Rider.
　Kerr, W. A. Practical Horsemanship.
　King, F. M. Longhorn Trail Drivers . . .

HORSEMANSHIP. *Continued:*
    Lagondie, J. G. Le Cheval et Son Cavalier.
    Lyall, J. G. The Merry Gee Gee . . .
    Montigny, E. L. X. Manuel des Piqueurs . . .
    Page, H. S. Between the Flags.
    Peters, J. G. A Treatise on Equitation . . .
    Senex [Pseud.] Observations on Horses . . .
    Smits, A. E. M. A Propos du Raid Bruxelles-Ostende.
    Thompson, C. Rules for Bad Horsemen . . .
    Tinker, E. L. . . . The Horsemen of the Americas . . .
    [Turquet de Beauregard, Y. L. M.] Saut d'Obstacles . . .
    Voigt, C. A. Famous Gentlemen Riders . . .
    Ware, F. M. First-Hand Bits of Stable Lore.
    Winter, G. S. . . . Bellerophon . . .

HORSES–INDIVIDUAL
    Anderson, C. W. Big Red.
    Blanchard, E. A. C., and Wellman, M. W. . . . Sir Archie . . .
    Breitigam, G. B. Morvich.
    Bruce, B. G. Memoir of Lexington.
    Clark, B. A Short History of the Celebrated Race-Horse, Eclipse.
    Cook, T. A. Eclipse & O'Kelly . . .
    Cooper, P., and Treat, R. L. Man o' War.
    Greenwood, Mrs. G. D. Gloaming the Wonder Horse.
    Hervey, J. L. Messenger the Great Progenitor.
    Huntington, R. History in Brief of "Leopard" and "Linden" . . .
    Lechmere, J. Pretty Polly.
    Lyle, R. C. Brown Jack.
    Rousouck, E. J. The Mighty Lexington at 7 Years of Age.
    Tattersall, G. The Cracks of the Day.
    Tattersall, G. The Pictorial Gallery of English Race Horses.
        (1844, 1850)
    Taunton, T. Famous Horses With Portraits . . .
    Taunton, T. H. Portraits of Celebrated Racehorses . . .
    Troye, E. The Race Horses of America.
    Vial de Sainbel, C. Essai sur les Proportions Geometrales de
        l'Eclipse.
    Watson, A. E. T. Galicia, Her Forbears . . .
    Watson, A. E. T. Prince Palatine . . .

HUMOR
    Anderson, J. S. The Turf in Caricature.
    Browne, H. K. The Derby Day.
    Cler, A. La Comédie à Cheval . . .
    Doré, G. Two Hundred Sketches . . .

HUMOR. *Continued:*
[Gérusez, V.] Paris à Cheval.
[Gérusez, V.] La Province à Cheval.
[Gérusez, V.] Sur le Turf.
Mason, G. F. Tit Bits of the Turf.
Merry, M. The Turf . . .
Rutherford, S. B. The Derby Dixienary.

HUNTER *see* BREEDS AND TYPES

HUNTING
[Apperly, C. J.] The Chace, the Turf . . .
Cox, H. E. de F. Chasing and Racing . . .
Dixon, H. H. Scott and Sebright.
Dixon, H. H. Silk and Scarlet.
Fawcett, W. Turf, Chase & Paddock.
Fitt, J. N. Hunting, Steeple-Chasing and Racing . . .
Griswold, F. G. Horses and Hounds . . .
Higginson, A. H. Try Back.
Smith, H. W. A Sporting Tour Through Ireland . . .

JOCKEYS
Acton, C. R. Silk and Spur.
Arcaro, G. E. I Ride to Win!
Cheltonian, A [Pseud.] Autobiographies of the Archers . . .
Chifney, S. The Narrative Statement of . . .
Donoghue, S. "Just My Story."
Fairfax-Blakeborough, J. Paddock Personalities.
Jockey's Guild, The. Year Book . . . (1945)
Khan, J. Racing Reminiscences . . .
Luke, H. Harry Luke's Reminiscences . . .
Neuter, A. de. . . . George Stern, Jockey . . .
O'Connor, W. S. Jockeys, Crooks and Kings.
Richards, G. My Story.
Sloan, J. F. Tod Sloan.
[Vosburgh, W. S.] Famous American Jockeys . . .
[Weeks, L. H.] The American Turf.
Yourell, M. Memoirs of a Jockey.

LAWS
Disney, J. The Laws of Gaming . . .
Edwards, F. Brief Treatise on the Law of Gaming . . .
Great Britain. Parliament. House of Lords. Select Committee
    to Inquire into the Laws Respecting Gaming.
Laws of Gaming, The . . .

LAWS. *Continued:*
New York. State Racing Commission. Annual Reports.
Oliphant, G. H. H. The Law Concerning Horses, Racing . . .

MEMOIRS *see* BIOGRAPHY

ORGANIZATIONS (Jockey Clubs, Société d'Encouragement, etc.)
American Jockey Club, The.
Black, R. Horse-Racing in France.
Black, R. The Jockey Club and Its Founders . . .
Gibert, C. C. A., and Massa, A. P. R. Historique du Jockey-Club
Français . . .
Irving, J. B. The South Carolina Jockey Club.
Kentucky Association. A Souvenir . . .
Société d'Encouragement Pour l'Amélioration des Races de
Chevaux . . .
Thoroughbred Horse Association. Reports.
United Hunts Racing Association. Calendar.

PERIODICALS, CONTINUATIONS, etc.
American Horse Breeder.
American Turf Register and Sporting Magazine, The.
Baily's Magazine.
Bulletin Hebdomadaire . . .
Il Cavallo.
Cultivator and Country Gentleman, The.
L'Éleveur. Journal des Chevaux.
Grandi Prove Ippiche, Le.
Horse, The
Horse and Hound.
Horse Review, The.
Illustrated Sporting News.
Journal des Haras . . .
Kentucky Farmer and Breeder.
New-York Sporting Magazine . . .
New York Sportsman, The.
Porter's Spirit of the Times.
Racing and Breeding.
Racing Illustrated.
Revue des Éleveurs de Chevaux de Pur Sang.
Spirit of the Times.
Sporting Magazine, The.
Sporting Mirror, The.
Sporting Review, The.
Sporting Sketches.

PERIODICALS, CONTINUATIONS, etc. *Continued:*
Turf Argentino.
Turf, Field and Farm.
Wilkes' Spirit of the Times.

PERIODICALS–CURRENT
Blood-Horse, The.
Bloodstock Breeders Review, The.
British Race Horse, The.
Maryland Horse, The.
Ruff's Guide to the Turf . . .
Thoroughbred Record, The.
Triangle Publications. Daily Racing Form Chart Book . . .

PEDIGREES
American Thoroughbred Breeders Association. Statistical
Summary.
Annals of the Turf; General Account . . .
Antwerp & Lamplighter [Pseud.] Modern Pedigrees.
"Australasian," The. Stallion Register . . .
Bayliss, M. F. The Matriarchy of the American Turf . . .
Becker, F. S. Charts of the Successful Sire Lines . . .
Becker, F. S. The Successful Female Lines . . .
Birch, F. E. Pedigrees of Leading Winners 1947-53.
Birch, F. L. Pedigrees of 150 Leading Winners . . .
Birch, F. L., and Birch, F. E. Pedigrees of 400 Leading
Winners . . .
Blood-Horse, The. Five Years of Speed . . .
Blood-Horse, The. Sires of American Thoroughbreds.
Blood-Horse, The. Stakes Winners . . .
Blood-Horse, The. Stallion Register.
Blood-Horse, The. Stallion Register and Mating Book.
Blood-Horse, The. Thoroughbred Broodmare Records . . .
Blood-Horse, The. Thoroughbred Sires and Dams . . .
Bobiński, K. Family Tables . . .
[Brignac, F. de.] Mères de Gagnants . . . (1956)
Brignac, F. de. Mères de Gagnants . . . (1942)
Bruce, S. D. The Horse-Breeder's Guide . . .
Bruce, S. D. The Thoroughbred Horse . . .
Chismon, Wm. Stallion Record . . .
Corbière, P. Étalons de Pur Sang de France.
Coussell, E. E. The Bruce Lowe Numbers . . .
Dawkins, G. H. Present Day Sires . . .
Du Hays, J. C. A. Les Courses en France . . .
Du Hays, J. C. A. Dictionnaire de la Race Pure . . .

PEDIGREES. *Continued:*

Estes, J. A. Thoroughbred Pedigrees.

. . . Étalons de Pur Sang. Répertoire 1957 . . .

Frentzel, J. P. Familien Tafeln . . .

Gasté, M. de. Race Pure.

Goodwin, W. J. Pedigree of the Thorough-Bred Horse . . .

Goos, H. Die Stamm-Mütter. (1897, 1907)

Halbronn, C. R. Les Étalons de France . . .

Halbronn, C. R. Guide de l'Éleveur . . .

Hermit [Pseud.] Les Chevaux de Deux Ans . . .

Herries, W. H. The Successful Running and Sire Lines . . .

Ireland. Irish Land Commission. . . . Return of Stallions . . .

Johnstone, A. Keylock's Dams of Winners . . .

Johnstone, A. Keylock's Dams of Winners . . . (1948-56)

Keylock, H. E. Dams of Winners. (1945)

Keylock, H. E. Dams of Winners. (1948)

Keylock, H. E. Dams of Winners. (1950)

LaBoyteaux, W. H. Thoroughbred Pedigree Charts.

Legoupy, A. Le Cheval de Demi-Sang Français.

Marchal, G. H. Les Souches des Poulinières Françaises . . .

Miranda Rosa, F. A. de. O Puro Sangue.

New Zealand Breeders' Association. Register of Thoroughbred Stallions . . .

Osborne, J. The Horsebreeders' Handbook . . . (1881)

Osborne, J. The Horse-Breeders' Handbook . . . (1890?)

Osborne, J. The Two Year Olds of 1899.

Palmer, J. H. Names in Pedigrees.

Petion, K. A. Genealogical Lists . . .

Poland. Society for Promoting Horsebreeding in Poland. Tabulated Pedigrees . . .

Pontet, T. Dictionnaire Généalogique . . .

Pontet, T. Répertoire Historique . . .

Reeves, J. H. The Orange County Stud Book . . . (1872)

Register of Thoroughbred Stallions . . .

Royal Dublin Society. Register of Thoroughbred Stallions . . .

Saint Saveur, . Les Grands Étalons . . .

Sharp, J. F. M. The Thoroughbred Mares' Record . . .

Templer, R. C. Sires of Winners.

[Teyssier des Farges, G. A.] L'Élevage du Pur Sang . . .

[Teyssier des Farges, G.A.] La Race Pure en France . . .

Thoroughbred Record, The. Annual Statistical Review . . .

Traces of the Turf.

Treacy, W., and Walker, K. American Thoroughbred Stallion Register . . .

[Vuillier, J. J.] Deuxième Tables de Dosages.

Vuillier, J. J. Les Croisements Rationnels . . . (1902-06, 1928)

PEDIGREES. *Continued:*
    [Vuillier, J. J.] Registre des Dosages du Haras.
    [Vuillier, J. J.] Tables de Dosages.
    Wackerow, C. Tables of Pedigrees of Thoroughbred Horses . . .
    Walker, W. H. The Sire and Family Number . . .
    Walker, W. H. . . . Stallion Register.
    Wall, J. F. Thoroughbred Bloodlines.
    Wanklyn, W. H. E. The Australasian Racehorse. A Record . . .
    Wanklyn, W. H. E. The Australasian Racehorse.
        Supplement . . .
    Wanklyn, W. H. E. The Great Sire Lines.

POETRY
    Budgell, E. A Poem Upon His Majesty's Late Journey . . .
    Cary, R. L. Sporting Ballads . . .
    Cary, R. L. Tales of the Turf . . .
    Dibdin, C. The High-Mettled Racer.
    Fothergill, G. A. Twenty Sporting Designs . . .
    [Fowler, A. A.] The Ballad of Myra Gray . . .
    Gordon, A. L. Racing Rhymes . . .
    [Gosden, T.] The Sportsman's Vocal Library . . .
    Harrison, S. Gentlemen, The Horse!
    Hood, T. Epsom Races . . .
    Ilwar, S. N. Racing Rhymes . . .
    Kipling, R. An Almanac of Twelve Sports.
    Lure of the Turf, The.
    Masefield, J. Right Royal. (1920, 1922)
    Paterson, A. B. The Man From Snowy River . . .
    Paterson, A. B. Rio Grande's Last Race . . .
    Peacock, T. The Stable Boy . . .
    Pierce, E. S. Poems of the Turf . . .
    Race in Four Cantos, A.
    Rae-Brown, C. Goneaways Race . . .

PORTRAITS
    Abbildungen Königlich Württembergischer Gestütts Pferde von
        Orientalischen Racen.
    A Comparative View . . .
    Cremière, L. Album du Centaure.
    Dubost, A. Newmarket . . .
    Famous Horses of America . . .
    Famous Sporting Prints.
    Fothergill, G. A. A Gift to the State.
    Gooch, T. Life and Death of a Racehorse . . .
    Hailey, C. A Generation of Derby Winners.
    Munnings, A. J. . . . Pictures of Horses . . .

PORTRAITS. *Continued:*
    Portraits of Broodmares . . .
    Portraiture of the Most Famous Racehorses . . .
    Roberts, J. The Sportsman's Pocket Companion.
    Schreiber & Sons. Portraits of Noted Horses of America . . .
    Sutcliffe, L. S. Photographs of Thoroughbred Mares.
    Sutcliffe, L. S. Photographs of 205 Thoroughbred Sires.
    [Teyssier des Farges, G. A.] Historique des Étalons . . .
    [Teyssier des Farges, G. A.] History of Celebrated English and
        French Thoroughbred Stallions . . .
    Vosburgh, W. S. Cherished Portraits . . .

RACING (By Country)
    Australia:
    Gould, N. On and Off the Turf in Australia.
    Haydon, T. Racing Reminiscences.
    Stainforth, M. Racehorses in Australia . . .
    Woodhouse, F. A Record of the Melbourne Cup . . .

    Canada:
    Lovers of the Horse . . .

    France:
    Black, R. Horse-Racing in France.
    Buffard, P. J. V. L'Élevage . . .
    [Caters, Louis de.] Les Courses de Chevaux . . .
    Cavailhon, E. Les Chevaux de Courses en 1889 . . .
    Cavailhon, E. . . . Les Courses et les Paris.
    Chapus, E. Le Turf . . .
    Delauney, J. F. Les Courses . . .
    Gayot, E. N. Guide du Sportsman . . .
    [Gérusez, V.] Sur le Turf.
    Henry, E. Les Courses.
    Laffon, F. G. Le Monde des Courses. (1887, 1896)
    Lafont-Pouloti, E. P. Memoire sur les Courses . . .
    Lagondie, J. G. Le Cheval et Son Cavalier . . .
    Mirabel, H. de V. Manuel des Courses.
    Noisay, M. de. Tableau des Courses . . .
    Noisay, M. de. Voilà les Courses.
    Parent, E. C. L. M. Manuel des Courses de Chevaux.
    Racing in France.
    Saint Albin, A. H. de L. de. Les Courses de Chevaux en France.
    Séguin, A. Observations sur les Courses . . .
    Stern, J. Les Courses de Chantilly . . .
    [Teyssier des Farges, G. A.] Les Courses en France . . .
    Thétard, H. Histoire et Secrets du Turf.
    Venancourt, D. de. La Vie Fiévreuse . . .

RACING (Great Britain). *Continued:*
Marsh, R. A Trainer to Two Kings . . .
Mason, W. H. Goodwood; Its House, Park and Grounds . . .
Mathematician [Pseud.] The Derby: a Record . . .
Moorhouse, E. The History and Romance of the Derby.
Moorhouse, E. The Racing Year. 1903.
[Mott, E. S.] The King's Racehorses . . .
Nevill, R. H. The Sport of Kings.
Newmarket. [Pseud.] Chapters From Turf History.
Orchard, V. R. The Derby Stakes . . . 1900-1953.
[Parsons, P.] Newmarket: or an Essay on the Turf.
Pownall, H. Some Particulars Relating to the History of
    Epsom . . .
Proctor, R. W. Our Turf . . .
Racing and Steeplechasing. (1886, 1889)
Racing Handbook and Horses in Training, The.
Richardson, C. The English Turf.
Richardson, C. Racing at Home and Abroad . . .
Rickman, E. On and Off the Racecourse.
Sheardown, W. Doncaster Races.
Siltzer, F. Newmarket: Its Sport and Personalities.
Sporting Life Turf Handbook. (1915)
Sportsman, The. British Sports and Sportsmen. Racing, Cours-
    ing and Steeplechasing.
Timeform. Racehorses of . . .
Watson, A. E. T. A Great Year . . .
Watson, A. E. T. The Racing World . . .
Watson, A. E. T. The Turf.
Watson, A. E. T. The Year's Sport . . .
Willmott-Dixon, W. Sporting Stories . . .

India:
Hayes, M. H. Indian Racing Reminiscences.
Hayes, M. H. Training and Horse Management in India.
Hobbs, H. The Romance of the Calcutta Sweep.
Khan, J. Racing Reminiscences . . .

Jamaica:
Jamaica Stud Book, The.

New Zealand:
Sutherland, E. G. The New Zealand Turf Historical Review.

United States of America:
American Race Horses.
American Racing Manual.
American Racing Record and Turf Guide.

RACING (United States of America). *Continued:*
  American Sporting Manual.
  Buck, H. A., and Burke, J. J. Horses in Training . . .
  Chapman, J. K. Chapman's Racing Record . . .
  Crickmore, H. G. The American Turf.
  [Crickmore, H. G.] Krik's Guide to the Turf . . .
  Davis, J. H. The American Turf.
  Goodwin Brothers. The Winning Stallions . . .
  Herbert, H. W. Frank Forester's Horse and Horsemanship . . .
  Higgins, D. W., & Co. Nominations to Stakes . . .
  Hildreth, S. C. The Spell of the Turf . . .
  Irving, J. G. The American Jockey Club.
  Irving, J. G. The South Carolina Jockey Club.
  Jockey Club, The. Round Table Discussion . . .
  Kentucky. General Assembly. Senate. Committee on Racing.
  Kentucky. State Racing Commission. . . . Biennial Report . . .
  Kentucky Association. Stake Books.
  Kentucky Jockey Club. Golden Anniversary of the Kentucky
    Derby . . .
  Kentucky Jockey Club. Kentucky Derby Lauded by the
    Press . . .
  Leach, G. B. The Kentucky Derby Diamond Jubilee . . .
  Menke, F. G. Churchill Downs . . .
  Menke, F. G. The Story of Churchill Downs . . .
  Merry, T. B. The American Thoroughbred.
  National Association of State Racing Commissioners. Statistical
    Reports . . .
  Newman, N. Famous Horses of the American Turf.
  O'Connor, J. L. History of the Kentucky Derby, 1875-1926.
  Pacific Coast Jockey Club. Inaugural Meeting. 1923. (Tanforan)
  Racing in America.
  Richardson, C. Racing at Home and Abroad . . .
  Ross, J. K. M. Boots and Saddles.
  Thayer, B. C. August in Saratoga.
  Thayer, B. C. Beautiful Hialeah.
  Thoroughbred Racing Associations of the United States. Two
    Year Olds of . . .
  Trevathan, C. S. The American Thoroughbred.
  Underwood, T. R. Thoroughbred Racing & Breeding.
  Vosburgh, W. S. "Cherry and Black" . . .
  [Weeks, L. H.] The American Turf.
  Westchester Racing Association. Belmont Park. (1947)
  Yates, L. B. Autobiography of a Race Horse.

RACING–HISTORY (By Country)
  France:
    Lee, H. Historique des Courses de Chevaux . . .

RACING—HISTORY (By Country). *Continued:*
Great Britain:
Browne, T. H. History of the English Turf.
Cooke, T. A. A History of the English Turf.
Hore, J. P. Sporting and Rural Records . . .
La Grange, E. de. Horse Racing Through the Ages.
Muir, J. B. Ye Olde New-Markitt Calendar of Matches . . .
Muir, J. B. W. T. Frampton and the "Dragon."
Prior, C. M. Early Records . . .
Prior, C. M. History of the Racing Calendar.
Rice, J. History of the British Turf . . .
Richardson, C. The English Turf.
Sporting Life, The. The British Turf and the Men Who Have
   Made It.
Stubbs, G., and Stubbs, G. T. Review of the Turf . . .
Whyte, J. C. History of the British Turf . . .

United States of America:
Culver, F. B. Blooded Horses . . .
Gittings, D. S. Maryland and the Thoroughbred.
Griswold, F. G. Racehorses and Racing.
Racing in America.
Sparrow, C. E. The Maryland Jockey Club . . .
Woodward, W. A Memoir of Andrew Jackson Africanus.

RACING CALENDARS (By Country)
Algiers:
Sport Algérien, Le. Chronique du Turf . . .

Australia:
Australasian Turf Register, The.
Inglis, G. Sport and Pastime in Australia.

Canada:
American Racing Calendar. (1873, 1876)
American Turf Register and Racing and Trotting Calendar.

France:
Bertrand, L. L'Hippodrome.
Bryon, T. J. Calendrier des Courses . . .

Great Britain:
Baily's Racing Register.
Cheny, J. An Historical List . . .
Heber, R. An Historical List . . .
Jackson, J. York Races . . .
Johnson, R. The Racing Calendar . . .

RACING CALENDARS (Great Britain). *Continued:*
    Orton, J. Turf Annals of York and Doncaster . . .
    Pick, W. An Authentic Historical Racing Calendar . . . (1786?)
    Pick, W. An Historical Account of All the Plates . . . (1770)
    Pick, W. Racing Calendar . . . (1802-27)
    Pick, W. The Sportsman and Breeders' Vade Mecum . . .
    Pick, W. The Turf Register . . . (1803-67)
    Pond, J. The Sporting Kalendar.
    Turf Companion, The.
    Turf Herald, The.
    Tuting, W., and Fawconer, T. The Sporting Calendar . . .
    Walker, B. An Historical List of Horse-Matches . . .
    Weatherby, C. The Racing Calendar Abridged . . .
    Weatherby & Sons. The Racing Calendar . . .

  India:
    Calcutta Turf Club. The Racing Calendar.

  Ireland:
    Sharkey, P. Irish Racing Calendar . . .
    Walker, B. An Historical List of Horse-Matches . . .

  New Zealand:
    Australasian Turf Register, The.
    Queensland Turf Club. The Queensland Racing Calendar . . .

  Tunis:
    Sport Algérien, Le. Chronique du Turf . . .

  United States of America:
    American Racing Calendar. (1840-41)
    American Racing Calendar. (1873, 1876)
    American Racing Calendar and Trotting Record.
    American Turf Register and Racing and Trotting Calendar.
    Brunell, F. H. Racing Form (Monthly Ed.)
    Crickmore, H. G. Racing Calendars. (1861-69)
    Goodwin' Brothers. Goodwin's Annual Official Turf Guide . . .
      (1883-1908)
    Triangle Publications. Daily Racing Form Chart Book . . .
    Watson, J. Watson's Racing Guide.

RIDING *see* HORSEMANSHIP

RULES OF RACING (By Country)
  France:
    Bryon, T. J. Manuel de l'Amateur . . .
    Séguin, A. Observations sur les Courses . . .

RULES OF RACING (By Country). *Continued:*
  Great Britain:
    Rous, H. J. On the Laws and Practise of Horse Racing.

  United States of America:
    American Jockey Club, The.
    Jockey Club, The. Rules of Racing . . .
    Kentucky. State Racing Commission. Rules of Racing.
    Rules and Regulations for the Government of Racing . . .
    South Carolina Jockey Club. Rules of . . .
    Sparrow, C. E. Maryland Jockey Club . . .

SALES CATALOGS
    Belmont, A. Reprint of Catalogue . . .
    Breeders' Sales Co., The. Thoroughbred Sales Catalogue, 1944- .
    Catalogues (Miscellaneous). 1879-86.
    Thoroughbred Sales Catalogs. 1917-39.
    Woodburn Sales Catalogues. 1860-76.

SHOEING *see* FARRIERY

SPORTS (Other than Racing)
    Apperly, C. J. Nimrod Abroad.
    [Bertram, J. G.] Sporting Anecdotes . . .
    Blaine, D. P. An Encyclopaedia of Rural Sports . . .
    Cobbett, M. R. Sporting Notions . . .
    Constable, H. S. Something About Horses . . .
    Daumas, M. J. E. Les Chevaux du Sahara . . . (1851, 1881)
    Daumas, M. J. E. The Horses of the Sahara . . . (1863)
    Dixon, H. H. Field and Fern . . . (North, South)
    Dixon, H. H. Saddle and Sirloin . . .
    Dixon, H. H. Scott and Sebright.
    Durand, E. Ponies' Progress.
    Egan, P. . . . Book of Sports . . .
    Egan, P. Sporting Anecdotes . . .
    Fairfax, T. The Complete Sportsman . . .
    Gordon, G. A. Sporting Reminiscences.
    Griswold, F. G. Sport on Land and Water.
    Griswold, F. G. Stolen Kisses.
    Haydon, T. Racing Reminiscences.
    [Hemyng, B.] Out of the Ring . . .
    Inglis, G. Sport and Pastime in Australia.
    Johnson, T. B. The Sportsman's Cyclopaedia . . .
    Lennox, W. P. Recreations of a Sportsman.
    Lynd, R. The Sporting Life . . .
    Russell, F. In Scarlet and Silk.

SPORTS (Other than Racing). *Continued:*
  Russell, F. Sporting Society . . .
  Sherer, J. Rural Life Described . . .
  Smith, H. W. A Sporting Family of the Old South.
  Sporting Anecdotes; Original and Select . . .
  Strutt, J. . . . On the Sports and Pastimes of the People of
    England.
  Walsh, J. H. British Rural Sports . . .
  Watson, A. E. T. King Edward VII as a Sportsman . . .
  Watson, A. E. T. Racecourse and Covert Side.
  Watson, A. E. T. Racing and 'Chasing . . .
  Watson, A. E. T. A Sporting and Dramatic Career.
  Watson, A. E. T. The Year's Sport . . .
  Wood, J. G. The Uncivilized Races of Men . . .

STABLE MANAGEMENT
  Daingerfield, K. Training for Fun . . . (1942, 1948)
  Darvill, R. A Treatise on the Care . . .
  Hayes, M. H. Stable Management and Exercise . . .
  Sharpe, H. The Practical Stud Groom.
  [Tongue, C.] Stable Practise . . .
  Wall, J. F. Practical Light Horse Breeding.
  Ware, F. M. Our Noblest Friend the Horse . . .

STANDARDBRED (Trotters)
  American Trotting Register Association. Index-Digest . . .
  Battell, J. American Stallion Register . . .
  Busbey, H. Recollections of Men and Horses.
  Busbey, H. The Trotting and Pacing Horse . . .
  Chester, W. T. Chester's Complete Trotting and Pacing
    Record . . .
  Splan, J. Life With the Trotters.
  U.S. Trotting Association. Annual Yearbook.
  Wallace, J. H. The Horse of America . . .
  Wallace, J. H. Wallace's American Trotting Register . . .
  Wallace, J. H. Wallace's Yearbook of Trotting.
  Woodruff, H. W. The Trotting Horse of America . . .

STEEPLECHASING
  American Race Horses.
  Blew, W. C. A. A History of Steeple-Chasing.
  Fawcett, W. Turf, Chase & Paddock.
  Fitt, J. N. Hunting, Steeplechasing and Racing . . .
  Gentleman, Un. Choses de Sport . . .
  Havrincourt, L. d'. Dressage en Liberté . . .
  Humfrey, J. The Steeplechase Horse . . .

STEEPLECHASING. *Continued:*
Mason, G. F. Heroes and Heroines of the Grand National.
Munroe, D. H. The Grand National.
National Steeplechase and Hunt Association. Records of Hunt Meetings.
Page, H. S. Between the Flags.
Racing and Steeplechasing. (1886, 1889)
Record of Hunt Race Meetings in America . . .
Richardson, C. Racing at Home and Abroad . . .
Rose, S. The Maryland Hunt Cup.
Russell, F. In Scarlet and Silk . . .
Smith, H. W. Life and Sport in Aiken . . .
Smith, H. W. A Sporting Tour Through Ireland . . .
Sportsman, The. British Sports and Sportsmen. Racing, Coursing and Steeplechasing.
Steeplechase Calendar, The.
Streett, W. B. Gentlemen Up.
[Turquet de Beauregard, Y. L. M.] Saut d'Obstacles . . .
Watson, A. E. T. The Turf.

STUDBOOKS (By Country)
Australia:
Australian Stud Book, The.

Brazil:
Jockey-Club Brasileiro. Stud Book Brasileiro. Guia de Pelagem Oficial.
Jockey-Club Brasileiro. Stud Book Brasileiro. Registro de Cavalos e Eguas . . .

Canada:
Canadian Thoroughbred Stud Book, The.

France:
Bryon, T. J. The French Stud Book . . . (1828)
Fleury, J. B. Le Stud-Book du Sud-Ouest . . .
Stud Book Français, Le. (1832 to date)

Great Britain:
General Stud Book, The. (1808, 1820 to date, 1834)
Introduction to a General Stud-Book, An. (1791)
Pick, W. The Turf Register . . . (1803-67)
Prior, F. M. Prior's "H-B" Stud-Book.
Supplement to the General Stud-Book, The. (1800)

Italy:
. . . Libro Genealogico dei Cavalli . . .

STUDBOOKS (By Country). *Continued:*
Jamaica:
Jamaica Stud Book, The.

Mexico:
Jockey Club Mexicano. Registro . . .

New Zealand:
New Zealand Stud Book . . .

United States of America:
American Stud Book, The. (1884 to date)
Bruce, S. D. The American Stud Book . . . (1868, 1873)
Edgar, P. N. The American Race-Turf Register . . .
Half Bred Stud Book, The.

STUDBOOKS—PRIVATE
Aga Khan. The Sheshoon, Ballymany . . .
Barnes, W. S. Souvenir Catalogue . . .
Belmont, A. Nursery Stud Thoroughbreds.
Blanc, E. Haras de Jardy . . .
Bradley, E. R. Catalogue of Thoroughbreds . . .
Bradley, E. R. Idle Hour Stock Farm Co. (1922?)
Bradley, E. R. Idle Hour Stock Farm Co. (1926?)
Chinn, P. T. Himyar Stud. (1920)
Chinn, P. T. Himyar Stud. (1927)
Dudley, W. S. Thoroughbreds . . . (1928, 1929)
Haggin, J. B. A. Catalogue of Stallions . . .
Haggin, J. B. A. Catalogue of Thoroughbreds . .
Hancock, A. B. Claiborne Farm. (1956)
Hancock, A. B. Ellerslie and Claiborne Studs.
Hancock, A. B. Thoroughbred Stallions . . .
Harris, N. T. Catalogue of Thoroughbreds . . .
Hart, H. S. Swingalong Stud. (1930, 1931)
Headley, H. P. Beaumont Stud. (1924, 1951)
Keiffer, L. E. Inverness Farm.
Kelly, E. The Madison Stud.
Kirkham Stud. Private Stud Book . . .
Koontz, F. B. Paulfred Farms . . .
Lorillard, P. P. Lorillard's Thoroughbred Stock. (1881, 1885)
Mackay, C. Thoroughbreds at Silver Brook Stud.
Madden, J. E. Pedigrees of Race Horses . . . at Hamburg
    Place . . . (1913, 1925)
Maple, J. B. Childwick Stud . . .
Markey, L. P. Bloodstock of Calumet Farm . . .
Platt, J. E. Bruntwood Stud . . .
Poniatowski, A. The Burlingame Stock Farm.

STUDBOOKS—PRIVATE. *Continued:*
    Pons, A. Season of 1930. Mereworth Stud Stallions.
    Sanford, J. Pedigrees and Family Histories . . . (1921)
    Schreiber, B. Catalogue of Thoroughbred Stallions . . .
    Shaffer, C. B. Coldstream Stud. (1928, 1930)
    Simms, E. F. Thoroughbreds . . . (1920)
    Sinclair, H. F. Rancocas Stock Farm.
    Stanford, L. Tenth Annual Catalogue . . .
    Whitney, C. V. Reference Catalogue . . .
    Whitney, H. P. The Thoroughbred Stud . . .
    Whitney, W. C. The Whitney Stud.
    Widener, J. E. Elmendorf Stud.
    Wood Park Stud.

TOTALISATOR
    Technique of Betting, The.

TRAINING
    [Bindley, C.] A Treatise on the Proper Condition . . .
    Brooke, G. F. H. Training Young Horses to Jump.
    Burch, P. M. Training Thoroughbred Horses.
    Chamberlin, H. D. Riding and Schooling Horses.
    Chifney, S. Genius Genuine. (1795)
    Chifney, S. Genius Genuine. (1803)
    Collins, D. The Horse-Trainer's and Sportsman's Guide . . .
    Daingerfield, K. Training for Fun . . . (1942, 1948)
    Darvill, R. A Treatise on the Care . . .
    Day, W. Le Cheval de Course . . .
    Day, W. The Racehorse in Training . . . (1880, 1925)
    Duval, C. L'Entraînement . . .
    Fillis, J. Breaking and Riding . . .
    Gayot, E. N. Guide du Sportsman . . .
    Gobert, H. J., and Cagny, P. Le Cheval de Course . . .
    Hayes, M. H. Riding and Hunting.
    Hayes, M. H. Stable Management and Exercise . . .
    Herbert, H. W. Hints to Horse-Keepers . . .
    [Higgins, F.] Flat-Racing Explained . . .
    Hontang, M. Psychologie du Cheval . . .
    Humfrey, J. Horse-Breeding and Rearing . . .
    Hunt, V. D. de V. The Horse and His Master.
    Lagondie, J. G. Le Cheval et Son Cavalier . . .
    Marshall, L. G. The Arabian Art of Taming and Training . . .
    Martinengo Cesaresco, E. The Psychology and Training . . .
    Meredith, G. W. L. Training Horses for Races . . .
    Minière, T. Osteolymphatisme . . .

TRAINING. *Continued:*
  Montigny, E. L. X. Manuel des Piquers . . .
  Muggridge, W. How to Train a Racehorse.
  Musany, F. C. M. L'Élevage, l'Entraînement . . .
  Museum of Foreign Literature and Science, The.
  Portefin, J. Le Cheval de Courses.
  Powell, W. J. Tachyhippodamia . . .
  Radcliffe, J. B. Amongst the Yorkshire Trainers . . .
  Rarey, J. S. The Art of Taming Horses.
  Rarey, J. S. The Modern Art of Taming Wild Horses.
  Rimington, M. F. The Reforming of Dangerous and Useless Horses.
  Summerhays, R. S. The Problem Horse.
  [Tongue, C.] Stable Practise . . .
  [Walsh, J. H.] Le Cheval Anglais.
  Warburton, F. T. The Race Horse.
  Ware, F. M. Our Noblest Friend the Horse.
  Wentworth, J. A. D. W. B.-L. Horses in the Making.
  Young, J. R. The Schooling of the Western Horse.

VETERINARY MEDICINE, SURGERY
  [Badcock, J.] Conversations on Conditioning . . .
  [Badcock, J.] . . . Farriery . . .
  [Badcock, J.] The Veterinary Surgeon . . .
  Cadiot, P. J. Roaring in Horses . . .
  Carver, W. Practical Horse Farrier . . .
  Clark, B. Veterinary Pamphlets . . .
  Codrington, W. S. Know Your Horse . . .
  Curot, E. Galopeurs et Trotteurs . . .
  Dadd, G. H. The Modern Horse Doctor . . .
  De Grey, T. The Compleat Horseman . . .
  Dollar, J. A. W. Surgical Operating Table . . .
  Farrier and Naturalist, The.
  Hanger, G. . . . To All Sportsmen . . .
  Hobday, F. T. G. Fifty Years a Veterinary Surgeon.
  Kendall, B. J. A Treatise on the Horse and His Diseases . . .
  Lawrence, R. The Complete Farrier . . .
  McGee, W. R. Veterinary Notebook . . .
  Magner, D. The Art of Taming and Educating . . .
  Markham, G. Markham's Masterpiece . . .
  Markham, G. Le Nouveau et Scavant Mareschal . . .
  Mason, R. . . . The Gentleman's New Pocket Farrier . . . (1848, 1863)
  Reeves, J. H. The Orange County Stud Book . . .
  Sherer, J. Rural Life Described . . .

VETERINARY MEDICINE, SURGERY. *Continued:*
>
Solleysel, J. de. The Compleat Horseman . . .
U.S. Department of Agriculture. Yearbook of Agriculture. Keeping Livestock Healthy. (1942)
U.S. Department of Agriculture. Bureau of Animal Industry. Special Report on Diseases of the Horse. (1890, 1903, 1916, 1942)
Vial de Sainbel, C. Elements of the Veterinary Art . . .
Vial de Sainbel, C. The Posthumous Works of . . .
Winter, G. S. . . . Hippiater Expertus . . .
Youatt, W. . . . Youatt on the Structure . . .

MISCELLANEOUS
>
Denhardt, R. M. Official Stud Book . . . (Quarter Horse)
Estes, J. A. Average Earnings Index . . .
[Finney, H. S.] A Stud Farm Diary.
Fothergill, G. A. A Gift to the State . . .
Gilbey, W. Racing Cups . . .
Hiatt, J. M. National Register of Norman Horses . . .
Ireland. Irish Land Commission . . . Return of Stallions.
Jennings, R. W. Taxation of Thoroughbred Racing.
Kentucky. State Racing Commission. Licenses.
Kentucky in Retrospect . . .
Knight, T. A., and Green, N. L. Country Estates of the Blue Grass.
Lectures Given at the . . . Annual Stud Managers Course.
Mason, W. H. Goodwood; Its House, Park and Grounds . . .
National Association of State Racing Commissioners. Bulletin.
National Association of State Racing Commissioners. Proceedings.
Official Horse Show Blue Book.
Omwake, J. The Conestoga Six-Horse Bell Teams . . .
Ranck, G. W. Guide to Lexington, Kentucky . . .
Ransom, J. H. Who's Who and Where in Horsedom . . .
Rasp, The.
Séguin, A. Le Régulateur des Classemens de Vitesse . . .
Stud Book Anglais, Le.
Trial of Mr. Samuel Emden . . .
Walker, W. Walker Foxhounds.
Washington. State College, Pullman. College of Agriculture . . . Stockmen's Handbook . . .
Wecter, D. The Saga of American Society.
Williams, R. D. The Foxhound.
Yates, N. W. William T. Porter . . .

www.ingramcontent.com/pod-product-compliance
Lightning Source LLC
Chambersburg PA
CBHW020608270326
41927CB00005B/231